MARXISM AND THE USA

MARXISM AND THE USA

Alan Woods

With appendices by Leon Trotsky, Frederick Engels, John Peterson, Thomas Trottier, and David May

NEW YORK

MARXISM AND THE USA
ALAN WOODS

First edition, 2005
Second edition, 2010
Reprint, 2020
Updated Introduction by John Peterson ©2019
Copyright © WR Books. All rights reserved.

Introduction by John Peterson
Proofread by Steve Iverson
Layout by Eric Norman, Emilia Miller, and Antonio Balmer
Cover design by Mark Rahman

United States distribution:
WR Books
PO Box 1575
New York, NY 10013

United Kingdom distribution:
Wellred Books
PO Box 50525
London
E14 6WG

Email: sales@wellredusa.com
MarxistBooks.com

Email: contact@socialist.net
WellredBooks.net

ISBN 190000724X

CONTENTS

Introduction to the Second Edition by John Peterson   vii

Author's Introduction   xi

Chapter I   "Blood From Every Pore"   1

Chapter II   The American Revolution   16

Chapter III   Rich and Poor   43

Chapter IV   The Second American Revolution   50

Chapter V   Labor and Capital   71

Chapter VI   Imperialism   95

Chapter VII   The Great Depression   113

Chapter VIII   World War II   123

Chapter IX   The Colonial Revolution   142

Chapter X   The Soul of America and the Future of Humanity   155

Appendix I   If America Should Go Communist by Leon Trotsky   183

Appendix II   Address of the International Working Men's Association to Abraham Lincoln drafted by Karl Marx   191

Appendix III The Need for a Labor Party—Selections from Frederick Engels   193

Appendix IV Shays's Rebellion and the American Revolution by John Peterson   202

Appendix V   When the Socialist Party Was a Factor in US Politics: Lessons in Party Building by Tom Trottier   213

Appendix VI The 75th Anniversary of the 1934 Minneapolis Teamsters Strike by David May   219

Bibliography   227

Index   229

INTRODUCTION TO THE SECOND EDITION

John Peterson

Marxism and the USA was the first title produced by the US section of the IMT, a modest milestone that reflected the growing interest in the ideas of Marxism in the "belly of the beast." The book was written at a time when George W. Bush was president, a time when many around the world—including many on the left—considered the US to be one reactionary bloc, devoid of class struggle or revolutionary potential. Woods aimed to dispel these misconceptions, draw on the marvelous traditions of struggle throughout US history, and inspire those new to the ideas of Marxism to learn more—and to get involved.

Providing one example after another, he showed how the ideas of socialism and communism are not recent, "foreign" importations, but have deep roots in the American tradition itself. He also debunks many of the common misconceptions Americans have about socialism, taking up the question of socialism and religion, freedom vs. dictatorship, an explanation of what happened in the Soviet Union, and more.

Authors such as Howard Zinn, Leo Huberman, John Dos Passos, Eric and Philip Foner, Herbert Aptheker, and others have analyzed US history from the perspective of the working masses, delving into little-known details and episodes and presenting them in an easy to understand style. Some, like Huberman, have focused on providing an economic history of the US in popular form (*We, the People*). Others, like Aptheker and the Foners, have offered a class perspective on specific periods or labor struggles.

Despite his later drift to the right, Dos Passos's *USA Trilogy* is a literary masterpiece, blending primary sources with fictional realism to portray the stormy years of bitter class struggle in the early twentieth century. For many American activists, Zinn's *A People's History of the United States* was their first introduction to the country's rich history of class struggle. And Gore Vidal, although not writing from a working-class perspective, has provided

penetrating insight into the foundations and founders of the American republic and its particular form of democracy.

However, none of the above writers present the broad sweep of this vast
topic from a consistently revolutionary Marxist perspective, and this is what
sets Woods's book apart. In this modest volume, he weaves together many of
the most important, and often not-well-known episodes of American history.
In a series of short and engaging pieces, he highlights the heroic revolutionary and labor traditions of this oft-maligned country.

As a young country, the history of the United States and its meteoric rise
to world prominence is compressed into a few intense centuries. The wealthiest country on earth certainly has its vast natural resources to thank, at least
in part, for its position. But above all, it was built on the backs of millions
of African slaves, European indentured servants, Native Americans, and the
endless stream of political and economic refugees who have searched for the
"American Dream" on its shores.

Unfortunately, most American students regard history as dry and dusty,
an endless and disconnected recitation of dates and individuals. But history
need not be "one damn thing after another," as the American Oliver Wendell
Holmes Jr. put it. It is a complex and contradictory process, driven forward
by the struggle over control of the surplus wealth created by the labor of the
masses. As Karl Marx explained in *The Communist Manifesto*: "The history of
all hitherto existing society is the history of class struggles." Or, as he further
elaborated in his introduction to *The Critique of Political Economy*:

> In the social production of their existence, men inevitably enter into defi-
> nite relations, which are independent of their will, namely relations of pro-
> duction appropriate to a given stage in the development of their material
> forces of production. The totality of these relations of production consti-
> tutes the economic structure of society, the real foundation, on which arises
> a legal and political superstructure and to which correspond definite forms
> of social consciousness. The mode of production of material life conditions
> the general process of social, political, and intellectual life. It is not the con-
> sciousness of men that determines their existence, but their social existence
> that determines their consciousness. At a certain stage of development, the
> material productive forces of society come into conflict with the existing
> relations of production or – this merely expresses the same thing in legal
> terms – with the property relations within the framework of which they
> have operated hitherto. From forms of development of the productive forc-
> es, these relations turn into their fetters. Then begins an era of social revo-
> lution. The changes in the economic foundation lead sooner or later to the
> transformation of the whole immense superstructure.

This concisely sums up the Marxist approach to history, also known as "historical materialism." Once we begin to understand history—not as a random series of unrelated episodes, but as an infinitely complex yet tightly interconnected chain of events involving mass social forces, in which cause becomes effect and effect becomes cause—a whole new world opens up. No longer does it appear to be more or less irrelevant collection of useless trivia. Instead, the experiences of past struggles of the working class come alive, ripe with lessons for our own fight to change the world today.

From the communistic traditions of the Native Americans, to the revolutionary-democratic beliefs of the Pilgrims; the Declaration of Independence and the revolutionary defeat the mighty British Empire; from Nat Turner's revolt to John Brown's implacable struggle against slavery; from the determined efforts millions of slaves to disrupt the Confederate war effort to Lincoln's revolutionary expropriation of billions of dollars of human property; from the early labor movement to the Flint sit-down strike, American history is full of tragedy and triumph, of individual sacrifice and collective struggle for "Life, Liberty, and the Pursuit of Happiness."

When *Marxism and the USA* first appeared, the comrades of the IMT were a tiny minority in the US, scattered far and wide across the country, still in the initial infant stages of developing our ideas, program, methods, and traditions. In the years since, we have made modest advances, with a clear program, growing experience, and connections with the labor movement, and well-established branches in a handful of major cities. This book played an important role in drawing together those initial disparate forces into a unified organization, based on shared political principles and aims. In the founding statement of the US section, published in 2002, we paid homage to the militant traditions of the US working class:

> The US working class has a proud and militant tradition. We look to the accumulated experiences of the American working class—the great railroad strikes, the mine wars, the formation of the Teamsters and the CIO, the Flint sit-down strikes, and more for inspiration. We rest on the traditions of William Sylvis, Albert Parsons, Mother Jones, Joe Hill, Elizabeth Gurley Flynn, Big Bill Haywood, Eugene Debs, John Reed, Louise Bryant, and the millions of rank and file workers who led and participated in the great struggles of the past. And we are confident that the greatest days of the US labor movement are still to come.
>
> We also base ourselves on the ideas of Marx, Engels, Lenin, and Trotsky, and on the further development of these ideas by the supporters of the In Defense of Marxism [www.marxist.com] website. The ideas of scientific socialism have been tarnished in the minds of millions by the horrific experience of Stalinism and the continued lies and distortions of the ruling

class. We believe that Stalinism was a historical aberration and a criminal totalitarian caricature of genuine socialism. We fight for international socialism, where the world working class has full democratic control over the means of production, distribution, and exchange, in harmony with the environment. Without democracy, there can be no socialism! A workers' government in the US would take over the vast wealth now owned by just a handful of individuals and democratically use it in the interests of everyone.

This edition includes several appendices. The 1934 Teamsters strike in Minneapolis was a watershed for the labor movement and the young forces of American Trotskyism. David May's article describing the struggle in context draws out the lessons to be applied today. Tom Trottier's overview of the early years of the Socialist Party of America is yet another example that socialist ideas have deep roots in the United States. And my own piece on Shays's Rebellion explores one of the seminal events of the post–American Revolutionary War period, which had a profound effect on the future development of the country.

Much has changed since Marxism and the USA was first published. GW is a distant memory, eight years of Obama have come and gone, and Donald Trump now sits in the White House. The 2016 elections unleashed the pent-up contradictions of the system, and socialism is now a household word.

Time and experience have proven Alan Woods's basic premise correct: the United States is a society torn apart by tremendous class contradictions, and sooner or later, the militant revolutionary traditions of the past will return on an even higher level. From Occupy to Black Lives Matter to the rise of DSA and the growing wave of teachers' strikes, eruptions of the class struggle are never far from the surface. To paraphrase W.E.B. DuBois, these more or less isolated eddies of the class struggle are swirling more and more into a mighty current. The revolutionary implications for the future are clear.

The US working class is destined to play a decisive role in the world socialist revolution. As the Russian revolutionary Leon Trotsky put it, when commenting on his brief stay in New York City before returning to Russia in March of 1917: "[The United States is] the foundry in which the fate of man is to be forged."

John Peterson

(Updated October 19, 2019)

AUTHOR'S INTRODUCTION

The present work began life as a draft introduction to the American edition of *Reason in Revolt*. Starting out from the idea that most Americans have been prejudiced against Marxism as an alien ("foreign") ideology, I started to explain that the history of the United States contains a great revolutionary tradition, beginning with the War of Independence that set up the USA in the first place. However, on delving more deeply into the subject, it became clear that it was much too extensive to be satisfactorily contained in the introduction to a book. I therefore put it to one side and wrote another one, the content of which was mainly of a scientific character.

Later on I showed a copy of the original draft to an American friend, who suggested that, suitably expanded, it could be published separately, and he very kindly furnished me with some interesting additional information. As a result, I felt obliged to introduce some more material on matters such as the American Revolution, the Civil War, and the history of trade unionism in the USA.

The subject is fascinating, and unfortunately very poorly known in Europe, where it has become a fashionable (and quite erroneous) idea that the USA, as the bastion of world imperialism (which Gore Vidal, the greatest living American writer, describes as "the Empire"), never produced anything of interest to socialists and revolutionaries. Actually, the reverse is true, as I hope I have shown in this long essay. Part of my intention was to combat the kind of senseless anti-Americanism that one encounters all too frequently in left circles. Marxists are internationalists and do not take up a negative stance in relation to the people of any country. We stand for the unity of all working people against oppression and exploitation. What we oppose is not Americans, but American capitalism and American imperialism.

The American people and above all the American working class have a great revolutionary tradition. On the basis of great historical events they are destined to rediscover these traditions and to stand once more in the front line of the world revolution, as they did in 1776 and 1860. The future of the entire world depends ultimately on this perspective. And although today it may seem very far off, it is not so incredible as one might think. Let us recall that before 1917 tsarist Russia was the bastion of world reaction, as the USA is today. Many people were convinced that the idea of socialist revolution in Russia was a crazy delusion on the part of Lenin and Trotsky. Yes, they were completely convinced, and completely wrong.

The rapacious greed of the big corporations and the ambitions of the ruling elite of "the Empire" are dragging the USA into one adventure after another. New nightmares can flow from such adventures. Fifty-eight thousand young Americans were killed in the quagmire of Vietnam. The aggressive policies of the Bush White House threaten many more casualties, American and others. Sooner or later this will impact back on the USA, producing a general reaction against a system that could produce such monstrosities. The mass demonstration in Seattle and other US cities have served notice on the establishment that the youth of America will not be prepared to remain silent forever.

The USA and the World

The terrible events of September 11, 2001 marked a turning point in the history of the United States and the whole world. Overnight, it became impossible for ordinary U.S. citizens to imagine that what was happening in the outside world was no concern of theirs. A general sense of insecurity and apprehension seized the national psychology. Suddenly, the world became a hostile and dangerous place. Ever since 9/11, Americans have been trying to make sense of the kind of world that could produce such horrors.

Many people have been asking themselves: what have we done that there should be such hatred against us? Of course, ordinary Americans have done nothing to deserve this kind of thing. And we regard it as a criminal act to kill innocent civilians, of whatever nation, to make a political point. What is not in doubt, however, is that the actions of the United States in the world—its government, its big corporations, and its armed forces—have aroused feelings of deep antipathy and resentment, and it would be as well for Americans to try to understand why this is so.

For much of its history, isolationism has played a central role in the politics of the USA. But the fact is that in the modern world no country can cut adrift from the rest of the world, no matter how big and powerful. Nowadays, the most decisive phenomenon of our times is precisely this: the crushing domination of the world market. It is often known by the latest buzzword, globalization. But in fact it is not new. Already over 150 years ago in that most contemporary of all works, *The Communist Manifesto*, Marx and Engels predicted that the capitalist system, beginning as a series of national states, would create a world market.

The participation of the USA in world economy and world politics has grown almost continuously for the last century. All attempts to pull America into a state of self-imposed isolation have failed, and will inevitably fail, as George W. Bush has found out very quickly. The United States has inherited the role that was previously held by Great Britain—that of the world's policeman. But whereas Britain's dominant role in the world took place at a time when the capitalist system was still in its ascending phase, America now finds itself ruling over a world that is mortally sick. The sickness is the product of the fact that capitalism on a world scale is in a state of irreversible decline. This expresses itself in a series of convulsions that are increasingly of a violent character. The terrible cataclysm of 9/11 was only one manifestation of this.

Anti-Americanism is, unfortunately, widespread. I say unfortunately because the present writer holds no ill feelings towards the people of the USA or any other country. As a Marxist, I am opposed to nationalism and chauvinist attitudes that sow hatred and conflicts between different peoples. But that does not mean that one can condone the actions of particular governments, companies, and armed forces that are pursuing actions that are harmful to the rest of the world. It just means that it is wrong to confuse the ruling class of any country with the workers and poor people of that country.

The phenomenon of anti-Americanism is strongest in poor countries in Asia, Africa, Latin America, and the Middle East. The reasons for this are related to the exploitation of the resources of these countries by voracious US multinational corporations, backed by the US military and the CIA, leading to the impoverishment of their people, the destruction of the environment, and the destabilization of their currencies, their economies, and even their governments. Such actions are not designed to promote love and respect for the USA in the world at large.

A couple of years ago *The Economist* concluded that the prices of raw materials were at their lowest level for 150 years—that is, since records began. The situation has varied somewhat since, but it has not changed the position of millions of workers and peasants of the Third World who are being forced to work for slave wages by big US corporations. One American golfer, Tiger Woods, for instance, earns more than the entire workforce of Nike in Indonesia.

The ruthless conduct of these big corporations is shown by the Bhopal tragedy in 1984, when 40,000 men, women and children were killed one night by the poisonous fumes from a Union Carbide plant situated too close to their homes. A recent report reveals that the area remains dangerously polluted to this day. This case is unusual only inasmuch as it hit the headlines.

The super-exploitation by rapacious corporations of what is known as the Third World is what causes a backlash in Africa, Asia, the Middle East, and Latin America which may sometimes take the form of a rejection of all things American, but which is at bottom an expression of anti-imperialism. The best way to put an end to the poverty and starvation in the Third World is to fight for the expropriation of the big corporations that are the enemies of working people everywhere—beginning with the workers of the USA, as we shall show.

Europe and America

Anti-Americanism is not confined to poor countries. Some Europeans have somewhat negative attitudes to America. They resent the subordinate role they have been compelled to accept on the world stage, and they fear the consequences of the colossal economic and military domination of the transatlantic giant. Behind the polite façade of diplomacy between the "allies" lies an uneasy and contradictory relationship, which manifests itself in periodic trade conflicts and diplomatic rows. On a different level, many Europeans resent what they see as the intrusion of an alien culture, brash and commercialized, which threatens to devalue and undermine their cultural identity. Behind the cultural resentments of the European intellectuals lies a deep-seated feeling of inferiority that seeks to hide behind a kind of cultural snobbishness. This feeling has a material basis, and in fact reflects the real state of affairs.

It is a simple fact that the history of the last hundred years is the history of the decline of Europe and the rise of the USA. As the Russian revolutionary Leon Trotsky predicted, the Mediterranean (which in the Latin tongue signifies "the center of the world") has become an unimportant lake. The center of world history has passed first to the Atlantic and finally to the Pacific—two mighty oceans, straddled by a colossus—the United States. The real relationship between Europe and America is summed up by the relationship between George W. Bush and Tony Blair. It is the relationship of the master and his lackey. And like a good English lackey, Mr. Blair does his level best to imitate the style and manners of his master, notwithstanding which, no one in their right mind can mistake the real relation between the two.

The airs of superiority that until recently were adopted by members of the British Establishment with regard to the values and culture of America are particularly comical. They resemble the airs and graces of the penniless English aristocrats in the 19th century in the presence of the wealthy bourgeois upstarts, a phenomenon well documented in the novels of Jane Austen and others. These airs and graces, of course, did not stop them from marrying off their daughters to the sons of the upstart money-grubbers at the earliest opportunity.

The negative attitude of Europeans towards American culture is the product of a misunderstanding. They are thinking of the made in the USA "cultural exports" that flood the markets of the world with bad music that makes you deaf, overpriced "designer clothes" produced by slave labor in the Third World that makes you indignant, and cholesterol-clogged fast food produced by slave labor in the high street that makes you obese. It is the kind of cheap and nasty commercialism that is the hallmark of capitalism in the period of its senile decay. That such monstrosities produce a feeling of revulsion in all thinking and feeling human beings is perfectly natural.

However, the concept of culture, above all in the modern world, is far broader than pop music, Coca-Cola, and McDonald's. It also includes such things as computers, the Internet, and many other aspects of science and technology. On this level, it is impossible to deny the impressive achievements of the USA. Moreover, it is precisely these scientific advances that are laying the foundations for an unprecedented cultural revolution, once they are correctly harnessed by a planned socialist economy on a world scale.

The present writer has no time for crude anti-Americanism. I am profoundly convinced that the colossal potential of the United States is destined to play a decisive role in the future socialist world order. But it must also be admitted that at the present moment in world history, the role of the USA on a world scale does not reflect its real potential for good, but only the rapacious greed of the big multinational companies that own America and control its actions in their own selfish interests. This author is a fervent admirer of the real America, and an implacable opponent of the other America, the America of the big banks and monopolies, the enemy of freedom and progress everywhere.

CHAPTER I

"BLOOD FROM EVERY PORE"

An "Un-American" Idea?

In order to understand the ideas of Marxism, it is first necessary to approach them without prejudice. This is difficult, because until now, the great majority of Americans have only heard of Marxism in connection with that monstrous caricature that was Stalinist Russia. Marxism ("communism") is therefore associated in the minds of many people with an alien regime, a totalitarian state where the lives of men and women are dominated by an all-powerful bureaucracy, and where individual initiative and freedom are stifled and negated. The collapse of the USSR apparently proves the inadequacy of socialism, and the superiority of the free market economy. What more needs to be said?

Well, there is a great deal more to be said. The monstrous bureaucratic regime of the USSR had nothing to do with the ideas of Marx and Lenin, who advocated a democratic socialist society, where men and women would be free to determine their own lives, in a way that they do not do in the USA or any other country today. This subject was very well explained in a marvelous book written by my friend and life-long comrade Ted Grant (*Russia, from Revolution to Counter-Revolution*). The fall of Stalinism in Russia did not signify the failure of socialism, but only a bureaucratic caricature thereof. It certainly did not signify the end of Marxism, which today is more relevant than ever before. It is my contention that only Marxism, with its scientific methodology, can furnish us with the necessary analytical tools whereby we can understand the processes that are unfolding on a world scale—and in the USA.

Whatever one thinks about Marxism, it has clearly had an enormous impact on the whole course of human history. Today it is impossible for any man or woman to claim to be properly educated, unless they have taken the trouble to understand at least the basic ideas of Marxism. This goes as much for those who are opposed to socialism as those who are for it. A serious barrier that confronts the American reader who approaches Marxism is the thought that this is a foreign import that has no place in the history, culture, and traditions of the United States. Although the infamous House Un-American Activities Committee and the late Senator Joseph McCarthy are now bad memories of the past, yet the psychological legacy remains, that "communism and revolution are not for us."

Actually, this is a serious misunderstanding of American history, which is not difficult to dispel. In fact, communism has far more ancient roots in America than capitalism. The latter has only existed for less than two centuries. But long before the first Europeans set foot on the soil of the New World (as they called it), Native Americans had been living in a communist society for thousands of years. The Native Americans did not understand private property (at least, not in our modern sense of the word). The state and money did not exist. There were neither police nor prisons. The idea of wage labor and capital was so alien to them that they could never be properly integrated in the new capitalist society that destroyed their old way of life, expropriated their ancestral common lands, and reduced them to an appalling state of misery and degradation—all in the name of Christian civilization.

This new way of life called capitalism, with its greed, absence of solidarity, and morality of the jungle—was really an alien system, imported from foreign lands. It can be argued—quite correctly—that this is precisely what made possible the opening up of America, the colossal development of industry, agriculture, science, and technology that have made the USA into the greatest economic power the world has ever seen. And since Marxism maintains that the key to all human progress lies in the development of the productive forces, this represented progress on a gigantic scale. Indeed, that is true. But there has been a price to pay for the progress that results from the anarchy of capitalism and the blind play of market forces. With the passing of time, an increasing number of people—not necessarily socialists—are becoming aware of the threat posed to the human species by the systematic destruction of the environment—the air we breathe, the water we drink, the food we eat. This apprehension is not lessened, but rather increased, by the remarkable progress of science and technology, which have advanced far more rapidly in the USA than in any other country in the world.

Before the Europeans arrived, America was a land of unspoiled prairies, pristine forests, and crystalline cascades and lakes. It was a land in which men and women could breathe freely. To the original inhabitants of America, the land was sacred and nature was respected:

> As the ecological patterns of this large geographic area varied enormously, each native group adjusted its lifestyle to benefit from the available resources. Such patterns reflected not so much economic prudence as a spiritual relationship with nature. Regardless of regional variations, the native peoples viewed the world as a balanced system in which all creation, animate and inanimate, existed harmoniously. Thus the biological world of edible plants or fish or game remained intimately attached to a spirit world. Humanity was but one part of that system. The acquisition of food, clothing, or shelter therefore depended upon maintaining spiritual relations with the rest of creation. From this perspective, the idea of owning parcels of land, bits of creation, was unthinkable (P.N. Carroll and D.W. Noble, *The Free and the Unfree, a New History of the United States*, 27–28).

How things have changed! The big companies that now dominate America have no concern for the environment—our common heritage. All is reduced to a question of profit for a few (a concept the Native Americans would have found incomprehensible). The advent of genetically modified crops undoubtedly contains the potential for important advances, but under the present system poses a deadly threat to the future of humanity.

There was a time when films about the "Wild West" inevitably presented Native Americans as bloodthirsty savages, and the white men as the bearers of civilization, destined to take over their lands and consign them to reservations where they would learn the benefits of Christian charity. Nowadays, this is no longer considered acceptable. Native Americans are presented in a more positive light. Yet in practice, the average American knows little about their culture and way of life. Actually, the man who did more than anyone else to write about the society and civilization of these peoples was the great American anthropologist, Lewis Henry Morgan. His famous book *Ancient Society* represented a revolutionary new departure in the study of anthropology and ancient history. He gave the first scientific explanation of the gens or clan as the basic unit of human society in prehistory:

> The simplest and lowest form of the council was that of the gens. It was a democratic assembly because every adult male and female member had a voice upon all questions brought before it. It elected and deposed its sachem and chiefs, it elected Keepers of the Faith, it condoned or avenged the murder of a gentilis, and it adopted persons into the gens...
>
> All the members of an iroquois gens were personally free, and they were bound to defend each other's freedom; they were equal in privileges and in personal rights, the sachem and chiefs claiming no superiority, and they were a brotherhood bound together by ties of kin. Liberty, equality and

fraternity, though never formulated, were cardinal principles of the gens (Lewis Henry Morgan, *Ancient Society*, 85).

And again:

A powerful popular element pervaded the whole organization and influenced its action. It is seen in the right of the gentes to elect and depose their sachems and chiefs, in the right of the people to be heard in council through orators of their own selection, and in the voluntary system in the military service. In this and the next succeeding ethnical period democratic principles were the vital element of gentile society (Morgan, 144).

Morgan's work was read with great interest by Marx and Engels and played an important role in developing their ideas about ancient societies. Morgan's writings about the Iroquois and other tribes were absolutely central to Engels's book *The Origin of the Family, Private Property, and the State*—one of the seminal works of Marxism. This, in turn, was the basis of Lenin's celebrated book *The State and Revolution*, which was written in 1917 and presents the genuine Leninist model of a socialist democracy, in which the old oppressive bureaucratic state would be dissolved and replaced by a direct democracy, based on:

• Free elections with right of recall of all officials.

• No official to receive a wage higher than that of a skilled worker.

• No standing army, but the armed people.

• Gradually, all the tasks of running the state to be done by everybody in turn (when everybody is a bureaucrat, nobody is a bureaucrat).

It is quite ironic that the source of some of the most basic writings of Marxism turns out to be—the United States. It is even more ironic that the democratic constitution that Lenin and Trotsky introduced into the young Soviet Republic after November 1917 had its roots in the writings of Lewis Morgan and is, in essence, a return to the old communist order of the Native Americans, though obviously on the higher foundations made possible by modern industry, science, and technology. So, in a way, one could argue that it was Russia that imported an old American idea, and not vice-versa!

Genocide of the First Americans

It is impossible to read today the accounts of the first contacts between Europeans and Native Americans without a profound sense of sadness. In every case the newcomers were greeted with the hospitality that was a sacred obligation for the people the haughty strangers regarded as "savages." Columbus wrote: "Of anything they have, if you ask them for it, they never say no." His journal is full of examples of the generosity of the unsuspecting natives, who were about to be enslaved and exterminated as a reward. "They ought to be good servants and of good skill," Columbus concluded.

The European colonization of the Americas had a devastating effect on the lives and cultures of the Native Americans. In the 15th to 19th centuries, their populations were decimated, by the privations of displacement, by disease, and in many cases by warfare with and enslavement by European settlers. The latter liked to portray their treatment of the Native Americans as the result of an admirable civilizing and humanitarian mission (just as the imperialists of our own period describe their missions in Iraq and elsewhere). They were bringing Christianity and civilization to a bunch of ignorant savages and naked heathens. In practice, however, their motives were simple greed and insatiable lust for gold and land.

A contemporary account describes the response of the most Christian Spaniards when the Aztec emperor distributed presents of gold among them:

> The Spanish burst into smiles; their eyes shone with pleasure . . . They picked up the gold and fingered it like monkeys; they seemed to be transported by joy, as if their hearts were illumined and made new (Quoted in P.N. Carroll and D.W. Noble, 40).

The first Native American group encountered by Columbus, the 250,000 Arawaks of Haiti, were enslaved and brutally treated. By the year 1550 only 500 were still alive and the entire people was totally extinct before 1650. This set the tone for the treatment of the First Americans for the next 400 years. When the Native Americans realized they were being expropriated and robbed, they reacted with predictable violence. A long and bloody conflict was born.

Here is a typical report of a Captain John Mason, who came across a Native American fort early one morning while the inhabitants were still asleep. Having blocked the exits, he then ordered his men to set fire to the wigwams:

> The captain also said: "We must burn them," . . . (and immediately stepping into the Wigwam where he had been before,) brought out a Fire-Brand and putting it into the Matts with which they were covered, set the Wigwams on fire . . . and when it was thoroughly kindled, the Indians ran as Men most dreadfully Amazed. And indeed such a dreadful Terror did the Almighty let fall upon their Spirits, that they would fly from us and into the very Flames, where many of them perished. And when the Fort was thoroughly Fired, Command was given, that all should fall off and surround the Fort; which was readily attended by all; . . . The Fire was kindled on the North East Side to windward; which did swiftly over-run the Fort, to the extreme Amazement

of the Enemy, and great Rejoycing of ourselves. Some of them climbing to the Top of the Palisade; others of them running into the very Flames; many of them gathering to windward, lay pelting at us with their Arrows; and we repayed them with our small Shot; Others of the Stoutest issued forth as we did guess, to the Number of Forty, who perished by the Sword . . .

And thus in little more than one Hour's space was their impregnable Fort with themselves utterly destroyed, to the Number of Six or Seven Hundred, as some of themselves confessed. There were only Seven taken Captive and about Seven escaped . . .

Of the English, there were two Slain outright, and about twenty wounded (Quoted in Leo Huberman, *We the People*, 26–27).

This amounted to outright genocide. Although there were honorable exceptions, most Europeans felt free to rob and kill the "primitive" people they found in their path. Europeans also brought diseases against which the Native Americans had no immunity. Usually it was unintentional, but sometimes they intentionally spread disease among the native tribes. This is probably the earliest example of germ warfare in history

Illnesses like chicken pox and measles, though rarely a cause of death among Europeans, often proved fatal to Native Americans. More deadly diseases such as smallpox caused the most terrible devastation in Native American populations. Nobody knows the exact percentage of the total Native American population killed in this way, but it is known that waves of disease often destroyed entire villages. Some historians believe that up to 80 percent of some Indian populations may have died as a result of European-derived diseases:

Sir Jeffrey Amherst—for whom Amherst College is named—had a plan for exterminating the Indians. He was commander in chief of the British forces in America in the 1760s, while the French and Indian War was going on. With all deference to historical perspective, the viewpoint of the age, and so on, his plan makes one more or less ashamed of the human race. His idea was to kill the Indians by spreading smallpox among them—and to spread it he proposed giving them blankets inoculated with the disease. The blankets were to be given as presents, accompanied by smiles and expressions of goodwill (W.E. Woodward, *A New American History*, 106).

In other words, the advent of "civilization" (read: capitalism) was disastrous for the Native Americans. Their tribal lands were plundered. They were killed like animals or herded into so-called reservations where they suffered a slow death from hunger, disease, alcohol abuse, or simple despair. Proud and ancient cultures were annihilated as the alien culture of Christianity was foisted on a defeated people. Having robbed them of their lands, the conquerors now proceeded to rob them of their soul.

The treatment of the Native peoples, along with the enslavement of the black Africans, constitutes a blot on the history of the USA. But the Europeans have no reason to feel in any way morally superior in comparison to Americans. This bloody barbarism constitutes a definite stage in capitalism, which Marx called the primitive accumulation of capital. In every country it bore the same hallmarks. In England we had the Enclosure Acts that robbed the peasants of their land and reduced them to beggary and starvation in their own country.

Marx pointed out that capitalism first came onto the stage of history dripping blood from every pore. The genesis of the capitalist system is the systematic expropriation of the property of the peasants, the Native Americans, the Scottish clans, and the peoples of the enslaved colonies, and, in Marx's words, this history "is written in the annals of mankind in letters of blood and fire":

> The spoliation of the church's property, the fraudulent alienation of the State domains, the robbery of the common lands, the usurpation of feudal and clan property, and its transformation into modern private property under circumstances of reckless terrorism, were just so many idyllic methods of primitive accumulation. They conquered the field for capitalistic agriculture, made the soil part and parcel of capital, and created for the town industries the necessary supply of a "free" and outlawed proletariat.

Capitalism always destroys every older social system with which it enters into contact. This destructive task has always been accomplished with the utmost barbarity and ruthlessness. In Scotland we had the so-called Highland Clearances, which deprived the free peasants of the Highlands of their ancestral lands and broke up the ancient clan system. Starving men, women and children were driven off their land like beasts and the estates turned into hunting preserves for the English aristocrats. To this day the North of Scotland is a wilderness. Many of the expropriated Scottish peasants were forced to emigrate to the United States and Canada.

The difference in the United States lies in the racial component. The First Americans were seen as inferior beings, not fully human, who could be conquered, enslaved, plundered, or killed without any qualms of conscience. In the early days a bounty was paid for the scalp of every Native American man, woman, or child handed in to the authorities. The first reported case of white men scalping Native Americans took place in New Hampshire colony on February 20, 1725. In spite of the movies, the Native Americans probably learned scalping from the Europeans and not vice-versa.

"Custer's Last Stand"

In the 19th century, the westward expansion of the United States led to a colossal increase in the numbers of Native Americans expelled from vast areas of their territory. Whole peoples were forced into marginal lands in areas farther and farther west, or simply by massacring them. The mask of hypocrisy was always available to salve the conscience of the Christian businessmen and politicians involved in this plunder. Numerous treaties were entered into during this period, but later violated or simply abrogated. When the natives resisted, it was reported at the time as the "Indian Wars." In fact, these wars had an entirely one-sided character.

This portrayal of the Native Americans as "savages" was perpetrated by countless novels, stories, and above all the cinema, where the white settlers were habitually portrayed as the victims, while the "Indians" were portrayed as bloodthirsty aggressors. The "Injun fighter" was always the hero. In turn these movie images fed racist prejudice that re-emerged time and time again in the bloody history of American imperialism. After all, racism is only the distilled essence of imperialism.

Among the military engagements of the "Indian Wars" one stands out as an example not only of the bravery of the Native Americans but also of their grasp of military tactics and strategy. I refer to the famous Native American victory at the Battle of the Little Bighorn in 1876. This episode has been subjected to an incredible campaign of falsification. It has entered the annals of Western history as "Custer's Last Stand" and has acquired virtually the status of a myth. At the time the press published prints of the gallant general surrounded by his faithful troopers, valiantly defending the flag until the last man was cut down by the "murdering redskins." This myth was later popularized in various Hollywood films, depicting Custer and his men as great heroes.

The achievements of the US cinema industry are well known and justly celebrated. But the American film directors have to this day shown themselves to be incapable of producing a single honest film about the Vietnam War. Some films have appeared that are quite good, cinematographically speaking. They at least attempt to show the Vietnam War as a barbaric war—although, generally speaking, the US soldiers are presented as the main victims of this barbarity.

This is a one-sided view, to put it mildly. The people of Vietnam suffered invasion by a foreign army; were killed by the hundreds of thousands by bullets, napalm, shrapnel, and chemical weapons ("defoliants"). Yet even in supposedly antiwar films they rarely appear as real human beings—usually they appear only as "collateral damage." The Vietnamese fighters who took on the might of the US military are never presented as what they truly were—heroic resistance fighters—but rather, as a shadowy and depersonalized enemy. In place of the "murdering redskins" of the old John Wayne movies we have the Vietnamese "gooks" or the Iraqi "terrorists." We really have not advanced very far!

The truth about the Battle of the Little Bighorn was very different from the fictional accounts. Recent research of the battlefield has finally nailed the lie. There was no "Custer's Last Stand." The US Cavalry was outmaneuvered and outfought by the Native American warriors, and cut down as they fled in panic. But this could not be admitted! How could the American public be informed that supposedly inferior "savages" had a better grasp of military science than an American general? How could they fight better than the crack troops of the Seventh Cavalry? In this way the lying propaganda of Custer's Last Stand was born. In one form or another it has been with us ever since.

The Native American victory at the Little Big Horn had to be avenged and was avenged with interest in the massacre at Wounded Knee in 1890. On January 31, 1876, the United States government ordered all remaining Native Americans to move into reservations or reserves. This was the end of a civilization. By the stroke of a bureaucrat's pen, the astonishing Prairie Culture that developed around the use of the horse for hunting, travel, and trading was crushed underfoot.

Nowadays many people in the USA realize that the image of the Native Americans as primitive savages is a travesty and a falsification of history. These peoples were not savages, but nations with a culture and a complex civilization from which we can learn many things. There is a natural desire to make amends. Naturally, all the rights of the Native Americans must be upheld. But the clock cannot be put back 150 years. When a way of life and a culture has passed into history it can no more be revived than a dead person can be brought back to life. We must march onwards to a higher stage of human civilization, while preserving and absorbing all that is valuable from the past.

It is very sad that the good name of America has been besmirched for so long by the taint of racism. After all, American history is the history of a gigantic melting pot that has absorbed people from many different nations, religions, and cultures. It is this rich ethnic mix in part that makes the American character so vital, energetic, and outgoing. Under socialism, the highest form of human civilization and culture, this stain will be erased once and for all, and the people of every ethnic background will have the possibility of a free development in conditions of complete liberty, equality and fraternity.

Forgotten Aspects of American History

In the 17th century, the Pilgrims began the task of taming the great American wilderness, displaying indomitable courage in the most difficult conditions. Who were they? They were political refugees fleeing from an oppressive regime in Britain. This regime was the result of the counterrevolution that took place after the death of Oliver Cromwell, when the English bourgeoisie compromised with reaction and invited Charles II back from France.

We must remember that at that time politics and religion were inextricably linked. Each different Church or sect represented not only differing interpretations of the Gospels, but a definite strand of political opinion, and, in the last analysis, the standpoint of a definite class or subclass in society. Thus, the Catholics represented open feudal reaction, and the Episcopalians were a disguised version of the same. The Presbyterians represented the wealthy merchants of the City of London, inclined to compromise with the monarchy. The Independents, typified by Cromwell, represented the more radical wing of the petty bourgeoisie, and so on.

On the extreme left wing there was a mass of sects, ranging from revolutionary democrats to communists: Fifth Monarchy men, Ranters, Seekers, Anabaptists, Quakers, and others were based in the lower levels of the petty bourgeoisie, the artisans and semi-proletarians, the fishwives and apprentices—in short, the masses. The Levellers and particularly the Diggers openly questioned the right to hold private property even at this time. In all these groups we see a fierce attachment to democracy, a hatred for the rich and powerful (whom they regarded as the agents of Satan and the "sons of Belial"), and an equally fierce attachment to equality. This was the spirit that inspired the English Revolution of the 17th century.

The revolutionary masses believed that they would establish the kingdom of God on this earth. We now know that this was an illusion. The level of historical development at that time was not ripe for the establishment of a classless society. The real function of the English (and later the American) Civil War was to clear the decks for the development of capitalism. But this would never have been possible without the active involvement of the masses, who were inspired by a very different vision.

Having come to power by basing himself on the revolutionary semi-proletarian masses, Cromwell brutally suppressed the left wing, and thus prepared the way for the return of the hated monarchy and its attendant bishops. The remnants of the Puritan left wing found themselves subjected to civil and religious persecution. That is why the "Pilgrim Fathers" (as they came to be called) went to America to found communities based not only on religious freedom but also on principles of strict equality and democracy.

The one hundred and two souls who set sail on the Mayflower were not men and women of property, but poor men and women from the lower classes of English society: small farmers, manual workers, artisans, weavers, carpenters, blacksmiths, and the like. Only a few were schoolteachers. As members of a dissident religious sect (the Brownites or Separatists), they were oppressed by poverty and the extreme difficulty in making a living in Restoration England. Politically, they were what we would call nowadays left-wing revolutionaries. Many of them emigrated to Holland, the only country in Europe that upheld religious toleration. But some of the more daring decided to make the long and dangerous crossing of the Atlantic in search of social, political, and religious freedom.

As Alexis de Tocqueville points out:

> Puritanism was not merely a religious doctrine, but it corresponded in many points with the most absolute democratic and republican theories (A. de Tocqueville, *Democracy in America*, 35).

But the Separatists were a more radical tendency than the run-of-the-mill Puritans. They advocated reform not only in religious but also in secular matters. This was enough for the authorities to regard them as dangerous subversives, much as the US authorities regard Marxists today. Worse still, they believed in holding property in common and sharing the products of labor. *In short, the Pilgrims were communists.*

The colony founded by these pioneers was based on a communal system. Whatever was produced was to go into a common fund and everyone was to be fed and clothed out of it. In other words, they based themselves on the communist principle: "from each according to his or her ability, to each according to his or her need." For the first seven years there was to be no private property in land. In the end it broke down, of course. It is impossible to construct a communist system on the basis of poverty and a low level of development of the productive forces. By 1623 the social differentiation was already so pronounced, and the objections to the communal system so general, that Governor Bradford abolished it and gave every family a plot of land.

However, even after that the Pilgrims organized their communities on extremely democratic and equalitarian lines:

> In Connecticut the electoral body consisted, from its origin, of the whole number of citizens; and this is readily to be understood, when we recollect that this people enjoyed an almost perfect equality of fortune, and a still

greater uniformity of opinions. In Connecticut, at this period, all the executive functionaries were elected, including the Governor of the State. The citizens above the age of sixteen were obliged to bear arms; they formed a national militia, which appointed its own officers, and was to hold itself at all times in readiness to march for the defense of the country (de Tocqueville, 37–38).

This model of popular democracy is not very different to the one implemented by the revolutionary people of Paris in the Commune of 1871, which in turn gave Marx the idea of what a workers' democracy (the "dictatorship of the proletariat") would look like. It was the model that Lenin cited in his book *The State and Revolution*, which formed the basis of the original soviet democracy of 1917 in Russia, before it was overthrown by the Stalinist political counter-revolution. But this historical parallel, for some reason, has never occurred to the official historians of the USA! According to these ladies and gentlemen the Pilgrims were only religious people, seeking the freedom to worship their God in their own way. Of course, this is partly true, but it does not convey the whole truth. These people were courageous revolutionaries fleeing from religious *and political* persecution in the Old World. They were very advanced in many ways. For example, they introduced compulsory public education, which they naturally justified in religious terms:

> It being one chief project of the old deluder Satan to keep men from the knowledge of the Scriptures . . . by persuading from the use of tongues, that learning may not be buried in the grave of our fathers, in the church and commonwealth, the Lord assisting our endeavors . . .

And so on.

If we look at the substance and not the religious form, this was an extremely advanced and enlightened reform. Schools were established in every village and town and the inhabitants were obliged to support them under pain of heavy fines. The municipal authorities were bound to enforce attendance at school and to impose fines on parents who failed to do so. It was at least two centuries before similar laws were passed in Europe.

These people practiced their own version of republican democracy at a time—let us not forget—when America was still under British rule and therefore formally a monarchy. They established a kind of regime of double power in which a republic and a citizen's democracy, complete with a people's militia, the election of all officials, and a general assembly of all the people, existed in every town and village. And this was at a time when absolute monarchies ruled the roost in all Europe and trampled the people's rights in the dust.

Class Struggle and Slavery

The class struggle existed from the beginning on American soil. The appearance of rich and poor had political consequences. The arrival of large numbers of poor people and indentured servants from England accentuated the differences. The existing landowners intended to become wealthy large landowners with estates worked by bonded labor. But the poor immigrants had other ideas and strove to get small plots of land to work for themselves. John Winthrop of Massachusetts expressed the attitude of the better-off colonists towards the newly arrived immigrants. He wrote of "the unwarrantableness . . . of referring matters of council or juricature to the body of the people, *quia* the best part is always the least, and of that the best part is always the lesser." Later he said that he favored a "mixt aristocracy."

Winthrop tried to restrict the number of voters. He had a law passed that limited the suffrage to church members. Then church membership was made exclusive. Political radicals could be expelled from the church and thus stripped of their political rights. Narrowness and intolerance began to take a hold. Under the guise of religious purity and Puritan rigor, there was an uninterrupted struggle going on between rich and poor, privileged and unprivileged.

As a matter of fact, the wages of English laborers were usually no more than what a slave owner paid for the food, lodging, and clothes of a slave. The generally held view of that time was that wages should be no more than what was necessary to keep the workers alive and able to reproduce. The subsistence-level theory of wages already existed in practice long before it acquired a theoretical expression in the writings of the classical economists at the start of the 19th century. This held that it was absolutely necessary to keep the working class in a state of abject poverty. The problem was that there was nothing to prevent a free worker from setting out for the vast western frontier, which was not far away, and establishing himself as a small farmer.

The British Virginia Colony was based on the cultivation of tobacco and the ownership of slaves. Plantation agriculture depended on slavery and a variant of it: the system of indentured labor. An indentured servant was bound to serve for a specified number of years. Some were convicts. They were sent to the Colonies as a kinder alternative to the punishments meted out by English law at a time when the theft of one shilling was punishable by death and a man could be hanged for pulling down a fence or poaching or stealing a sheep. However, as there were few other choices available for a poor laborer, so most indentured servants renewed their contracts for as long as they could.

This led to the creation of the plantation owners' greatest fear: a permanent class of poor, discontented, and armed laborers. Their fears were realized with Bacon's Rebellion, a class revolt led by Nathaniel Bacon that succeeded in burning Jamestown to the ground in 1676. After this experience plantation owners sought to replace white indentured laborers with what they hoped would be a less rebellious form of labor—African slaves.

The introduction of slaves from Africa was the answer of the plantation owners to the annoying tendency of the free workers' efforts to improve their lot and fight against exploitation. Even before 1700 most of the slaves were in the Southern Colonies. But New England had its fair share. In Rhode Island in 1756 there were 35,939 whites and 5,697 black Africans. Most of the slaves in the colonies north of Virginia were house servants, but not all. One man in Philadelphia ran his iron foundry with thirty slaves. During the 18th century so active was the slave trade with the New England Colonies that the price of newly landed slaves fell to thirty pounds.

The number of black slaves increased enormously in South Carolina after the introduction of rice growing in 1696. From 1700 on the number of blacks always outnumbered the white population. On the eve of the American Revolution the proportion was two to one. The slave owners lived in terror of a slave uprising. The punishments for black slaves were barbaric in the extreme. They were often burned alive for offenses for which whites were hanged. In 1739 there was a slave insurrection. It was brutally put down but not before 21 whites and 44 slaves were killed. As a result the assembly approved a draconic slave code. It became a penal offense to teach a slave to read and write. Slaves were not allowed to hold meetings, even church services, unless a white person was present. At the same time some concessions were made: the hours of work should not exceed fifteen, and Sunday should be a holiday.

The slave trade was an important and very profitable industry. The prosperity of towns like Liverpool was based upon it. In 1771 there were 107 slave ships from Liverpool on the African coast, and a further 60 or 70 from America. They were generously financed by wealthy corporations in the City of London and the British government actively supported and aided the slavers. Considerable fortunes were made from the slave trade, including that of the family of William Gladstone, the future leader of the British Liberal Party.

In the South the whole socioeconomic system was based on slavery. The luxurious lifestyle of the landowners was entirely based on the labor of the slaves. George Washington, a big landowner, had numerous indentured servants. A letter to his agent in Baltimore dated 1774 states that four men convicts and a man and his wife had been purchased on his account for the sum of 110 pounds sterling. The four men had to serve for three years and the married couple four years. This works out at five and a half pounds per year for each one. Even Thomas Jefferson, the author of the Declaration of Independence, who wrote that "all men are created equal," owned more than 200 black slaves, whom he never freed, though others, including Washington, did.

The continued existence of slavery increasingly acted as a drag on the progress of America even after it had won its independence. Marx explained that no people can be free if it keeps another people in chains. Slavery was a heavy burden on the American people. It exercised a constant downward pressure on the wages of free labor and a permanent threat to democratic rights. Its existence tended to degrade the status of all manual labor. Any free worker was just one step above the bonded servant or slave. Even the American Revolution did not abolish this cancer. For that, a second American Revolution would be necessary.

CHAPTER II

THE AMERICAN REVOLUTION

[W]hat country can preserve its liberties, if its rulers are not warned from time to time that [the] people preserve the spirit of resistance? Let them take arms. The tree of liberty must be refreshed from time to time, with the blood of patriots and tyrants.—Thomas Jefferson, Letter to Col. William S. Smith, 1787

Nowadays, the public in the USA is taught to fear and hate revolutions. Like communism, they are regarded as un-American, something alien and a threat from without. In actual fact, from its very beginnings America has always been nourished by foreign revolutions, with waves of immigrants fleeing political repression in search of a better life. However, the above quotations show clearly that revolution is an idea that is far from foreign to the native soil of the USA, which owes its very existence to a revolution. When the American colonists raised the flag of revolt against the English Crown, this was a very revolutionary act. It was this that served as the source of inspiration for the French Revolution that broke out just over a decade later. Thus, the flame of revolution in Europe was first kindled in America.

The young American bourgeoisie was rankling under the onerous rule of a foreign power based some thousands of miles away, which could introduce painful taxes, limits on trading, and other burdens that hampered the free development of the American bourgeoisie. These fetters had to be broken and they were broken by revolutionary means. The imposition of the Stamp Act in 1765 was the event that set the whole process in motion. But it was only the accident through which necessity revealed itself, as Hegel would have said. In fact there were many other Acts that stoked the fires of resentment: the Navigation Acts, which regulated and restricted American commerce, the prohibition of settlement beyond the Appalachian Mountains, and the Tea Act, designed to prevent the East India Company from going bankrupt.

A revolution necessarily means the eruption of the masses onto the arena of politics and can only succeed in its objectives to the degree that it involves the mass of "ordinary people" in activity. The American Revolution was no exception to this rule. In order to succeed, the bourgeois leaders must arouse the masses and lean on them to strike blows against the enemy. Although the official histories emphasize (and overemphasize) the role of men like George Washington, what really guaranteed the success of the revolution was the active involvement of the masses—the artisans, carpenters, apprentices, the small farmers and trappers, and the elements of the lower middle class, lawyers and journalists inspired with revolutionary ideas, who spurred them on to action.

The bad conditions and absence of rights produced a ferment of discontent in the lower orders of society. So when the merchants of the colonies rebelled against the impositions of the British administrations that hampered trade and made their life impossible, the lower classes joined in with gusto. Trotsky explains that poverty alone is not enough to make a revolution. If that were the case, the masses would always be in revolt. But it is not the case. The "mob" in America already existed before 1776, but was capable of doing nothing more than to cause occasional disturbances. Now things were different. The poor and dispossessed now had a focal point for their discontent, a banner and a rallying cry, even if it was not exactly their own.

A decisive role was played by revolutionary agitators like Samuel Adams of Boston, the most outstanding figure of the American Revolution. His energetic agitation for the revolutionary cause struck a responsive note among the masses. He was the most able of the class of agitators but there were many unsung heroes like him whose names have not come down to us. The immediate target of the agitation was the hated Stamp Act which required all legal documents, licenses, commercial contracts, newspapers, pamphlets, and playing cards to carry a tax stamp. Stamp distributors were hanged in effigy and their houses torn down. Packages of stamps were burned in bonfires to wild cheering and the beating of drums.

The class basis of the American Revolution was well understood by the British colonialists. General Thomas Gage, who was head of the British troops in America, wrote in worried tones to the King's Secretary of State on December 21, 1765:

The Plan of the People of Property has been to raise the lower Classes to prevent the execution of the Law . . . with the view to terrify and frighten the people of England into a Repeal of the Act. And the Merchants, having Countermanded the Goods they had written for unless it was repealed, they make no Doubt that many Trading Towns and principal Merchants in London will assist them to accomplish their Ends.

The Lawyers are the Source from whence the Clamors have flowed in every Province. In this Province, nothing Publick is transacted without them, and it is to be wished that even the Bench was free from blame. The whole body of Merchants in general, Assembly Men, Magistrates, etc., have been united in this Plan of Riots, and without the influence and Instigation of these the inferior People would have been very quiet. Very great Pains were taken to rouse them before they stirred. The Sailors are the only People who may be properly Stiled Mob, are entirely at the Command of the Merchants who employ them.

These lines undoubtedly contain an error. It is always a characteristic of the police (or military) mentality that it attributes strikes, disturbances, and revolutions to the work of "agitators" who are so inconsiderate as to stir up the masses. The latter would otherwise, according to this view, continue meekly to submit to the yoke. Agitators there were, of course, and very talented ones, such as Sam Adams. But to imagine that they could have such a dramatic effect on the masses, unless the latter were already prepared to hear their revolutionary message, is a self-evident stupidity. The relatively small number of revolutionary agitators, organized in illegal societies like The Sons of Liberty, only succeeded because the people were already preparing to move, motivated by their own experience.

Role of the Masses

If ye love wealth greater than liberty, the tranquillity of servitude greater than the animating contest for freedom, go home from us in peace. We seek not your counsel, nor your arms. Crouch down and lick the hand that feeds you; May your chains set lightly upon you, and may posterity forget that ye were our countrymen. —Samuel Adams

The official histories of the Revolution, as always, play down the role of the masses and concentrate on the upper strata—the wealthy Boston merchants and landowners like Washington, who were pursuing their own interests, as General Gage understood quite well. But in order to succeed in their struggle ~lonial administration, they were compelled to rely on the masses, e fighting. It was the workmen in the towns who organized in)erty, wrecked the houses of the hated stamp agents, and threw their furniture onto the streets and burned them. It was they who tarred and feathered informers. It was they who translated the speeches of the leaders into action. Later on it was the small farmers and trappers who played the decisive role in fighting against the English army of occupation.

The fact is that the American Revolution would never have succeeded unless the masses had intervened in a decisive way. It is a matter of record that the wealthy American merchants who had set the ball rolling with their clash with the City of London on questions of trade and taxation soon recoiled from the Revolution when they saw that the poor people were getting active and taking matters into their own hands. The aims of the wealthy merchants and landowners, however, were narrow and egotistical. They aimed to destroy the rule of the British Crown in order to replace it with their own rule. This was not a very inspiring prospect, and hardly a program to set the masses on fire. More idealistic slogans were necessary. Cromwell promised the masses in England the installation of the reign of God on earth, no less, while Robespierre proclaimed the rule of Reason and Liberty, Equality, Fraternity. The American Revolution also required a banner to rally around and a program they believed in.

All this is not to say that the men who led the American Revolution did not believe what they preached. They sincerely believed that they were fighting for the sacred principles of Liberty set forth so movingly in the Declaration of Independence. A man like Thomas Jefferson, the most outstanding of the well-known leaders of the Revolution, was a product of the Age of Enlightenment, well schooled in the ideas of Locke, Hobbes, Newton, and Bacon. For such a man, the fact that the American colonies were ruled by a despotic foreign power must have embittered the very depths of his being.

However, while the speeches were being made on the top, the mainspring of the revolt came from the bottom. Before the revolution the workers—the "men of no property"—were generally deprived of political rights. Power was in the hands of wealthy merchants and magistrates who could do pretty much anything they liked. The rate of wages was decided usually by an association of owners or masters in the same trade. These were almost always on a subsistence level. The workers had no say in the matter. Associations of workers were forbidden by law. Those who owned no land had no right to vote in any of the colonies. James Truslow Adams wrote:

> It was only as the Revolution approached that these unfranchised elements . . . wrested political control of the colonial government from the class of propertied freemen, and then largely by illegal, violent, and terroristic methods.

The merchants were terrified that the masses would "go too far" and therefore attempted to reach a compromise with the enemy. In the moment of truth the rich American "patriots" had much more in common with their class brothers in England than with the working class and poor farmers of their own country. Many wealthy citizens deplored the actions of the "mob." Such a man was Henry Laurens, a wealthy planter and merchant of South Carolina. For this "leader of public opinion," things were getting out of hand. He asked "what would become of our estates without law, particularly ours who depend on commerce?"

While the respectable merchants fretted and dithered, the masses took decisive action from below. Hitherto the bourgeois had restricted themselves to a *voluntary* boycott of British goods. But the "Boston Tea Party," when a group of colonists, thinly disguised as Mohawks, resorted to direct action, dumping British tea chests into the sea, threw down a bold challenge to the British. British public opinion was outraged. London reacted by attempting to starve Boston into submission through the imposition of a naval blockade that closed the port. But this only radicalized the whole situation. Once a revolution has aroused the masses, they are not easily intimidated even by the greatest power on earth.

Even in the moment of its birth, America was faced with the crying contradiction between rich and poor—*that is, with the class question*. From the very beginning there has been a contradiction between the theory and practice of American democracy, an immense gulf between words and deeds. While the people were fighting for the Rights of Man, the merchants and landowners of America were really only concerned with the rights of the rich. Gouverneur Morris expressed the feelings of the rich when he wrote:

> ... These sheep, simple as they are, cannot be gulled as heretofore. In short, there is no ruling them ... the heads of mobility [the mob] grow dangerous to the gentry and how to keep them down is the question.

It has been *the question* for the American ruling class ever since. As early as 1772—before the outbreak of hostilities with England—Sam Adams wrote in *The Boston Gazette*:

> Is it not High Time for the People of this Country, explicitly to declare whether they will be Freemen or Slaves ... Let us ... calmly look around us to consider what is best to be done ... Let it be the topic of conversation in every social Club. Let every Town assemble. Let Associations and Combinations be everywhere set up to consult and recover our just Rights.

What is this but a call for the setting up of what the Russians were later to call *soviets* (which in the Russian language signifies "committee" or "council")? The American revolutionaries set up something that approximates to soviets—that is, revolutionary committees—over one hundred years before the Russian workers thought of it. They established their Liberty clubs and Committees of Correspondence, which kept the revolutionary fighting groups in contact with one another.

The town laborers detested the whole colonial system and looked forward eagerly for its destruction. They could hardly be worse off! One of the most famous of the revolutionary secret societies was The Sons of Liberty. To disguise their identity they blackened their faces and dressed up as Indians or used other disguises. They used passwords and secret signs. Their favorite weapon was tar and feathers. They also tore down houses. Unpopular customs officers and Tories (that is, supporters of British rule) would end up tarred and feathered or have their house demolished, or both.

The activities of The Sons of Liberty and other similar groups gradually became bolder, to the point where armed clashes with the redcoats became inevitable. On March 5, 1770, a clash between a mob and British soldiers led to the "Boston Massacre" when the redcoats panicked and fired into the crowd, killing four people. The murderers were let off with minor punishments. This was the spark that lit the fuse. Sam Adams worked incessantly, day and night, writing letters to far-flung settlements denouncing these deeds. Paul Revere—a Boston engraver and a member of The Sons of Liberty—produced an engraving of the massacre that was distributed far and wide.

The irony was that the masses who led the revolt were fighting for demands that would benefit merchants like Laurens, not themselves. These men of no property would never have to put a Stamp Act tax-stamp on a document in their lives. Not for the first or the last time, the masses were fighting and risking their lives to fight someone else's battle. As W.E. Woodward correctly points out:

> The discontent of the workingman was very real, and very bitter, though it had long been inarticulate. This dissatisfaction had nothing to do with British rule, though the illiterate mob was made to believe that Britain was the cause. The protest of the working classes was, in reality, an unconscious revolt against their position in the colonial world.
>
> The chief defect of colonial civilization—in respect to the common man—was not overregulation; the free white men of the time had more personal liberty than the common people in England. Its deficiency lay rather in underregulation, in a general neglect of all social problems. The higher

classes had no time to give to the consideration of such matters. Their entire attention was fixed on land and money. They never made any serious attempt to better working conditions, or to establish minimum wages or hours of labor, or to consider the poor as anything else than servile dependents on the rich (Woodward, 131).

The Declaration of Independence

In 1774 the delegates for the Continental Congress assembled in Philadelphia. Hostilities had already broken out and the delegates, although all from the wealthier classes of society, were under pressure to adopt a more radical stand. *Originally the majority of the upper class Americans did not want independence.* But the mood of the masses made all thought of compromise impossible. The situation was explosive and this favored the most radical elements in Congress. As a result, on July 4, 1776, the Thirteen United States of America declared their independence from Great Britain.

The task of drafting the declaration was given to a committee composed of John Adams (cousin of Samuel Adams and future president), Benjamin Franklin, Thomas Jefferson, Robert R. Livingston, and Roger Sherman. Thomas Jefferson, a 33-year-old Virginian landowner and left-winger, was charged by the committee to write the declaration. He wrote one of the most inspiring revolutionary documents in history.

Here was an act of tremendous boldness and one that required great courage. The revolutionaries had thrown down the gauntlet to the most powerful imperial state in the world. Their lives were now forfeit and could only be saved by outright victory and they knew it. There could now be no turning back, as Benjamin Franklin pointed out when he uttered the famous words, "We must hang together, or assuredly we shall all hang separately." Later, when Jefferson was the American ambassador in France, he wrote:

> If our country, when pressed with wrongs at the point of the bayonet, had been governed by its heads instead of its hearts, where should we have been now? Hanging on a gallows as high as Haman's. You began to calculate and to compare wealth and numbers: we threw up a few pulsations of our warmest blood: we supplied enthusiasm against wealth and numbers: we put our existence to the hazard, when the hazard seemed against us, and we saved our country.

The Declaration of Independence, with its ringing endorsement of the idea of liberty and equality for all, was a clarion call to the downtrodden and oppressed everywhere. It was as revolutionary in 1776 as *The Communist Manifesto* would be in 1848.

This document seems the more remarkable because of the state of the world in which it was written. In 1776 there were kings on the throne of England, France, Austria, and most of the other great powers of Europe. Russia was ruled by a tsar (or tsarina), the Ottoman Empire by the sultan, and China by its imperial dynasty. Democracy was therefore a novel and highly revolutionary doctrine.

This epoch-making document still has the power to inspire today. In it the idea of liberty is magnificently expressed. Life, liberty, and the pursuit of happiness are proclaimed as *inalienable rights*. But no citizen of Russia, China, or the Ottoman Empire could say the same thing. Nor could the citizens of France, Austria, or Prussia; and even England was a monarchy ruled, in practice, by a corrupt and reactionary oligarchy of wealthy landowners. The Declaration shook the world. When it was announced, it caused a tremendous stir in every American city. It was read aloud to exited groups of citizens on the streets of Philadelphia. Here was something really worth fighting and dying for! "And for the support of this Declaration," Jefferson concluded, "we mutually pledge to each other our Lives, our Fortunes, and our sacred Honor."

The document would doubtless have been even more radical had it not been for the fact that it had to be subscribed by all thirteen colonies, including the slaveholding colonies from the South. In fact, the most obvious and glaring weakness of the document is that it does not deal with the issue of slavery at all. There was a considerable slave population—539,000, or one-fifth of the total population of the colonies. It seems that Jefferson wanted to include a reference to slavery and made several proposals for its abolition, but all were rejected. Finally, following the protests of the slaveholding states, all mention of the institution of slavery was omitted from the final draft. Jefferson began to temporize on the issue, postponing it to some unspecified future date. In this way, the seeds were laid for a bloody Civil War and a second American Revolution.

On the thorny question of religion, however, Jefferson was implacable. He insisted that, though the citizen had the right to hold any belief he or she chose, governments did not have the right to favor any faith. Therefore the state and religion must be radically separated. At the time when this democratic principle was proclaimed, the states had their own laws on religion, mostly of a retrograde character. Some states prohibited Roman Catholicism. In Jefferson's own state, Virginia, heresy was a capital offense. The radical separation of the state and religion is a basic democratic principle, but it is now under attack from the so-called religious right. These people wish to introduce religion into the schools and interfere with the curriculum to teach the Book of Genesis instead of the scientific theory of evolution. These elements wish to throw America back to the Dark Ages, to the age of superstition and the Salem witch trials, and to ditch an essential feature of the Declaration of Independence.

Today the principles of the Declaration of Independence are the heritage of every American citizen. All Americans believe in these principles—at least, they would like to believe in them. Yet, if we are to be honest, there are contradictions in the very text of the Declaration and the American Constitution itself. When it is said that all men are created equal, this is clearly not in accordance with the facts. Although we may come into this world in a more or less equal state as human beings, there is inequality from the very start. The world is divided into rich and poor, and the former rule over the latter, exploit and oppress them. This was already the case when Thomas Jefferson wrote the Declaration of Independence, and it is a million times truer today.

In the 18th century, it was still possible to dream of a democratic republic comprised of small farmers (this was Jefferson's ideal), in which the differences between rich and poor would be reduced to a minimum. Over 200 years since the American Revolution, the USA is entirely dominated by a handful of giant corporations that act effectively as a law unto themselves, much as the old aristocracies of 18th century Europe did. Although theoretically the U.S. is a democracy and a republic, in fact all the important decisions are taken by small groups of unelected persons. Moreover, the power of the president, and the clique that surrounds him, is colossal and tends to constantly encroach on the rights of the citizens, the law, and the Constitution itself.

For the wealthy merchants in Congress, freedom meant first and foremost freedom of trade and free enterprise. But free enterprise, as Marx explains, always begets monopoly, and today, the USA is more monopolized than any other country on earth. In place of Jefferson's democracy of small farmers we have the dictatorship of big business. The roots of this contradiction can already be found in the 18th century, as we shall show.

First Shots of the Revolution

The revolutionary agitation gathered strength continually, impelled by the movement from below. There were attempts at compromise but they all broke down. It is not a question of the incompetence of Lord North or the madness of George III, as some historians have tried to imply. Once the contradictions in society have reached a critical point, nothing can prevent an explosion. It is not a question then of this or that action by this or that government minister but of profound forces that, having matured over a long period, must break out onto the surface. Actually, the intention of the leaders was not to win independence from London but to reach a compromise that would lead to the abolition of the Stamp Act and other restrictive measures. When the First Continental Congress met it was overwhelmingly composed of wealthy landowners and merchants. The men of no property—the workers, artisans, and dirt farmers—were conspicuous by their absence. The outlook of the majority was conservative:

> The spirit of colonial independence had not yet sunk deep into their convictions. Independence was too great a leap to take at once; they were less radical in temperament than the people who had sent them there. Why? Because all of them—or nearly all—represented some kind of vested interest and they moved with the customary caution of men of property. They regarded the Congress as a meeting of protest rather than of rebellion (Woodward, 145).

We find a similar situation at the beginning of the French Revolution and the English Revolution. These were objectively bourgeois revolutions, but in practice the bourgeois elements that stood at the head of the movement in the initial stages were striving for a compromise with the old order. In every case the Revolution only succeeded to the degree that the leadership was taken out of the hands of the bourgeoisie and passed to the masses of proletarians, semi-proletarians, and plebeians. If the bourgeois elements had retained control, it would have led to defeat. But that was not to be the case.

Events on the ground soon destroyed all attempts at compromise at the top. On April 18, 1775, events were brought to a head by the attempt of the British army to arrest two revolutionary leaders—John Hancock and Sam Adams. Warned in time by Paul Revere, who rode out of Boston ahead of the troops, the pair escaped. Revere also warned the local militia commander at Lexington that they were in danger of losing their powder. The British, under the command of Major Pitcairn, arrived at Lexington to be confronted by some fifty armed Minutemen of the Massachusetts militia on the village green. When ordered to disperse, they stood their ground. In the ensuing fire fight, eight militiamen were killed. The first shots of the American Revolution had been fired.

The British may have won the first round but it was a pyrrhic victory. On the way back, the redcoats found themselves under fire from an invisible enemy. Farmers came straight from the fields, their clothes still caked in mud, and hid behind trees as they shot down one British soldier after another. By the end of the day, the militia had lost 93 men and the redcoats 293. Once the revolution began it attracted all the slumbering forces of revolt that had lain dormant in the entrails of society. There were the backwoodsmen, for instance. They were not concerned with things like the Stamp Act but rather with the issue of land. *For such men as these, revolution was not just to kick out the British but also to break the power of the land companies—most of which were owned by Americans.* These were the men who formed the most combative sections of the revolutionary militia—the sharpshooters whose guerrilla tactics drove the redcoats to desperation, attacking without warning and then disappearing back into the impenetrable forest.

Despite everything, the leaders continued to resist the demand for independence. Although the colonies had been advised to form temporary governments, Congress insisted that these provisional governments were to "continue only during the present unhappy and unnatural conflict" (See Woodward, 150).

There were many traitors who did not want the revolution to succeed. Benedict Arnold was not an isolated case. Even those in Congress who reluctantly accepted the need to fight (when the British left them with no alternative) were more afraid of the masses than the British redcoats. In their heart of hearts many of them desired some kind of deal. In fact, most of the American aristocracy were pro-British Tories. The strength of a revolution lies in the energy, the conviction, and the active participation of the masses. The period of revolutionary ascent always corresponds to the period of greatest activity of the masses. That is why a revolution is democratic by its very nature. The same is true of any strike. A strike will succeed to the degree that the rank-and-file workers take the running of the strike into their own hands. Bureaucratic control is the kiss of death.

The psychology of the American elite was brilliantly conveyed by Gore Vidal in his novel about the American Revolution, *Burr*:

> "I hate the enemies of England." There was real passion in her voice. "I hate what your Virginia dolt is doing to our world."
> I assured her that it would still be *our* world when the war ended; but without the inconvenience of paying taxes to England. She would not believe me.
> "It will not be ours but theirs, those wild men from the woods, from the water frontage, from the worst stews of the towns. They'll take *everything*" (Gore Vidal, *Burr*, 135).

These lines perfectly express the mentality of the wealthy Americans who were terrified by the forces unleashed by the Revolution. The men of property—even those who hated the English—were afraid that by rousing the mass of poor and dispossessed Americans to fight the English, they would put in danger the sacred rights of private property. The American ruling class in its heart has always feared democracy and done its best to curtail democratic rights because they fear that a real "government of the people, by the people, and for the people" would lead to the overthrow of the dictatorship of money. All their actions have been governed by this fear—from 1776 right up to the present day.

Expropriation of Property

The ideals expressed in the Declaration of Independence were extremely revolutionary for their day: "We hold these truths to be self-evident: *that all men are created equal*." This proclamation of equality was like a revolutionary manifesto. In earlier documents the "inalienable rights" of man were usually stated to be "life, liberty, and *property*." The last point was of particular interest to the wealthy merchants and landlords who now stood at the head of the Republic. However, Thomas Jefferson substituted for this the phrase, "life, liberty, *and the pursuit of happiness*," leaving out any reference to property.

This was clearly a significant change that represented the pressure of the lower classes. In fact, the revolutionary government took measures that violated the sacred rights of property when it confiscated the estates of the pro-English landowners—the Tories. The estates were then broken up and sold to small farmers. In the process many of the big estates were broken up and something like an agrarian reform was carried out. This, along with independence, was one of the main gains of the Revolution. W.E. Woodward writes:

> The seizable property of the Tories, or loyalists, must have been about one-third of the total property value of the colonies. This is merely an estimate, and it is probably too low. Nearly all Tory property was confiscated, and the Tories were treated with the utmost rigor. Washington called them "abominable pests of society," and declared they should be treated as traitors. Their confiscated property was usually sold at auction, and it seldom brought more than a small fraction of its current value. The proceeds went into the state treasuries (Woodward, 166).

The amounts of land confiscated by the revolutionaries were considerable. The Fairfax estate in Virginia covered six million acres. The Phillipse estate in New York extended for 300 square miles. Sir William Pepperell could ride for 30 miles along the coast of Maine without ever leaving his own land. Yet despite the demand from Britain that the loyalists should be given compensation, not a single cent was ever paid to them:

> Then came the question of compensation to the loyalists whose property was confiscated during the war. The American commissioners declared that the loyalists' property had been confiscated by the various states, and that Congress had no power to compel the states to make restitution. As a

compromise the Americans agreed to include in the treaty a clause which would "recommend" the states to compensate the Tories. It was also agreed that private debts owed to British creditors were still valid. The compensation clause was futile; none of the states paid any attention to it (Woodward, 211–12).

The same point is made by other authors:

Loyalists were tarred and feathered, ridden on rails, flogged, even executed. The term "lynch law" probably originated from the proceedings of one Charles Lynch, a justice of the peace in Virginia, who achieved a certain notoriety for his treatment of Tories.

In addition to the brutal treatment they received, Tories had their property snatched from them by the newly formed revolutionary governments. Many Tories were forced to seek shelter behind British lines. These actions reflected not only a tradition of social antagonism but also a strong desire among revolutionaries to achieve a united front. By the war's end, nearly one hundred thousand colonial inhabitants had gone into exile in Canada and England. Their banishment brought profound psychological alienation—"a dismal gloom," reported one unhappy exile from London (Carroll and Noble, 117)

George Washington Restores 'Order'

The main concern of Congress was to keep control of the movement and limit its scope. On June 15, 1775, three days before the Battle of Bunker Hill, the Continental Congress assumed control of the militia that was besieging Boston as well as all the other men under arms in the colonies. Colonel George Washington, a rich landowner, was promoted to the rank of general and made commander in chief. This choice was no accident. The gentlemen in Congress needed an aristocrat as a guarantee against the "mob" in Boston. Discipline was to be restored. Order was to prevail. The wealthy property owners in Congress were more frightened by their own supporters than of the British army.

Washington must have been shocked at what he saw in camp. As befits a revolutionary army, there was an egalitarian spirit and a marked lack of rank. Ordinary soldiers spoke to their officers on familiar terms. They did not bother to shave and talked in the ranks. Men could come and go as they pleased. Washington soon sorted that out. He introduced courts martial. Lieutenant Whitney was convicted of "infamous conduct in degrading himself by voluntarily doing the work of an orderly sergeant."

Did these methods give better results? Actually, they did not. The men who Washington criticized so bitterly were the same American militiamen who had inflicted a terrible defeat on the British army at Bunker Hill—a defeat so resounding that after it the redcoats stayed under cover for nine months. The American troops never achieved such a result anywhere else, despite all Washington's discipline and courts martial.

George Washington was in fact a very mediocre figure. His role in the American Revolution has been greatly exaggerated, while the role of real revolutionaries like Sam Adams has been played down. "Discipline is the soul of an army" was one of Washington's favorite maxims. True—but the discipline of a revolutionary army is not the same as the discipline of any other army. Broadly speaking, every army reproduces the structures and is motivated by the spirit of the society that produced it. The army of a democracy will not be the same as the army of a fascist regime. The army of a class society needs a ferocious discipline—a reign of terror in fact—because it is maintained by force.

The discipline of a revolutionary army, on the contrary, is a voluntary discipline because it is necessarily an army of volunteers. The armies of the French Revolution, although they were composed largely of untrained volunteers, dressed in rags and barefoot, swept the best trained and equipped mercenaries in Europe before them and scattered them like the wind. The difference is that they knew what they were fighting for. They believed in it and were willing to die for it. This made them virtually invulnerable.

A revolutionary army must be run on democratic lines. This does not at all contradict the requirements of discipline in the battlefield. The Russian Red Army under Trotsky was very democratic. The Bolsheviks abolished the saluting of officers and all the outward trappings of command: the medals and gaudy uniforms. The officers and men ate in the same canteens and the soldiers were no longer required to use the polite form (*vy* in Russian, like *vous* in French or *usted* in Spanish) when addressing an officer. But when in battle strict discipline was expected and all orders had to be obeyed. The Red Army became a formidable fighting force while maintaining the norms of proletarian democracy. By the way, a similar regime existed in Oliver Cromwell's Model Army during the English Revolution in the 17th century.

The aristocratic Washington, who was very much in favor of pomp and circumstance, medals, and smart uniforms, and who tried to impose strict (bourgeois) discipline in an army of revolutionary volunteers, did not make them a more effective fighting force but rather the opposite. In the same way the Stalinists in Spain in the Civil War of the 1930s, using the same arguments as Washington, actually destroyed the basis of the revolutionary army and undermined its fighting spirit, leading to its defeat at the hands of Franco's fascist army.

Far from improving the military efficiency of the revolutionary forces, Washington committed a major blunder. The strength of the revolutionary army lay in its guerrilla tactics, combining flexibility with great mobility. They could inflict considerable casualties on the British and then vanish into thin air. The farmers' boys and backwoodsmen were fine sharpshooters, but could not stand a bayonet charge by regular troops. Washington attempted to turn them into regular soldiers and made a mess of it. Charles Francis Adams, who was a soldier in the revolutionary army as well as a historian, wrote:

> Washington measured himself and his army up against his adversary at the point where they were strongest and he was least so. He offered infantry to infantry; oblivious of the fact that the British infantry were of the most perfectly organized kind, while his own was at best an extemporized force.

The main problem was not military but political. Both Washington and the bourgeois and landlords in Congress lacked the will to pursue the fight against the British to the finish. They admitted there was a war but denied it was a war against the king! As a result the war dragged on inconclusively for years. Washington was a careerist, more suited for political intrigues and maneuvers at the top than fighting the enemy. As Gore Vidal wittily (and correctly) says, ". . . though Washington could not defeat the enemy in battle, he had a fine talent for defeating rival generals in the Congress" (Vidal, 73)

There can be no doubt that the British were actually winning the war before the French came in on the American side. The French were motivated not by the love of liberty (they lived under an absolutist monarchy a hundred times more oppressive than the British equivalent), but by hatred of England, their old rival. This tipped the balance in favor of the American colonists. Britain was already worn down by the costs of a prolonged war that was draining them financially and disrupting trade, especially when Spain and Holland also joined in.

In 1781 the British General Cornwallis found himself trapped in Yorktown, with the American forces in front of him, and the French fleet at his rear. There was no escape. He was forced to surrender. At this time the ruling administration in London was led by men who were unenthusiastic about continuing the war. They added up their sums and concluded that it was costing them more to hold down the American colonies than what they could ever hope to get back. They decided to pull the British army out. The war was over.

Washington's alleged military skills therefore had little or nothing to do with the victory. The war itself was really mainly a series of inconclusive skirmishes. As a military chief his record was very poor. In the first three years he lost every single engagement, except for a small victory at Trenton, and that was achieved more by luck than judgment. In a Christmas Eve skirmish in the middle of a snowstorm, he managed to defeat a whole brigade of Hessians. It helped a little that the Hessians, who had been celebrating the festive season, were blind drunk at the time and did not know what they were doing.

Other revolutionary generals were more capable and more successful than Washington. And the most successful actions of the revolutionary forces were carried out by the guerrillas, whom he despised. The reason that Washington's image has been boosted by the official historians of the Revolution is that he represented the most conservative wing of the leadership—a "moderate," a respectable man of property—a man in the image of the present-day rulers of the USA, with whom the modern bankers, capitalists, and Republican leaders can feel comfortable.

The attempts of Washington to control the revolutionary army from the top and impose a ferocious military discipline were not dictated by military necessity but rather by the wish of the bourgeois and landowners in Congress to police the revolutionary masses and prevent the revolutionary movement from getting "out of hand." Even in the course of hostilities, the men of property were preparing for the moment of victory, when it would be necessary to reassert their "sacred right to rule" and crush the very people who had won the victory.

The New Oligarchy

> *Democracy has never been and never can be so desirable as aristocracy or monarchy, but while it lasts, is more bloody than either. Remember, democracy never lasts long. It soon wastes, exhausts and murders itself. There never was a democracy that did not commit suicide.*—John Adams

The fears of the "Moneyocracy" were fully confirmed by what happened after the British were driven out. With the removal of the common enemy, the class divisions emerged with renewed force. The wealthy upper class was itself divided between the Whigs, who supported the Revolution, and the Tories, the most conservative wing of the bourgeois and landowning aristocracy, who had supported the British Crown. But after the defeat of the English and the departure of the Redcoats, the Tories had no alternative but to throw in their lot with the winning side.

Although the right to vote was extended to include new layers of property owners, it was still highly restrictive. A new oligarchy was being created, in which the rich and powerful joined forces in a reactionary bloc against democracy and the demands of the lower orders. They attempted to give the most restrictive interpretation to the Constitution, stressing property rights above all else. Their model was the principles of the British government—that is, an aristocratic constitution that excluded the bulk of the people from government. The common people had shed their blood to drive the British out, while the American ruling class conspired in Congress to reintroduce the corrupt and undemocratic British system of government. For them, all the rights and privileges were the monopoly of the rich, while all the obligations and duties were for the poor. As long as the rich were all right, everybody was assumed to be all right. (The same idea is basically behind what is today called the "trickle-down" theory.)

A section of the bourgeoisie favored a strong central state, while others wanted a weaker center. From this arose the Federalists and anti-Federalists. Some of the Whigs became anti-Federalists, while others like Hamilton (who was really a monarchist in disguise) became strong Federalists. Tory Federalists became Republicans, while anti-Federalist Republicans became Jeffersonian Democrats. The Tories were in favor of strong central government in order to protect property, although previously they had been opposed to any government since they supported the British Crown.

The fact is that Alexander Hamilton and John Adams were conspiring to reintroduce an English-style monarchical system. The differences between Jefferson and Hamilton were between the right wing of the bourgeoisie, who wanted a deal with the counterrevolutionaries, and the more radical wing that was prepared to lean on the masses for support, but without surrendering an atom of real power. Of the 13,000 men who lived in New York City, only 1,300 owned enough property to qualify as voters. In the election of 1789 there were over 200,000 residents in New York State, of whom only 12,000 were eligible to vote for governor. In Massachusetts the property qualifications for voters were twice as high as under British rule. The Federalists were firm supporters of oligarchic rule and in essence opposed to democracy:

> Supporters of the new Constitution—people who styled themselves Federalists—argued that state governments were too susceptible to popular control, that the masses did not respect the interests of property, that liberty threatened the stability of the republics. The Federalists appealed to people with interstate interests—merchants, commercial farmers, public creditors, and urban workers whose livelihoods depended upon the prosperity of their employers. They also attracted politicians who lacked power within the existing state governments, men who hoped to supplant the entrenched political groups. As defenders of property, the Federalists saw a strong national government as a bulwark against the caprice of popular politics.

"In framing a government which is to be administered by men over men," Madison declared, "the great difficulty lies in this: you must first enable the government to control the governed; and in the next place oblige it to control itself." These lines strikingly express the attitude of the oligarchy to the people. The first task of government is not to represent the people, but to *control* them. The real attitude of the ruling elite was shown by the words of John Adams, who together with Hamilton had founded the Federalist Party (though he later described Hamilton as "the bastard son of a Scotch peddler").

Party lines constantly shifted and the arguments between the rival factions were acrimonious at times, but in the last analysis, the entire ruling class was united against the demands of the workers and the poor. Having aroused the masses to fight against Britain, it was not easy to get them to accept the rule of a privileged oligarchy after the redcoats had left. In fact, for all the talk of "Liberty," the victory of the Revolution had only transferred power from a corrupt and reactionary colonial government to an equally corrupt and reactionary American oligarchy.

The Revolution proclaimed the inalienable Rights of Man, but these did not include women, slaves, Native Americans, or the great majority of the population who owned little or no property. When the revolutionary armies were disbanded, there was no money to pay the arrears of wages. Some of the men were paid off in land warrants, which were later sold to speculators for paltry amounts. Half the members of Congress had their pockets full of these warrants. George Washington was one of the big buyers. As president, Washington tried to give the impression of standing above classes and party strife. But in practice he represented the oligarchy, whose interests and psychology he shared:

> He was a practical man, not troubled much by unrealizable ideals. His intellectual outlook was that of an industrialist or a banker. It was what we call today the "banker-mind." The banker stands for stability, and Washington was for that. The banker is for law and order, for land and mortgages, for substantial assets—and Washington believed in them too. The banker wants the nation to be prosperous; by that he means that he wants the common people to have plenty of work and wealthy people to have plenty of profits. That was Washington's ideal (Woodward, 255–56).

Shays's Rebellion

In every great revolution we see more or less clearly defined stages, which recur with a strange regularity and with uncanny similarity. The initial stage, which corresponds with the first awakening of the masses and the growth of their self-awareness, is characterized by a mood of euphoria and a spirit of unity. But gradually this illusory unity dissipates and there is a growing division between the more revolutionary elements and the more moderate party. The period of revolutionary ascent is marked by a movement to the left, in which the more revolutionary wing and the most audacious leaders gain the upper hand and sweep all before them.

However, as Trotsky explains, revolution is a powerful devourer of human energies. As the masses become exhausted by their exertions and sink into passivity, the conservative wing tends to regain control and elbow the revolutionaries to one side. This happened in every bourgeois revolution in history, and corresponds to the inevitable dialectic of such a revolution. The Declaration of Independence stated that all men were born free, and proclaimed the equality of all men as "self-evident." These were ideals worth fighting and dying for. But once the British had been defeated, the American bourgeoisie soon made it clear that all men were not equal, and that they intended to rule and exploit the people, just as the British had done before them.

There is a stage in every great revolution when the masses—or at least the most militant section of the masses—begin to feel that they have been cheated of the fruits of victory, that power is slipping through their fingers and they have to act to prevent this from happening. A desperate minority moves to take power and is crushed. This marks a decisive turning point in the revolution, where the conservative wing crushes its former allies and proceeds to consolidate its power as a new ruling class. This stage in the American Revolution was Shays's Rebellion.

When the cannons had fallen silent and the smoke had finally cleared from the battlefields, the small farmers, workers, and artisans who had done all the fighting looked around them and saw that they had gained nothing from the Revolution. They were crushed by debts and taxes. Interest rates were charged at up to forty percent. Poor settlers, crossing the mountains in search of land, found the best farming country in the hands of land companies. All the power was in the hands of the rich—the merchants, the landowners, the moneylenders. Runaway inflation made money worthless. To make matters worse, the war was followed by a deep trade depression that lasted from 1783 to 1788. Prices and taxes soared. As a result, thousands languished in debtors' prisons. In Massachusetts alone, 90 percent of those in prison were debtors. The discontent of the masses reached boiling point.

There were serious uprisings in Massachusetts. In New Hampshire a mob of several hundred men marched to the legislature with clubs, stones, and guns to demand relief. The rebels assumed (erroneously) that the problem was a shortage of currency. "Print money and lower the taxes" was their slogan. But there is no doubt that the high taxes fell disproportionately on the poor. They particularly targeted the courts where moneylenders would secure eviction orders against poor farmers who had fallen into debt. In the *New York Picket* of September 11, 1786, we read:

> On Tuesday the 29th [of August] ... the day appointed by law for the sitting of the Court of Common Pleas ... there assembled in the town from different parts of the county four or five hundred people some of whom were armed with muskets, the others with bludgeons, with the professed intention to prevent the courts from proceeding to business ...

This movement culminated in what was known as Shays's Uprising—an armed insurrection led by Captain Daniel Shays, a former officer in the revolutionary army, and now, like so many others, a ruined small farmer. About 1,000 men, armed with muskets, swords, and clubs, succeeded in closing the courts for several months. Leo Huberman writes:

> The upper classes throughout the country were thoroughly frightened at this armed uprising of the poor people. There was no money in the treasury to pay the state troops, so a number of rich people contributed enough to do so. Shays and his followers headed for Springfield, where there was a public storehouse containing 7,000 muskets and 13,000 barrels of gunpowder, stoves, camp kettles and saddles. They were stopped by the state troops, a few shots were fired, and the mob dispersed (Huberman).

It was at this time that Thomas Jefferson made his famous remark that the Tree of Liberty must be watered from time to time by the blood of patriots. He also wrote that "a little rebellion now and then is a good thing, and as necessary in the political world as storms in the physical." However, this view was anathema to the majority of the American ruling class. Again, Gore Vidal accurately expresses the views of the oligarchy in the following imaginary dialogue between George Washington and Aaron Burr, a controversial figure in the American Revolution and the central figure in his novel of that name:

> Washington spoke through me, but not to cut me off: he was going deaf and did not hear half what was said to him. "When word came to me of the treasonous acts of a certain Captain Daniel Shays—a dirty fellow once known to me—it was apparent that we must have a strong government to protect our property. Mr. Hamilton concurred with me and we summoned a constitutional convention at which I, at great personal sacrifice, let me say, presided. I regard, Sir, that convention as the most important event of my own career. Because had we not invented this federal government, *they* would have taken away *everything*."
>   The face was dark with sudden color. The hands that were stretched to the fire trembled. "By now that Massachusetts rabble would have divided all property amongst the worthless classes. Not even your French have dared go so far. This is not natural, I said at the time. This must be stopped. We did

not fight and win a war with a despot across the sea to be in turn tyrannized by a bloody mob whose contribution to our victory, if I may say so, was considerably less than that of those gentlemen who sacrificed all that they had in order that we be a separate nation. So what we won in that war we mean to keep, Colonel Burr. And I am sure that you agree with that sentiment."

The true significance of Shays's Rebellion can only be understood in class terms. Later, General Knox wrote to George Washington to explain the dangerous character of the ideas of the insurgents. In particular, Knox said that the rebels believed that "the property of the United States has been protected from . . . Britain by the joint efforts of all *and therefore ought to be the common property of all.*" He added: "Our government must be braced, changed, or altered to secure our lives and property" (Quoted in Woodward, 228, my emphasis—AW).

The rebellion was crushed and fourteen of its leaders, including Shays, were sentenced to death, though later pardoned. In Shays's rebellion, the masses, feeling that the power that they have fought and died for is slipping from their hands, tried desperately to seize the initiative again. But the movement was doomed to defeat. The class nature of the American Revolution of the 18th century was objectively bourgeois. It could not go beyond the limits prescribed by the capitalist mode of production. Consequently, the attempt of Shays to do so was condemned in advance to failure, as the similar attempt of the English Levellers and the left wing of the Puritans was condemned to defeat over a century earlier in England.

The challenge thrown down by Shays terrified the oligarchy that was quietly concentrating political and economic power into its own hands. They understood the need to create a strong state power immediately as a bulwark against the masses. At the same time, they were under the pressure of the masses.

The Constitution

When the 55 delegates met in 1787 to revise the Articles of Confederation, not one of them was from the working class or the class of small farmers. The class that had done all the fighting and dying in the revolution was rigorously excluded from the decision-making process. So were a number of the most prominent revolutionary leaders. Patrick Henry was not there. They asked him to serve, but he would have nothing to do with it. Nor was Samuel Adams, the most outspoken of the revolutionaries. Nor was Christopher Gadsden of South Carolina, organizer of mechanics and laboring men. Their day had passed; the moving spirits of the convention did not want any organizers of rebellion, or leaders of the populace. Thomas Jefferson, idealist and demo-crat, was in France serving as the American ambassador.

The men who drafted the American constitution were all moneylenders, merchants, manufacturers, bondholders, or slaveholders. They met behind closed doors, and all the delegates were pledged to secrecy. When the Con-stitution was finally announced most people were surprised. They knew nothing about it. The secrecy with which the Constitution was drawn up is no accident. It is possible to draw a parallel between this phase of the American Revolution and the Thermidorean counterrevolution in France, that is to say, the beginnings of a conservative reaction against the egalitarian spirit of the revolution in its flood tide. In the sense that it marked the inevitable stage of stabilization when the men of money, the big landowners and wealthy mer-chants grabbed power out of the hands of the plebeian radical wing, this is a fair comparison. That is precisely why the proceedings had to take place behind the backs of the people.

Gradually, the voice of the radical elements was drowned out by the men of property. Hamilton was openly contemptuous about democracy. He was not the only one. Listen to what Madison had to say: "In future times a great majority of the people will not only be without landed, but any other sort of property. These will either combine under the influence of their common situation; in which case, the rights of property and the public liberty will not be secure in their hands, or, which is more probable, they will become the tools of opulence and ambition; in which case there will be equal danger on another side."

These lines are perfectly clear. The fierce debates that raged over the Con-stitution were the parting shots of class conflict. The central contradiction may be simply stated: *most of the authors of the Constitution did not believe in the equality of man, but the common people certainly did.* It required a second revolution (the Civil War) to get the question of the suffrage included in the Constitution in the Fifteenth Amendment of 1870. But at that time the ques-tion was left up to the individual states. This meant that three quarters of the free white men in all states except two or three were excluded from voting because they did not posses enough property. However, at the proposal of Jefferson and other left-wingers, a Bill of Rights was approved.

The discussions on the Constitution dragged on for months. The disputed questions were numerous: should large states have more say in the national government than small states? Should black slaves be counted as white people? And so on. But there was one question upon which they all agreed: that those with little or no property should not have too much power. In the end, the Constitution of the United States was only approved after bitter argument and even then was only passed by a narrow margin by those few who were eligible to vote, as these figures show:

	For	Against
New York	30	27
New Hampshire	57	47
Massachusetts	187	168
Virginia	89	79

The American republic at its birth was a revolutionary power that owed its existence to the workers and small farmers and was, at least in the beginning, under their pressure. Later, as the lava of revolution cooled, the big landowning and merchant interests prevailed. But in the beginning, the American Revolution was a beacon of hope to the entire world.

America and the French Revolution

The international significance of the American Revolution was far greater than what most people realize today. The connection between the American and French Revolutions was very close. That great English-American revolutionary Thomas Paine lived in France and developed the most radical ideas. The proclamation of *The Rights of Man* was a most revolutionary idea for its time. People like Thomas Paine were the most advanced revolutionary democrats of their day. The ideas of liberty, equality, and fraternity that they advocated shook the ruling classes of all Europe.

What is even less understood is the impact these revolutionary ideas from America had on the infant workers' movement in Britain. Tom Paine's writings were passed from hand to hand in underground workers' groups known as corresponding societies. Nowadays, the British establishment likes to parade its democratic credentials. But this is a blatant lie. The British ruling class fought tooth and nail against democracy. They opposed every attempt to establish the right to vote. This was conquered in struggle by the British working class, which paid a heavy price in martyrs, with imprisonment, deportation, and even death as its reward. In those dark days when the working class of Britain was struggling to win the most elementary rights, when the trade unions were illegalized by Pitt's notorious Combination Acts, the flame of freedom was kept alight, not only by the example of revolutionary France, but by the revolutionary democratic ideas of Thomas Paine, who for generations was the hero of British workers.

The American Revolution provided a stimulus for the French Revolution of 1789–93. But in its turn the French Revolution had a considerable impact on America. The news from Paris exacerbated the split between right and left inside Washington's cabinet, especially after the execution of Louis XVI and Marie Antoinette in April 1793. Jefferson, who stood on the left, welcomed it, but the conservative wing recoiled in horror, probably picturing themselves on the steps of the guillotine. Although the French Revolution appalled the American conservatives, much as the Russian Revolution did later, it inspired the left wing and reaffirmed their revolutionary identity and aspirations. Even before 1789, Thomas Jefferson was strongly anti-monarchical in his views. He was sent as ambassador of America to Paris—probably to get him out of the way.

While in Paris he had occasion to note that France was divided between sheep and wolves, with an abyss separating rich and poor. Among all that aristocratic gang he felt like "a savage from the woods of America." It was not therefore surprising that Jefferson greeted the revolution enthusiastically. "Was ever a prize won with so little human blood?" he asked, answering the attacks of the enemies of the revolution who (as they always do) tried to portray it as an orgy of bloodletting.

The French Revolution opened up a deep rift that expressed itself on party lines. The Jeffersonians were pro-French in foreign policy and advocated a loose confederation of states in America with less power for the center. It based itself on the support of the small farmers and proletarian and semi-proletarian elements in the cities. The Federalists, on the other hand, were pro-British (their opponents called them "the English Party"), stood for a strong central government, and represented the interests of the big merchants and manufacturers.

In October 1789 Jefferson returned to America. Revolutionary France was attacked by the reactionary powers of Europe: England, Austria, Sardinia, and the Netherlands. The Democratic-Republicans wanted war against England, whereas the Federalists wanted war against France. The Democratic-Republican Party at that time stood on the left. They were pro-French, anti-British, and argued for greater egalitarianism. The leaders included Thomas Jefferson, James Madison, George Clinton, and Aaron Burr.

The Federalists were the right wing and included many former Tories. This was the party of the oligarchy par excellence, and was backed by Alexander Hamilton, John Adams, John Jay, and (surreptitiously) by Washington himself. However, realizing that for America to unite with Britain against France was politically impossible, Washington insisted on strict neutrality.

The impact of the French Revolution in America was tremendous. It gave fresh heart to the revolutionaries and the left wing and threw the conservatives into a panic. They feared that the example of the Jacobins would lead to a second revolution in America that would lead to the overthrow of the oligarchy. This did not happen because the vast open spaces to the west provided a safety valve. The energies of the downtrodden that in France were the mainspring of the revolution, in America could be channelled into the movement to the West. Nevertheless, the contradictions remained and would burst to the surface in the Civil War.

The French Revolution, with its slogan Liberty, Equality, Fraternity also inspired an uprising of black slaves in Santo Domingo. This terrified the big landowners of the Southern states even more. Gabriel Prosser led an uprising of slaves in America, which was put down with great ferocity. Thousands of black slaves were slaughtered in Virginia.

The war in Europe had serious repercussions in America. Both the British and French seized American vessels. This was used as an excuse to bring in the Alien and Sedition Act that gave the executive the power to arrest and deport any foreigners and arrest citizens for criticizing the government. Here we see the beginnings of an attempt to limit and even undermine the democratic rights established by the Constitution and the Bill of Rights. The Act was used to harass, arrest, and imprison anti-federalist elements. We see exactly the same thing now with the antidemocratic Patriot Act legislation introduced after 9/11. Jefferson and others attempted to resist the attacks on democracy by insisting on states' rights. Although the same demand was later filled by a reactionary content—to defend the right of the Southern states to keep slaves—at this time it had a progressive character.

Federalists and Anti-federalists

The struggle between Federalists and anti-federalists was in essence the struggle between the American Thermidorean counterrevolutionaries and those who sought to uphold the original aims of the American Revolution. Thomas Jefferson even spoke openly of the need for a second revolution. This was actually what took place in the Civil War. The third—and greatest— American revolution is currently in the process of being prepared. The victory of the conservative faction led to a state of affairs which had very little to do with the revolutionary-democratic ideals of 1776. P.N. Carroll and D.W. Noble point out:

> The importance of the legislatures made questions of political representation more pressing than ever before. In organizing republican governments,

American politicians assumed that the legislatures represented specific constituencies and spoke for that amorphous group they called "the people." They agreed, nevertheless, that the power of the people could easily degenerate into anarchy and destroy the governmental balance. To reduce the likelihood of mob rule, the state constitutions restricted political participation to male property owners and often established still higher property qualifications for officeholding. Despite occasional demands for wider democracy, the older habits of elitist politics prevailed. Consequently political representation remained with the more affluent citizens even though there is some evidence that members of state senates were slightly less wealthy than the councillors of the colonial period.

The conservative nature of these changes tells much about the American Revolution. Despite the revolutionary implications of the Declaration of Independence—the demands for government by consent of the governed and the assumptions about political equality—power generally remained in the hands of moderate leaders who were concerned as much with the interests of property as with the cause of liberty (Carroll and Noble, 120–21).

Needless to say, the Federalists attacked Jefferson viciously, using exactly the same kind of language the US reactionaries later used against socialists. When he stood against Adams in the election of 1800, it was said that a Jefferson victory would destroy religion and undo the bounds of society, and that a vote for Jefferson was a vote against God, etc. However, the people showed that they would not be bullied and voted for Jefferson, risking the wrath of the Almighty in the hopes of achieving justice in this life.

Even the geography of the new capital was a reflection of the class struggle. By moving the capital of the republic to Washington, the Federalist faction clearly intended to remove the government and presidency from the pressure of the masses of New York. The new capital, conveniently situated near to the conservative agrarian states of the South, was a place where hardly anybody lived. The scale and style of the White House and Capitol suggested grand imperial ambitions. Jefferson, who was allergic to monarchy, commented ironically that the White House was big enough to house "two Emperors, one Pope, and the Chief Lama."

To his credit, Jefferson immediately took measures to counteract the Federalists' attempt to move in the direction of monarchy. He banned the use of his image on coins, forbade the celebration of his birthday and opened up the White House to anyone who wanted to visit him. He dressed so modestly that a visiting diplomat took him for one of the servants. This is quite in the spirit of the Bolshevik leaders who, after the October Revolution, would take no more wages than those of a skilled worker, walked the streets without armies of bodyguards, and were easily accessible to anyone who wanted to meet them.

When the famous English writer Arthur Ransome visited Moscow in 1919 he met Bukharin, who at that time was a key figure in the revolutionary government. He gave Bukharin a packet of sugar, and the Bolshevik leader was delighted because he did not have any sugar. This was absolutely typical of all the Bolshevik leaders at that time. The situation only changed after the Stalinist political counterrevolution, itself the result of the isolation of the revolution in conditions of frightful poverty and backwardness.

This democratic, egalitarian spirit of the founders of the American republic stands in stark contrast to the conduct of America's present-day political leaders. Thomas Jefferson was a true son of the Enlightenment with a classical education and a healthily skeptical attitude to religion. He dressed like a servant and when he died he did not have enough money to pay his debts. George W. Bush is an illiterate billionaire who cannot utter a single coherent sentence and has a brain that is chock-full of the crudest religious superstition. He also has pretensions to imperial grandeur to rival those of Nero or Caligula. We leave it to the reader to decide whether this represents progress or regression.

CHAPTER III

RICH AND POOR

I think our governments will remain virtuous for many centuries, as long as they are chiefly agricultural; and this will be as long as there shall be vacant lands in any part of America. When they get piled upon one another in large cities, as in Europe, they will become corrupt as Europe.—Thomas Jefferson

The conquest of independence for the American colonies, although it was a great step forward, did not mark the final victory of democracy in America. Power was in the hands of a wealthy oligarchy:

> The most serious problem inherited from the Revolution was its failure to carry out its declaration of the equality of all men. We have pointed out that half-consciously the leaders of the Revolutionary period confined the application of equality to those men whom they recognized as parties to the social contract and members of the political community. Even among them equality was never rigorously asserted. Property qualifications for voting and unequal representation of sections in the state legislature gave distinct advantages to the wealthier men and the wealthier areas. Literacy tests as the years passed were substituted for property tests as a more defensible means for disfranchising the poor, but with almost the same effect. Those inequalities have persisted to the present day, operating now primarily to give white men an advantage over Negroes, and rural areas an advantage over urban areas at the ballot (Dan Lacy, *The Meaning of the American Revolution*, 282–83).

The ideal of many of the founding fathers, especially Thomas Jefferson, was that of a democratic republic of small farmers. "Those who labor in the earth," he wrote, "are the chosen people of God." To further this aim, in 1804 Jefferson purchased the vast territory of Louisiana from France for the immense sum (for those days) of 15 million dollars (double the total Federal budget)—the biggest land deal in history. By the stroke of a pen, Jefferson removed Britain, France, Russia and Spain from a massive swath of North America, and provided a huge area of land for the expansion of the population.

As usual, the losers were the Native Americans who were deprived of their ancestral lands and pushed to the west. Although he was an advanced democrat in many ways, Thomas Jefferson was incapable of thinking of them as human beings with the same rights as the European settlers. There was no place in his agrarian scheme for the First Americans whose lands were expropriated. "The backward [tribes] will yield," he wrote in 1812, "and we shall be obliged to drive them, with the beasts of the forests, into the Stony [Rocky] Mountains" (Quoted in Carroll and Noble, 137).

However, Jefferson's dream of a free agrarian republic was already obsolete before he died. The development of capitalism in America, made possible by the Revolution, signified the rapid growth of industry in the North and East that brought in its wake a growing gap between rich and poor, workers and capitalists. The dream of an agrarian paradise became the nightmare of industrial capitalism. As far as democracy was concerned, it was fine in theory but in practice was little more than a fig leaf to disguise the rule of a wealthy elite:

> The government in Washington had grown, through successive administrations, into a pleasant little oligarchy. A handful of men ran everything, and when they departed from the scene they chose their successors in the manner of one who writes a last will and testament. Jefferson chose Madison and Madison chose Monroe (Woodward, 361).

The rich and powerful vied with each other to get their hands on the pork barrel of political power, just as they do today. The only important business in Washington was office-holding and related matters, just as it is today. No wonder Jefferson remarked shortly before his death: "I like the dreams of the future better than the history of the past."

In a Few Hands

A Whig journalist in the early years of the 19th century wrote:

> Ours is a country, where men start from an humble origin, and from small beginnings rise gradually in the world, as the reward of merit and industry, and where they can attain to the most elevated positions, or acquire a large amount of wealth, according to the pursuits they elect for themselves. (Quoted in Carroll and Noble, 155).

So much for the self-satisfied rhetoric of the American dream. The reality, however, was very different. Not only were the Native Americans, black

slaves, and women excluded from this dream, but also the grow
of propertyless industrial workers laboring in the sweat shops of ￼ ￼ cities of
the northeast.

The conquest of formal democracy and the proclamation of the Rights of
Man did not prevent the concentration of economic and political power into a
few hands. The position of the working class did not improve but worsened,
as shown by the following "Appeal to the Working People of Manayunk to the
Public," published in *Pennsylvanian*, August 28, 1833:

> We are obliged by our employers to labor at this season of the year, from 5
> o'clock in the morning until sunset, being fourteen hours and a half, with an
> intermission of half an hour for breakfast, and an hour for dinner, leaving
> thirteen hours of hard labor, at an unhealthy employment, where we never
> feel a refreshing breeze to cool us, overheated and suffocated as we are, and
> where we never behold the sun but through a window, and an atmosphere
> thick with the dust and small particles of cotton, which we are constantly
> inhaling to the destruction of our health, our appetite and strength.
>
> Often we feel ourselves so weak as to be scarcely able to perform our
> work, on account of the over-strained time we are obliged to labor through
> the long and sultry days of summer, in the impure and unwholesome air of
> the factories, and the little rest we receive during the night not being suffi-
> cient to recruit our exhausted physical energies, we return to our labor in
> the morning, as weary as when we left it; but nevertheless work we must,
> worn down and debilitated as we are, or our families would soon be in a
> starving condition, for our wages are barely sufficient to supply us with the
> necessaries of life. We cannot provide against sickness or difficulties of any
> kind, by laying by a single dollar, for our present wants consume the little
> we receive and when we are confined to a bed of sickness any length of time,
> we are plunged into the deepest distress, which often terminates in total
> ruin, poverty, and pauperism.
>
> Our expenses are perhaps greater than most other working people, be-
> cause it requires the wages of all the family who are able to work (save
> only one small girl to take care of the house and provide meals) to furnish
> absolute wants, consequently the females have no time either to make their
> own dresses or those of the children, but have of course to apply to trades
> for every article that is wanted (J. Kuczynski, *A Short History of Labor Condi-
> tions under Industrial Capitalism*, vol.2, 25).

The condition of women workers was underlined in a report by the National
Trades' Union Convention in September, 1834:

> Mr. Douglass observed that in the single village of Lowell, there were
> about 4,000 females of various ages, now dragging out a life of slavery and
> wretchedness. It is enough to make one's heart ache, said he, to behold
> these degraded females, as they pass out of the factory—to mark their wan
> countenances—their woe-stricken appearance. These establishments are

the present abode of wretchedness, disease and misery; and are inevitably calculated to perpetuate them—if not to destroy liberty itself.

Another report states:

It has been shown that the number of females employed in opposition to male labor, throughout the United States, exceeds 140,000 who labor on an average from 14 to 15 hours per day, without that pure air and wholesome exercise which are necessary to health, and confinement with the consequent excess of toil, which checks the growth of the body, destroying in effect the natural powers of mind, and not infrequently distorting the limbs.

Even more ghastly was the position of children:

"If children must be doomed to those deadly prisons," said the New Haven delegates to the above mentioned convention, "let the law at least protect them against excessive toil and shed a few rays of light upon their darkened intellect. Workingmen! Bitter must be that bread which your little children earn in pain and tears, toiling by day, sleeping by night, sinking under oppression, consumption and decrepitude, into an early grave, knowing no life but this, and knowing of this only misery."

The class struggle has accompanied the American Republic ever since it was born. In 1778, when the ink was scarcely dry on the Declaration of Independence, journeymen printers of New York City combined to demand an increase in wages. The first strike of wage earners took place in Philadelphia as early as 1786 when the printers fought for a weekly minimum wage. The first general strike—that is, the first strike of a considerable number of workers in a large number of trades in one big strike movement—took place in 1827, again in Philadelphia. In this period, many trade unions were formed and there were numerous strikes.

The bosses ferociously resisted the right of workers to organize in unions and go out on strike. In 1806 members of the Philadelphia Journeymen Cordwainers were tried for criminal conspiracy after a strike for higher wages. The charges were (1) combination to raise wages, and (2) combination to injure others. Bankrupted as a result, the union disbanded. This was not an isolated case. Wherever possible the employers brought in scab labor to break strikes and appealed to the courts to declare trade unions illegal. Far from trade union organization being recognized as a democratic right, the unions were dragged through the courts and prosecuted for "conspiracy in restraint of trade"—a phrase copied from English common law. For decades, strikes, boycotts, and other forms of working class struggle were subject to legal action on the grounds of "conspiracy."

Andrew Jackson

Andrew Jackson was a self-made frontiersman from Tennessee. The son of a poor family from the West, one of his biographers says of him:

> He became imbued with the doctrine that . . . the banker is vastly overpaid for his services in expediting commerce, and that for bankers in Philadelphia and New York to have the power of life and death over business enterprises in Tennessee is criminal injustice.

There was growing discontent among the propertyless masses, small farmers, frontier settlers, and religious minorities. Although Jackson was an outsider to politics, he got a surprisingly large popular vote when he ran for president in 1824. The WASP elite was alarmed. The ruling class in the USA has, contrary to the well-known mythology, never been fond of democracy. One of them, James Kent of New York, voiced the real feelings of the rich and powerful concerning democracy:

> It is not to be disguised that our governments are becoming downright democracies. The principle of universal suffrage, which is now running a triumphant career from Maine to Louisiana, is an awful power, which, like gunpowder, or the steam engine, or the press itself, may be rendered mighty in mischief as well as in blessings.

In the election of 1828 Jackson swept the board. Overnight the flood tide of democratic protest had swept away the old Massachusetts and Virginia dynasties. Jackson ("Old Hickory") became the first west-of-the-mountains president. On his inauguration day he allowed the people of Washington—"from the highest and most polished," reported a disgusted Justice Story, "to the most vulgar and gross in the nation"—to enter the White House and consume ice cream and cake, lemon and punch. This turned into a riot and was dubbed "the reign of King Mob" by Judge Story. For the conservatives the American people have always been "King Mob"—people to be feared, not trusted.

Andrew Jackson claimed to represent the interests of the small man, the farmer, and the unsettled West. In reality, the Jacksonian Democrats inaugurated an alliance between the Southern slavocracy and Northern, urban political machines. In this era, the Democrats were characterized by the lack of a clear program, aims, and perspectives. The only common denominator of Jackson's party was Jackson himself. And he was always better at saying what he was against than what he was in favor of. Nevertheless, the masses looked upon Jackson as their man in the White House—the People's Champion.

That is, of course, unless you were Native American. An energetic advocate of westward expansion (later termed "manifest destiny"), Jackson, like his predecessors, looked down on the peoples who originally lived in those lands. He was an active proponent of their removal—more often than not by brute force. His signing into law of the "Indian Removal Act" legalized the wholesale killing, enslavement, and land theft that had begun with the arrival of the first Europeans. The infamous episode of the "Trail of Tears," during which the Cherokee were herded from Georgia to Oklahoma, was a direct result.

Jackson had no clearly defined political program, but he spoke for millions when he denounced the most obvious symptoms of capitalist robbery and exploitation: paper money, chartered corporations, and banks. The Jacksonian Democrats condemned the moneyed aristocracy that had robbed the people of their birthright. This was the period of intense struggles over issues like tariffs and the Bank of the United States. The masses hated the Bank, which had received a charter for twenty years in 1816. Jackson himself shared the common view of all bankers as a bunch of parasites and slick swindlers. During the panic and ensuing depression of 1819 and 1820, the Bank had deflated the currency, denied credit to merchants and local banks, and rapaciously levied on assets in cases where loans were in default. In other words, it acted as banks always act. As W.E. Woodward put it:

> It was an inveterate foe of everybody who owed it money unless the debtor was a member of Congress or the editor of a newspaper. . . . Its funds were intelligently mobilized; its drafts were readily honored in all commercial centers, and in Europe; its notes never fell below their par value; it provided a stable currency. But it was in the hands of men who carried it on as a private enterprise, a magnified pawnbroker's shop endowed with extraordinary privileges. In spirit it was antisocial and greedy (Woodward, 398).

The fact that an outsider from the West could overthrow the old political dynasties, the cliques of landowners who had been in power ever since the Revolution was in itself of tremendous symptomatic importance. The Jacksonian period was a period of tremendous ferment and unrest that came from the unresolved contradictions that lay within the foundations of American society:

> It was like a chemical mixture which has never composed itself, but wherein its biting acids continually fume and struggle. The social chemistry of America was in a state of extreme tension (Woodward., 393).

Jackson's confrontation with the Bank of the United States led to what is known as the Bank War. It expressed the conflict between rich and poor, the oligarchy and democracy, but also the contradiction between the Northern free states and the slaveholding states of the South, as opposition to the Bank ultimately reflected a reactionary rejection by the Southern slaveholders of the progressive development of capitalism in the young United States. Following his reelection in 1832, Jackson abolished the Bank. This was a utopian attempt to fight against tendencies that were irresistible. Capitalism, market forces, and banks were firmly entrenched. But the Bank War showed that The Revolution had left many unpaid bills. These now demanded to be paid.

The contradiction between North and South expressed itself again as a struggle over tariffs. This in turn led to an attempt at secession by the state of South Carolina after the adoption of the Tariff Act of 1828. A pragmatic populist, Jackson had to back down on the tariff question, which he supported, but denounced the secessionist leaders and appealed to the people of South Carolina to repudiate their leadership. "Their object is disunion," he thundered. "Disunion by armed force is *treason*." Here already were the first rumblings of the Civil War.

CHAPTER IV

THE SECOND AMERICAN REVOLUTION

I believe that to have interfered as I have done, as I have always freely admitted I have done, in behalf of his [God's] despised poor, I did not wrong but right. Now, if it is deemed necessary that I should forfeit my life for the furtherance of the ends of justice, and mingle my blood further with the blood of my children and with the blood of millions in this slave country whose rights are disregarded by wicked, cruel, and unjust enactments, I say let it be done.—John Brown

The growth of capitalism was expressed in the rapid development of the textile factories in England and the Northeastern United States, beginning in the last decades of the 18th century. This in turn led to an insatiable demand for raw cotton. The perfection of the cotton gin in 1793 guaranteed rich profits for the Southern planters. Thus, slave labor entered as an important component part of the accumulation of capital. It made fabulous fortunes, not only for the Southern slave owners, but for the most Christian industrialists of the North and Britain. America, which proclaimed the sacred principle of liberty, was stained by the evil of slavery. Men and women, torn from their homes and lands in black Africa by the monstrous trade in human beings, were bought and sold like chattel by Christian gentlemen who worshipped the Lord in church every Sunday, and tortured, beat, raped, and killed their slaves every other day of the week.

Although the African slave trade was already illegal, the Southern planters continued to import slaves after 1808. It is estimated that as many as 150,000 slaves were sent to the New World every year, compared to 45,000 towards the end of the 18th century. And although many of them were not shipped directly to the USA, most of them must have ended up there. In the *Charleston*

Courier of April 12, 1828 we read:

> As valuable a family ... as ever was offered for sale, consisting of a cook about 35 years of age, and her daughter about 14 and son about 8. The whole will be sold together or a part of them, as may suit a purchaser.

The slaves were regarded as chattel or animals, as the following description of a slave sale shows:

> About a dozen gentlemen crowded on the spot while the poor fellow was stripping himself, and as soon as he stood on the floor, bare from top to toe, a most rigorous scrutiny of his person was instituted. The clear black skin, back and front, was viewed all over for sores from disease; and there was no part of his body left unexamined. The man was told to open and shut his hands, asked if he could pick cotton, and every tooth in his head was scrupulously looked at.

The class outlook of the slave owners was well expressed in the comments of Senator Hammond of South Carolina:

> In all social systems there must be a class to do the mean duties, to perform the drudgeries of life ... we call them slaves. We are old-fashioned at the South yet; it is a word discarded now by ears polite; I will not characterize that class in the North by that term; but there you have it; it is there; it is everywhere; it is eternal ... The difference between us is that our slaves are hired for life and well compensated; there is no starvation, no begging, no want of employment among our people, and not too much employment, either. Yours are hired for the day, not cared for, and scantily compensated, which may be proved in the most deplorable manner, at any hour in any street of your large towns. Why, sir, you meet more beggars in one day, in any single street of the city of New York than you would ever meet in a lifetime in the whole South. Our slaves are black, of another inferior race ... your slaves are white, of your own race; you are brothers of one blood.

These lines are interesting because they let slip the smiling mask of the ruling class to reveal the brutal hypocrite that hides beneath it. In order to defend the indefensible—chattel slavery—the Southern slave owner points an accusing finger at the Northern capitalist. The attempt to prettify chattel slavery is, of course, absurd. Yet there is just a grain of truth in this attack against the hypocrisy of the Northern capitalists. The pro-slaver says to them:

> Why do you condemn us, when in reality you are just as bad as us? Our slavery is open and self-evident. We do not hide it. But your slavery is just as bad, if not worse, except it is hidden and hypocritical.

We need not accept the logic of the slaver to understand that the attitude of every exploiting class in history—slave owners, feudal lords, and capitalists—to the exploited class is very similar. The Northern manufacturers were luke-warm about abolition because they feared—not without reason—that any attempt to challenge the "sacred rights of property" in the South would set an unwelcome precedent for the working class in the North.

There were a number of slave revolts that were put down with the utmost savagery. The whites were always concerned with intimidating the blacks, in-culcating in them a sense of inferiority and fear of their masters. By all man-ner of cruelty, the blacks, both free and slaves (and many were free in some states) had to be *put in their place*. A few thousand wealthy slave owning fam-ilies ruled the South, while four million black slaves did all the work, the gap being filled by a population of poor whites who could always be depended upon to support their masters against the slaves.

In order to end this abomination and finish the job begun in 1776, a new revolution was necessary: a long and bloody Civil War. This took great cour-age and determination. The name of Abraham Lincoln will forever have a place of honor in the annals of the long struggle for democracy. In the course of this struggle, he grew in stature as a man and a leader. The initiative for this epic struggle, however, came from below, from the militant abolitionists and the slaves themselves. A movement that began as a small minority, despised as "extremists" and "subversives," shunned by the "moderate mainstream" succeeded, by heroic efforts, in turning America upside down.

The expansion of the United States created conditions for a struggle be-tween the North and South as they advanced westward in parallel lines. In 1818 the state of Missouri applied for admission to the Union. Slavery existed in Missouri, and New England and the North were opposed to the extension of the slave system. They therefore opposed the acceptance of Missouri or any other state that accepted the institution of slavery. The reason for this opposition was not wholly humanitarian. On the one hand, slavery had no place in the capitalist industrial economy of the North. On the other hand, the Northerners and New Englanders feared that they would come under the political domination of the Southern slave states.

When Missouri applied for admission there were eleven free states and eleven slave states, so that its admission could tilt the delicate balance one way or the other. On the other hand, Maine, which was free, had also applied to join the Union, and this was blocked by the South for the same reason. The deadlock was broken by the so-called Missouri compromise. The southern border of Missouri is the 36 degree 30 minutes parallel of latitude. According to the compromise, the northern limit of slavery (from the Mississippi west-wards) was to be that parallel, with the sole exception of Missouri, which, although north of the line, was admitted as a slave state. In return, Maine was also admitted.

Such a geographical compromise obviously had an extremely tenuous and fragile nature and could be upset by the slightest disturbance. Like all such agreements, it merely expressed the balance of forces at a given moment. As soon as the balance of forces changed, it would be torn to shreds. The whole logic of the situation was tending to war. The main result of the Missouri Compromise was to create a powerful Southern self-consciousness, born out of suspicion and hatred of the North. On the other hand, the acceptance of Missouri as a slave state outraged public opinion in the North and gave rise to increasingly militant antislavery groups, opposed to compromise and inclined to direct action. In the words of W.E. Woodward:

> The Civil War was built up as a house is built, brick upon brick. One of its cornerstones was the Missouri Compromise (Woodward, 354).

There was a militant anti-slavery tendency that used revolutionary methods to free the slaves. The struggle between slaveholders and abolitionists erupted into open civil war in 1856, when John Brown led his militant abolitionist forces into Kansas to do battle with the slavers. In October 1859, John Brown led a band of 18 armed men, of whom four were black, to capture the Federal arsenal at Harper's Ferry, Virginia. The raid failed and Colonel Robert E. Lee, the future commander of the Confederate forces, led a detachment of US Marines which captured John Brown. Amid a lynch-mob atmosphere, Brown was sentenced to death by hanging, the sentence being carried out in December 1859. His execution had far-reaching consequences and only exacerbated the accumulated social contradictions. During the war, the song "John Brown's Body," which includes the line "John Brown died that the slaves might be free," would become a rallying cry for the Union troops.

The defeat of the South—that bastion of landowning reaction—and the emancipation of the slaves was undoubtedly a progressive task, and one that merged imperceptibly with a war of emancipation of the black slaves. But the bourgeoisie dragged its feet, looking for a compromise up to the very last moment when the first cannon balls were fired at Fort Sumter on April 12, 1861. It was the pressure from the antislavery militants and the working class and lower middle class that forced the North into action. The workers of the Union were prepared to sacrifice their lives in this cause. And the workers of Europe instinctively understood this and took a truly internationalist position in relation to the Civil War—*The Second American Revolution*.

The Civil War

Historical legend presents the picture of the "antislave" North conducting a campaign for freedom against the slaveholding South. Like all historical legends, however, this is a gross oversimplification. The fact of the matter was that a significant section of the capitalist class in the North and also of the political establishment—including in Lincoln's own party—did not want to fight against slavery and were in favor of reaching a compromise with the Southern slave owners. Lincoln himself was originally a compromise candidate between the openly abolitionist wing and the compromisers on the right wing.

Like every other serious conflict, at bottom the American Civil War was a class struggle. The Northern manufacturers necessarily had to come into conflict with the Southern landowning classes. The conflict of interest between the two lasted for sixty years and finally ended in civil war. However, the mutual hatred between the Northern capitalists and the slave owners of the South, grounded in economics, was only half the story. There was a genuine sense of moral outrage among sections of the Northern working class and middle class against the evils of slavery. The abolitionists waged an energetic campaign of agitation and propaganda aimed at arousing public opinion in the North.

Pamphlets and books like Harriet Beecher Stowe's *Uncle Tom's Cabin* caused widespread indignation against the institution of slavery and prepared the ground for more active revolutionary measures. A section of the abolitionist movement was inclined to direct action. The execution of John Brown brought matters to a head. Historian Lloyd Lewis explains that the incident at Harper's Ferry "was to the South a gathering thunderhead on the Northern sky, promise of the hurricane to come." Fearful of slave uprisings and interference from Northern abolitionists, the South began to organize militias that would form the basis of the Confederate Army. Mass antislavery rallies and demonstrations took place in the North.

It was this mass agitation that led, the following year, to the election of Abraham Lincoln. This was taken as a signal for the secession of the slave states. Lincoln was immediately faced with a serious crisis provoked by the secession of South Carolina on December 20, 1860. This was followed in early 1861 by the secession of Texas, Georgia, Alabama, Mississippi, Louisiana, and Florida. Virginia, Arkansas, Tennessee, and North Carolina followed, making a total of eleven states. The immediate cause was the old argument over tariffs. The South produced nothing that needed tariff protection, whereas the

Northern capitalists needed a tariff barrier to protect their infant industries against competition from Europe.

The ruling class in the South had no interest in developing industry. The Southern slave owning aristocracy based itself on backwardness. The big landowners were quite happy to remain as England's cotton field and in return they would import English manufactured goods without the imposition of a tariff that would only benefit the manufacturers of the North. The secession was a direct challenge to American nationhood. If accepted, it would undermine everything the American people had fought for since Independence. But from the standpoint of the South it was a defensive war "for Southern rights."

When South Carolina and ten other slave states declared themselves to be no longer part of the Union, Lincoln's main priority was to prevent the breakup of the Union. As a minority president, Lincoln was compelled to do deals with other parties and groups. He could not even rely on the support of all members of his own party. On the contrary, the upper circles of the party were constantly conspiring to remove him and replace him with some political baron. Therefore he was obliged to tack and compromise. But compromise was in vain.

In vain did Lincoln attempt to reassure the slave owners that his government would "not interfere with the institution of slavery in the states where it exists." He was merely echoing the position of an important section of the Northern bourgeoisie that wanted to avoid a conflict with the South. This fact explains why Lincoln was so cautious at the beginning. His own views were quite clear from the beginning when he said: "*A house divided against itself cannot stand; this government divided into free states and slave states cannot endure, they must all be free or all be slave; they must be one thing or the other.*" But he did not have a firm base of support. This only came in the course of the war itself, which galvanized and hardened public opinion. By the end of this terrible conflict, however, Lincoln was not the same man as at the beginning. From a political tussle to preserve the Union, the Civil War evolved inexorably into a revolutionary war against slavery.

The industrial bourgeoisie of the North wished to consolidate its power by destroying the outmoded slave system in the South. It suited their interests. But they did not pursue the task with any enthusiasm. On the contrary, a significant section of the Northern capitalists would have been willing to reach a compromise with the Southern reactionaries. They feared a war that would disrupt trade and preferred to confine themselves to a series of parliamentary maneuvers, like the "Missouri Compromise." But the logic of the situation ruled out any compromise, and these parliamentary intrigues and political struggles culminated in the civil war that the bourgeoisie had hoped to avoid.

While the South was eager for war and immediately began its preparations, the North dragged its feet and was unprepared for the conflict when it finally erupted in the attack on Fort Sumter. But as soon as it became clear that war was unavoidable, Lincoln acted with tremendous determination. He ordered the removal of two million dollars of Southern funds from the Treasury and the confiscation of Western Union's files. He also suspended the right of *habeus corpus*, by executive order, although according to the Constitution only Congress has the right to do this. Thousands of men were arrested and held indefinitely without even charging them with any offense. These measures were strictly unconstitutional. They were *dictatorial* measures. But they were absolutely necessary in the given situation.

Under the Constitution the power to raise armies and to declare war is invested in Congress. Lincoln paid no attention to this. He immediately assumed the authority to create armies and to wage war on the secessionist states. A drastic measure, certainly. But what else could he have done? Nor did the freedom of speech fare any better. Lincoln's subordinates raided the offices of newspapers and stopped their publication, in spite of the First Amendment of the Constitution. This states that the federal authority shall not abridge the freedom of speech or of the press.

The Maryland Legislature was due to convene on September 17, 1861. The military commander of the district was instructed by the secretary of war to arrest all the members who were *suspected* of disloyalty. Many were arrested and thrown into prison, although none of them was actually charged with having committed acts of treason or disloyalty. There were many such actions. In his inspired historical novel *Lincoln*, Gore Vidal writes:

> Currently, by Seward's order, the mayor of Baltimore and the mayor of Washington were both in prison, where they would remain without trial until such time as he or the President was inspired to let them go. As a Lawyer and as an office-holder, sworn to uphold the Constitution and its Bill of Rights, not to mention those inviolable protections of both persons and property so firmly spelled out in *Magna Carta* and in the whole subsequent accretion of the common law, Seward found that he quite enjoyed tearing up, one by one, those ancient liberties in the Union's name. Never before had anyone ever exercised such power in the United States as he did now, with Lincoln's tacit blessing. Although, officially, the secret service was under the military, regular reports were made to Seward, in whose name letters were opened, copies of telegrams seized, arrests made (Vidal, 273).

Nowadays it is assumed that everyone was behind Lincoln (in the North at least). But this is very far from the truth. Most of the rich hated him. There were constant conspiracies to get rid of him, and a constant avalanche of calumnies and insults in the press. *Harpers Weekly* described the President as a *"Filthy story-teller, Despot, Liar, Thief, Braggart, Buffoon, Usurper, Monster, Ignoramus, Abe, Old scoundrel, Perjurer, Robber, Swindler, tyrant, Field-Butcher, Land Pirate."* This was typical. It was also in the Civil War that the (then) revolutionary measure was introduced to tax the incomes of the rich to finance the war. No wonder the rich denounced Lincoln as a dictator and called for his removal! Nowadays he would have been called a communist as well.

However, unless Lincoln had been prepared to override the private interests of the capitalists, the Union would never have won the war. In every war situation, certain liberties are suspended or curtailed. The same is true in a revolution, although the degree to which such "exceptional" measures is necessary depends on many things. If the Southern slave owners had been prepared to accept the will of the majority and obey the democratically elected government, Lincoln would never have had to take the measures he did to curtail democratic rights. But the slave owners' rebellion forced him to do so.

To those who argue that a socialist revolution necessarily means the abolition of democracy, we answer: not so! Marxists stand for democracy and are its most fervent defenders. We will make use of all the democratic openings to present our ideas and fight to win the majority. We stand for a democratically elected socialist government. We do not advocate violence. But we are also realists and know that the ruling class will never surrender its power, wealth, and privileges without a fight with no holds barred. What happened in the American Civil War proves this.

If a democratically elected socialist government is faced by another slave owners' rebellion, we reserve the right to act in the same way that Abe Lincoln acted. To do anything else would be to accept the right of capital to continue its dictatorship forever and deny the right of the people to determine its own destiny. Of course, it goes without saying that any suspension or curtailment of democratic rights must be only temporary, for the duration of the emergency, not a moment longer. That was the case in Britain and the USA during the Second World War, which most people thought was a war for democracy (in fact, it was not, but that is another matter). The workers in the USA and Britain had democratic traditions but were prepared *voluntarily* to accept certain limitations for the duration of the war and *for that only.*

Nobody nowadays condemns Abraham Lincoln for his actions during the Second American Revolution, when he took measures against big business, confiscated wealth, and arrested counterrevolutionaries without trial. Few people even remember such things. Yet they throw their hands up in horror at the actions of Lenin and Trotsky in 1917 in Russia. Why such a hypocritical difference should be made between the two is not clear.

The Problem of Leadership

At the start of the war, in fact, things went very badly for the Union. The South had better generals, who were not afraid to go on the offensive, making up with courage and energy for their numerical disadvantage compared to the more populous and wealthy industrial North. The white population of the South believed they were fighting a defensive war—a war for self-determination and independence, in fact—and they fought with conviction. As a result the Confederate forces won victory after victory.

By contrast, at the beginning of the war the Union forces did not display the necessary determination and energy. They were continually forced onto the defensive by the Confederates who fought better and had far more capable generals. Even the celebrated defense of Fort Sumter, which Union propaganda made a great deal of at the time, was little more than a charade. Major Anderson, the Fort's defender, declined to haul down the flag after the first volleys but stated complacently that even if he were not attacked he would have to hand over the Fort in a few days, as there would be nothing to eat. The resistance was merely formal. The surrender of Fort Sumter seems to have been quite an amicable affair. Major Anderson had dinner with General Beauregard, the Confederate commander, and then the Union flag was hauled down to the accompaniment of a salute and full military honors.

This was typical of the attitude of most Union commanders at the beginning of the Civil War. It is strikingly similar to the position at the start of the English Civil War in the 17th century, when Royalist and Parliamentarian commanders often exchanged letters on the eve of battle professing their friendship for each other and their abhorrence of the conflict that pitted one against the other. In a civil war above all, political questions predominate over military ones. At bottom, the problem was not military but political. The Northern general staff simply reflected the opinions of most of the ruling class, which did not believe in the war and was looking for a compromise.

The Confederates, quite naturally, had a poor opinion of the North's military potential. When Lincoln announced his appeal for 75,000 volunteers, the Confederate cabinet met the news with roars of laughter. Actually, the Union army increased rapidly to the point where it was already the strongest army in the world, with close to 200,000 well-trained troops in the area of

Washington alone. But this advantage was initially thrown away by a succession of incompetent Union generals. General McClellan was one of the most notorious cases. His supine inactivity exasperated Lincoln, who wrote him a stream of letters like the following:

Major-General McClellan,

I have just read your despatch about sore-tongued and fatigued horses. Will you pardon me for asking what the horses of your army have done since the battle of Antietam that fatigues anything?

This angry correspondence culminated in a laconic outburst of despair:

My dear McClellan; if you don't want to use the army I should like to borrow it for a while.

Yours respectfully, A. Lincoln.

At one point McClellan came within six miles of the rebel capital Richmond, but failed to take the city although his army outnumbered the Confederate forces by at least five to one and their commander had been seriously wounded. The real reason for this situation was not just that McClellan was a bad general (which he was). The real reason was that he was intriguing against Lincoln. McClellan, who secretly aspired to become a dictator, an American Bonaparte, was, like a significant section of the Northern ruling class, in favor of doing a deal with the South to end the war. Most of the other generals in the Union army were not much better. General Hooker, ironically nicknamed "Fighting Joe" is another example of a useless Northern general. He was a champion at the art of whisky drinking, though not at the art of war. At the battle of Chancellorsville he led 130,000 Union troops against Lee's Confederate army of only 60,000. Yet Lee managed to inflict the greatest defeat on the Northern army in the history of the war. General Hooker is today remembered for something not directly connected with the military profession but with a rather older one. His camp, according to a contemporary witness, resembled something in between a brothel and a casino. So addicted were the general and his staff to the sins of the flesh that the female visitors to his camp were known as "Hooker's girls," or simply hookers.

General Sherman was a more effective, if extremely brutal, commander. He had been removed from command early in the war because his superiors thought he had gone mad. His "crime" was to predict that hundreds of thousands would die in the coming conflict—a prediction that tragically came true. Politically he was a reactionary who believed in slavery. In December 1859, when the abolition uproar was at its height, he wrote, "I would not if I

could abolish or modify slavery." And in July 1860, he wrote, "All the Congress-
es on earth can't make the negro anything else than what he is; he must be
subject to the white man, or he must amalgamate or be destroyed. Two such
races cannot live in harmony save as master and slave."

He is quoted as saying (correctly) that the war did not begin professionally
until after Vicksburg and Gettysburg (that is, not until July 1863). Paradoxically, General Robert E. Lee, the Southern commander, was opposed to slavery.
Before the war he wrote that it was a "moral and political evil" and hoped it
would be abolished. But his loyalty lay with his state of Virginia, and he fought
with great valor and ability to establish a nation that would have been based
on that same "moral and political evil," while Sherman's army emancipated
the slaves as it marched through Georgia. The personal and moral values of
the individuals were subordinate to the class content of the struggle. This was
basically a war between two incompatible socio-economic systems—capitalism and slavery. Capitalism won and that changed everything.

The war dragged on and the cost in lives was without precedent. In a single campaign, the Union army under Ulysses S. Grant lost 50,000 dead and
wounded. And these figures do not include the Confederate casualties. This
further strengthened the capitulationist trend of the Northern bourgeoisie.
The mood of the capitalists was to sell out and get peace at all costs. The
so-called Peace Democrats were on the rise, reflecting the bourgeois' lack of
enthusiasm for the war. War was bad for business (although not in all cases).

But the Northern employers should not have worried. In the long run
the South could not prevail. The industrial might of the North, its far greater
wealth and bigger population proved decisive. Industrial output in the state
of New York alone was four times that of the entire Confederacy. The population of the United States at the beginning of the war was about 31.5 million. Of
these about 8.7 million were in the Confederacy, from which we must deduct
3.6 million slaves. The Confederate army had to be drawn from the white population of just over five million, plus some reinforcements from three Southern states that did not secede: Maryland, Kentucky, and Missouri. By contrast,
the Union had a population of about 23 million.

That means the North could put four times as many men on the field and
take many more losses without affecting their fighting capacity. In addition
the North had command of the sea and was able to blockade the Southern
ports more or less effectively from the beginning. The blockade caused
shortages that led to food riots even in Richmond, the Confederate capital.
This shows the falsity of the propaganda of the pro-Confederate historians,
according to whom the entire population of the South were united in their

enthusiasm for the Confederate cause. The initial enthusiasm wore off and by 1864 the Confederacy was held together by arbitrary and despotic measures backed up by state repression.

As the war dragged on there were also problems in the North. After years of hardship there was discontent among a layer of the masses. The Conscription Act, which allowed the sons of the rich to buy their way out of military service, provoked riots in New York, where the measure was seen as "a rich man's war and a poor man's fight." In what turned out to be a prolonged war of attrition, the North was able to tolerate the terrible casualty rate far better than the South. However, to win the war it was necessary to adopt a revolutionary policy that would rouse the masses in the North to fight with the spirit of conviction.

Role of the Working Class

War is undoubtedly terrible, and civil wars are more terrible than any other. Yet war is also a source of profit to some, and great fortunes can be coined by the few from the blood, sweat, and tears of the many. The American Civil War was no exception. In the spring of 1864 it was possible for a speculator to take $600 in gold, exchange it for $1,000 in dollars, buy a $1,000 bond with the dollars and get $60 a year interest on the bond or a 15 percent profit on his initial investment. All measures to limit this profiteering proved futile. Despite its fundamentally revolutionary character, the Civil War led inexorably to increased centralization of power and wealth in a few hands. This explains the resentment of the masses, as expressed in outbursts like the New York riots.

Bondholders plundered the treasury, crooked manufacturers plundered the army, speculators plundered the whole population and made their fortunes out of blood, death, and misery. In his *Life of Thaddeus Stevens*, James A. Woodburn writes:

> One may well doubt whether there was ever a more outrageous fleecing and robbery of a patriotic people than that perpetrated through the influence of capitalists and money lenders by the manipulation of government finance during and immediately following the American Civil War.

Lincoln realized that the masses would not be prepared to give their lives willingly just to prevent the South from seceding. He therefore proposed a most revolutionary measure. On September 22, 1862, president Lincoln summoned the cabinet and took them by surprise. He told them he had an important paper to read. But when they came into the room it appeared the President was reading a humorous story—which he often did. Then he closed his book and informed them that he had been thinking a lot about the relation between the war and slavery. "I think the time for action has now come and I have got you together to hear what I have written down." This was the Emancipation Proclamation. It read as follows:

> I, Abraham Lincoln, President of the United States of America, do proclaim that on the first day of January, 1863, all persons held as slaves within any State, or designated part of a State, the people whereof shall then be in rebellion against the United States, shall then be, thenceforward and forever, free; and the executive Government of the United States, including the military and naval authorities thereof, will recognize and maintain the freedom of such persons, and will do no act, or acts, to repress such persons, or any of them, in any efforts they may make for their actual freedom.

It must be realized that this proclamation, like so many of Lincoln's acts during the war, was an executive order, issued under the war powers conferred on the president by Congress. In effect, he went over the heads of Congress and the cabinet to speak directly to the American people. He understood that in order to win the war it was necessary to inspire and motivate the masses by adopting a revolutionary program. The Civil War would not be won by guns and bayonets alone, but by the moral force behind the guns and bayonets. As long as people in the North suspected that this was a rich man's war in which the poor were called on to fight and die for the interests of the wealthy merchants and industrialists of the North, the war could not be won. He therefore decided to appeal directly to the masses.

In order to wage war against the slaveholding South, Abraham Lincoln relied upon the support of the mass of American workers and small farmers. After some initial hesitation (he was afraid of losing the support of the four border states of Delaware, Kentucky, Maryland, and Missouri, where slavery still existed), he accepted the recruitment of black soldiers into the Union armies. He also openly espoused the cause of labor, making comments that nowadays would automatically make him suspect of subversion and communism. He said, among other things:

> All that harms labor is treason to America. No line can be drawn between these two. If any man tells you he loves America, yet hates labor, he is a liar. If a man tells you he trusts America, yet fears labor, he is a fool.

He also defended the right to strike as a democratic right of working people:

> I am glad to see that a system of labor prevails under which laborers can strike whenever they want to . . . I like the system which lets a man quit when he wants to and wish it might prevail everywhere.

After two years of bloody fighting, the Emancipation Proclamation freed the slaves in those states fighting against the Union. Later the slaves were also freed in the neutral border states. No longer were four million human beings to be held in bondage. Inspired by the message of freedom, the workers of the North threw themselves enthusiastically into the struggle. Many trade union locals were dissolved for the duration of the conflict, as the entire workforce was often away at war. In the conflict between Northern industrial capitalism and Southern landlordism and slavery, it was clear which side the workers supported. American trade unionists also played a decisive role in the fight against slavery, as Northern workers signed up in droves for the Union Army.

The victory of the North was due only to a small extent to the military capabilities of General Ulysses S. Grant. Although undoubtedly a better general than his predecessors (he could hardly be worse!) Grant was no military genius. As W.E. Woodward expresses it: "Grant just happened to be swimming with the tide and he was a man who swam extremely well in that particular kind of tide" (Woodward, 563). Later he proved to be a spectacularly incompetent president at the head of a voraciously corrupt administration. As a general, he combined a muleheaded stubbornness with an indifference to the horrific scale of casualties on his own side. These qualities, however, were sufficient to wear down the South and bring it to its knees.

The Battle of Gettysburg was the decisive turning point. The battle was fought over three days of bloody slaughter from July 1 to the 3, 1863. The Confederates lost 20,000 men, killed, wounded, or captured. The Union army had 23,000 casualties. But these losses were far more serious to the South than to the North. In the end, the wealth, population, and industrial muscle of the Union was decisive and the Confederates' early victories proved unsustainable. But it was above all the courageous decision of Abraham Lincoln to fight a revolutionary war against the slave-owning South that tipped the balance. Lincoln's "Gettysburg Address" is one of the great revolutionary democratic documents of all time. With its clarion call of government of the people, by the people, for the people, it stands alongside the Declaration of Independence as a landmark in the struggle for democracy.

By the spring of 1864 the Confederacy was on its knees. One hard blow would be enough to topple it. Congress created the grade of lieutenant general and Lincoln immediately conferred this rank on Grant. The victory of the Union was not in doubt. But the losses in the Union army were horrendous, in large measure because of the way Grant conducted himself. We see the character of the man in the short but bloody battle of Cold Harbor, where the Union forces lost 7,000 men in an hour, compared to 600 of Lee's men. The army was on the brink of mutiny. Some regiments refused to participate in what was obviously a suicidal assault on the rebel capital.

More successful was Sherman's advance through Georgia and the Carolinas, which was accompanied by a merciless scorched earth policy. Sherman's army burned everything in its path. The actions of a section of the soldiery were a disgrace to the Northern cause. But this burning and plundering was enthusiastically greeted by sections of Northern public opinion. Especially bloodthirsty (as is often the case in times of war) were the preachers. Phillip Brooks, a devout Massachusetts pastor and author of *The Influence of Jesus*, when he heard about the torching of Columbia, exclaimed: "Hurrah for Columbia! Isn't Sherman a gem?" Despite its savagery, Sherman's campaign severely weakened the already enfeebled South. Grant's forces overwhelmed Lee's defenses. Finally, Lee faced Grant at Appomattox, about 80 miles from Richmond, with a force of only 28,000 starving and exhausted men against Grant's army of 72,000. Lee was compelled to surrender.

Lee presented himself to Grant dressed in a splendid uniform of Confederate grey made from English cloth and handed Grant a handsome sword with a jewel-studded hilt. Grant was dressed in the travel-stained uniform of a private to which the shoulder straps of a lieutenant general had been attached. The contrast had a deep symbolic value. The aristocratic slave owning gentry of the South were overthrown by the capitalist North. The past was defeated by the future.

The victory of the North was a revolutionary victory. It transformed the face of the United States. At a stroke the rule of the slave owners was overthrown. The reactionary class of Southern planters was deprived of two billion dollars worth of property, with not a single cent in compensation. *Thus, there is nothing "un-American" about the expropriation of tyrants and oligarchs, which was carried out both in 1776 and in 1865. The United States was established at birth with an act of revolutionary expropriation. In the same way, a socialist USA in the future will be established by the expropriation of the property of the big banks and corporations that exercise their dictatorship over the people and have turned democracy into an empty word.*

By the end of the war, Abraham Lincoln was a changed man. He was drawing ever more radical conclusions. Lincoln's revolutionary measures earned him the love and admiration of the working class in the USA and internationally. But it aroused the bitter hatred of the ruling class—and not only in the South. Even at the height of the war, Lincoln did not have a firm base of support in his own party. A section put forward the cowardly and reactionary scoundrel McClellan as the presidential candidate. Lincoln's popular majority was tiny—only half a million votes. In spite of everything, Lincoln was reelected and the Thirteenth Amendment for the unconditional abolition of slavery was passed. It was a new dawn for the American people. But Lincoln also took measures in the interests of the poor farmers in the North. The Homestead Act was the first in American history to give public land free of charge to citizens who agreed to settle on it. What new measures he would have passed had he lived we shall never know. The slave owners took their revenge for their defeat. On April 14, 1865, Abraham Lincoln was shot down in cold blood by a Confederate assassin.

International Repercussions of the Civil War

At the outbreak of the Civil War there was a considerable amount of British capital invested in American enterprises, including the railroads, banking, coal, timber, and land. The sympathies of the British ruling class were with the South. A reactionary coalition of textile manufacturers, landowners, and imperialists put heavy pressure on the British government to recognize the Confederate States. *The Times* of London could hardly conceal its glee when commenting on how short-lived the Union of American states had been.

The Confederates were confident in their belief in the power of King Cotton. And since Britain took five-sixths of all the exports of American cotton, and there were about 400,000 workers in English cotton mills who depended on cotton for their livelihood (making a total of about two million with their families and dependents), they were convinced that within three months Britain would recognize the South, smash the blockade, and if necessary, fight the Union to guarantee supplies of cotton to British mills. During the Civil War several Confederate warships were built in English shipyards or purchased from British subjects. Their crews were mostly made up of English sailors. Three of these vessels—the *Alabama*, *Florida*, and *Shenandoah*—did a lot of damage to Northern commerce. Yet none of these vessels ever entered a Confederate port. This open connivance of the British government with the rebels constituted a flagrant provocation and a blatant breach of neutrality.

In fact, Britain came close to declaring war on the Union in November 1861 when an American ship, the *San Jacinto*, stopped the *Trent*, a British mail packet boat, off the coast of Cuba and seized two Confederate commissioners on their way to London. A military intervention by Britain would have drastically changed the balance of forces to the disadvantage of the Union. If the British government finally backed down it was mainly for fear of the reaction of British public opinion, and especially the working class.

While the British ruling class openly sympathized with the slave owners of the Confederacy, the working people of Britain wholeheartedly backed the Union. This was quite remarkable if we bear in mind that the Civil War in America badly disrupted the trade in cotton and caused a depression in the cotton mills of Lancashire and terrible unemployment and suffering for the workers. The English radical John Bright toured Lancashire explaining the plight of the American slaves:

> The jobless mill hands resolved to stick by their black brothers in the Southern states of America, although their allegiance compelled them to feed at soup kitchens and live on charitable relief (Woodward, 527–28).

In this war against the forces of reaction, the International Workingmen's Association (the First International) sided unequivocally with the North against the South. It is not generally known that Karl Marx wrote two letters to Abraham Lincoln on behalf of the IWA, expressing his admiration and support for the latter in his fight against slavery. Thus, in this decisive moment in American history, Marxism stood shoulder to shoulder with the American people, and not just in words. Members of the IWA fought in the ranks of the Union army, and thus fulfilled their internationalist duty. Working-class revolutionaries like Anneke and Weydemeyer—the latter a close friend of Marx—served with distinction in the ranks of the Union army.

An Interesting Comparison

Recently the author of these lines was invited to participate in a television documentary about the French Revolution. The filmmakers were charming and intelligent young Americans, who apparently wanted to know what the Marxist perspective on the French Revolution was. During our preliminary conversations, they asked me whether I considered the French Revolution to be justified, in view of all the violence and bloodshed it involved. I think they were a bit surprised at my answer. I drew their attention to the fact that America won its independence through a revolution, and that in that revolution they did not treat the British very gently. Moreover, the second American Revolution was a very violent and bloody affair. Yet nobody has ever asked me whether the American War of Independence was justified, or whether Abraham Lincoln was right to use violence against the Southern slave owners.

In the French Revolution of 1789–93, almost two million died out of a population of only 26 million—that is, about 7.7 percent. Yet few French people (excepting a handful of eccentric people nostalgic for the good old days of Louis XVI) would argue that they would have been better off under the *ancien régime*. Even fewer Americans would argue that, in order to avoid bloodshed, they should have remained under the blessed rule of George III!

The critics of Bolshevism also frequently raise the question of revolutionary violence. Actually, the October Revolution was a relatively peaceful affair, particularly in Petrograd, since the Bolsheviks had the support of the overwhelming majority, and practically nobody was prepared to fight for the old regime. The real bloodbath began in the Civil War, which was the exact equivalent of the slaveholders' rising in the USA. Soviet Russia was invaded by 21 foreign armies of intervention: British, French, German, Poles, Czechs, Japanese—and Americans. Many people were killed unnecessarily because of this, and the Russian people suffered terrible hardship. Incidentally, this was when the parties that opposed the Bolsheviks were banned—since every one of them took up arms against the Soviet government.

Lenin and Trotsky originally had no plans to prohibit other parties. After the October Revolution the only party that was outlawed was the fascist and antisemitic Black Hundreds. But in the same way that Abraham Lincoln was obliged to take drastic measures against the rebels during the Civil War, so Lenin and Trotsky were compelled to act against parties that not only agitated against the Revolution but took up arms against it. It is not generally realized that, relative to population size, many more people were killed in the American Civil War than in the civil war in Soviet Russia. Yet very little is said on this subject, and certainly nobody ever accuses Abe Lincoln of being a bloodthirsty monster as they accuse Lenin and Trotsky with tedious regularity. Let us make a brief comparison of the two.

Because of the chaotic character of the period, there are no exact figures for casualties in the Russian Civil War. But the total deaths incurred in both the First World War and the subsequent Civil War adds up to about three million. If we assume that one-third of these died during the Civil War (which is certainly an exaggeration), the result would be one million. Since the population of Russia was 150 million at that time, that is 0.7 percent. In the American Civil War, according to the most accurate figures I could find, the total killed (not including wounded) on both sides was 558,052 out of total population of 34,300,000. That would mean 1.63 percent of the population was killed. That is already more than in the Russian Revolution. However, if we include the wounded—many of whom were horribly crippled and deformed—then the percentage of the total killed *and* wounded would actually be 2.83 percent of the population. In other words, a lot more blood was shed in the American Civil War.

	Population (millions)	Enrolled (thousands)	Enrolled (percent)
Union	26.2	2,803.3	10.7%
Confederate	8.1	1,064.2	13.1%
Combined	34.3	3,867.5	11.1%

	Combat Deaths	Other Deaths	Wounded	Total Casualties
Union	110,070	249,458	275,175	634,703
Confederate	74,524	124,000	+137,000	335,524
Combined	184,594	373,458	+412,175	970,227

The Civil War in the USA was a revolution, just as much as the French Revolution of 1789–93 or the October Revolution in Russia. Many people lost their lives in it, yet nobody considers it a "crime." In fact, while naturally regretting the loss of life, the historians are unanimous in agreeing that it was worth it, that is to say, *the end justified the means*. Yet this is supposed to be the original sin of Bolshevism!

We might add that there is no reason to suppose that the Socialist Revolution in America will be a bloody affair. The USA is not tsarist Russia! The American working class is an overwhelming majority of the population. It could easily take power, brushing aside the resistance of the big corporations, on one condition: that it is organized, disciplined, and determined to overcome all obstacles. There is one other condition that would guarantee a peaceful transformation: a courageous and farsighted leadership that would not be afraid to adopt the most audacious measures to disarm the ruling class and render it impotent. The American workers need a revolutionary party and a leadership like that of Abraham Lincoln and Sam Adams: men and women who are not hypnotized by the power of the oppressors, their rules and regulations, but prepared to rely only on the revolutionary initiative and power of the masses.

How Capitalism Failed African Americans

The Second American Revolution was a tremendous step forward, but it never realized its promise to black Americans. The real winners in the Civil War were the Northern capitalists who opened up new markets and obtained a huge new supply of dirt-cheap labor. Nearly a century and a half after the abolition of slavery in the USA, we are very far from achieving genuine equality for all, regardless of race, color, or sex. Despite a number of advances achieved through the struggles of black people in the 1960s, the position of blacks remains one of clear disadvantage. Michael Moore points out that in the USA today:

· About 20 percent of young black men between the ages of sixteen and twenty-four are neither in school nor working—compared with only 9 percent of young white men. Despite the "economic boom" of the nineties, this percentage has not fallen substantially over the last ten years.

· In 1993, white households had invested nearly three times as much in stocks and mutual funds and/or IRA and Keogh accounts as black households. Since then, the stock market has more than doubled its value.

· Black heart attack patients are far less likely than whites to undergo cardiac catheterization, a common and potentially lifesaving procedure, regardless of the race of their doctors. Black and white doctors together referred white patients for catheterization about 40 percent more often than black patients.

· Whites are five times more likely than blacks to receive emergency clot-busting treatment for stroke.

· Black women are four times more likely than white women to die while giving birth.

· Black levels of unemployment have been roughly twice those of whites since 1954.

· In the first nine months of 2002, the US unemployment rate averaged 5.7 percent, compared with the first nine months of 2000, when it averaged 4 percent. About 2.5 million more workers are unemployed now than in 2000. But the unemployment rate for African-Americans has risen about 60 percent faster than for all workers. Some 400,000 more are now out of work than were out of work in 2000, a two-year rise of 30 percent.

Capitalism has failed all Americans, with the exception of the tiny minority that own and control the means of production and treat the country and its government as their private property. But the biggest losers are the twenty percent at the bottom of the pile, and of these the biggest majority are blacks and Latinos. Despite the attempts to disguise this situation by the kind of tokenism that allows a handful of privileged blacks like Colin Powell or Condoleeza Rice to figure prominently on the stage, the position of the great majority of working class and poor black people has not been substantially improved.

The conclusion is clear. The only way to eliminate racism is by pulling it up by the roots. The black slaves were first brought into the USA as a form of cheap labor serving the wealthy Southern planters. As a result of the Second American Revolution, they are formally free. But they remain as before cheap labor at the disposal of big business. The link between racism and capitalism was eventually clearly understood by Malcolm X and the Black Panthers, who attempted to organize on class lines and link the struggle of blacks for advancement to the general struggles of the American working class. This represented a deadly menace to the establishment that has thrived for so long on the policy of divide and rule. That is why the Black Panthers and Malcolm X were targeted and ruthlessly hunted down and killed.

Marxists consider the basic principles of the American Revolution to represent a great historic advance, but also consider that the only way to breathe life into these great principles is by overthrowing the rule of the big banks and monopolies that exercise a dictatorship over the people and have turned the idea of democracy into an empty shell. The overthrow of the dictatorship of big business demands the utmost unity in struggle of all working people—black and white, Native American and Irish, Hispanic and Asian, Arab and Jewish, white and blue collar, men and women, old and young. We make no distinction on grounds of color, sex, or creed. It is necessary to unite all the oppressed, underprivileged, and exploited people under the banner of the labor movement and socialism.

On the basis of a genuine socialist society—which has nothing to do with dictatorship or totalitarianism—the idea of the Rights of Man and Woman will cease to be an empty phrase and become a reality. Not only life, liberty, and the pursuit of happiness, but a genuine freedom to develop the potential of human beings to the full—this is the meaning of socialism.

CHAPTER V

LABOR AND CAPITAL

"Give Me Your Huddled Masses"

The emigration of the Pilgrims was the first influx into America of people fleeing from a defeated revolution, but by no means the last. Over the last two centuries we observe the following phenomenon: after every defeat of a revolution in Europe, there was a big influx of refugees into America. That rich mosaic of peoples that fused together to form the modern American nation was formed in the first place out of Poles, Hungarians, Germans, Italians, Russians, Scandinavians, Jews, Irish, and Asians, with the admixture of the descendants of African slaves and more recently, people from Latin America.

Where did these people come from? If we leave aside the Native Americans and the millions of black slaves forcibly torn from their native lands and shipped to the plantations of the South, and consider the European immigrants who formed the central core of the population of the USA in the 19th century, the great majority were, like the Pilgrims, political refugees fleeing from either victorious counterrevolution or national oppression. The defeat of the Polish uprisings of 1830 and 1863, the crushing of the German revolution of 1848, the persecution of Jews and revolutionaries by Russian tsarism, the defeat of numerous uprisings of the Irish people against their British tormentors—all these things provided America with a steady flood of human material that made it what it is today.

The opening up of the West was undoubtedly a historically progressive development (although it was a terrible tragedy for the native peoples who were regarded as an obstacle to be removed). Americans refer proudly to the "pioneer spirit" that made this development possible. But where did this spirit come from? In order to conquer the vast open spaces of North America, to clear the dense forests, to brave the innumerable dangers of an untamed and hostile environment—all this required a special kind of people, motivated by a special kind of spirit. If we examine this question more closely, it will immediately become evident that those heroic pioneers who threw themselves with such energy into the opening up of America were to a very large extent revolutionaries who, having lost all faith in the possibility of changing the Old World, looked for and found a new life in the New World. The very same energy and courage with which they fought against the ruling regimes in Europe was now turned to other purposes. *Thus, the celebrated American "pioneer spirit" was to a very large extent the product of a revolutionary psychology and spirit that simply found a different outlet.*

This fact was already understood by the great German philosopher Hegel, who pointed out that if France had possessed the prairies of North America, the French Revolution would never have taken place. Here we also find the historical explanation for the celebrated "American Dream," the idea that it is possible for anyone to succeed on the basis of individual initiative and work. In a period when America possessed vast expanses of uncultivated land, this vision was not altogether without foundation. The apparently unlimited possibilities meant that the idea of revolution was subsumed and absorbed. In place of the struggle between the classes, there was the struggle of individual men and women against nature, the unceasing fight to tame the wilderness and carve a living out of mother earth. This is the true origin of that element of rugged individualism that has for so long been regarded as the basic ingredient of the "American character."

W.E. Woodward writes:

> Like those who were better off, the average laboring man or farmer was an individualist too. He detested authority and was inclined to be rowdy and pugnacious. His class consciousness was dissipated by his individual self-assertiveness. The working class had no leaders, and it is doubtful if any set of leaders, however gifted, could have organized the laboring men of that time into a permanent association or a working class political party. Laborers' revolts took the form of spontaneous and senseless riots which usually began and ended in a few hours.
>
> The spirit of our early civilization was the spirit of the pioneer. It pervaded all classes of society. Four out of five men were pioneers in something or other, or the sons of pioneers. A feeling for adventure, a pride in single-handed accomplishment, was a necessity of social life.
>
> Through the generations the pioneering spirit has persisted in its various sublimated forms, long after the need for it has passed away. It has become so thoroughly infused in the American character that it has acquired

the dignity of an honored tradition, and in that role it adds enormously to our present-day vexations and befuddlements. You may observe it in the ardent worship of individualism; in the widespread opposition to collective efforts for human betterment; in the stubborn attempts to preserve, in individualistic patterns, activities which are inherently social. There is a time and a place for the pioneer, the individualist, but in a modern, compact, highly organized society, he is not helpful but destructive (Woodward, 252).

In the 19th century, the famous French sociologist and historian Alexis de Tocqueville wrote a well-known book called *Democracy in America*, which ever since has enjoyed the status of a classic. His basic thesis is that democracy in the United States had such profound roots because the difference between rich and poor was relatively small, and certainly much less than in Europe. He also observed that many rich Americans had started out poor and worked their way up the social ladder. When de Tocqueville wrote his book, this was largely true. With the exception of the South—where slavery still ruled supreme and a wealthy white aristocracy existed—in most of the states of the Union, there existed a remarkable degree of equality between citizens. Of course, there were still rich and poor. But even the poorer citizens felt that it was still possible to "get on" with a little effort. Class divisions existed—there were the so-called range wars between the big ranchers and smallholders that sometimes assumed a violent character. But in general, until the last decades of the 19th century, the class struggle, although clearly present, remained relatively undeveloped.

This had certain consequences. For example, for a long time the state was relatively weak, and America was not cursed with the heavy burden of bureaucracy and militarism that weighed so heavily on most nations in Europe. However, all that began to change with the rapid development of industrial capitalism towards the end of the 19th century. The growth of the big trusts, the search for markets and the commencement of America's involvement in foreign adventures, beginning with Spanish-Cuban-American War of 1892–98, marked the inexorable transformation of the USA into a country dominated by giant monopolies and the most powerful imperialist state the world has ever seen.

The Golden Calf

"To think," he said to Gallatin, "what has happened to our country since your father's day! Since the time of Jefferson!"

Gallatin was astonished. "But surely everything is so much better now, Mr. Tilden. The country is so big, so very rich . . ." This was some weeks before the panic. "Railroads everywhere. Great manufactories. Floods of cheap labor *from poor old Europe. America is El Dorado now, while in my father's time it was just a nation of farmers—and not very good farmers at that."*

"You misunderstood me, Mr. Gallatin." Tilden's sallow cheeks now each contained a smudge of brick-colored red. "I speak of corruption. Of judges for sale. Of public men dividing among themselves the people's money. Of newspapers bought, bought by political bosses. Even the Post.*" Tilden nodded gravely to me, knowing that I often wrote for that paper. "The* Post *took a retainer from Tweed. That's what I mean by change in our country, this worship of the Golden Calf, of the almighty dollar, this terrible corruption"* (Gore Vidal, 1876).

American capitalism in the nineteenth century was a historically progressive force, and the victory of the North laid the basis for the economic expansion and domination of the US on a world scale. It freed up a massive labor pool for capitalist enterprise, and allowed for the domination of a handful of industrialists, paving the way for the giant trusts and monopolies of the 1890s. While the working class was fighting and dying in the war against slavery, the monopolists-to-be were busily enriching themselves in the lucrative war industry. The early fortunes of Carnegie, Mellon, Armour, Gould, Rockefeller, Fisk, Morgan, Cooke, Stanford, Hill, and Huntington were made during this period.

The triumph of capitalism in the USA signified an unprecedented development of the productive forces. This is best shown by the explosive growth of the railroads:

In 1860 there were 30,000 miles of railroad track in the USA. In 1880 there were three times as much—90,000 miles. By 1930 the figure was 260,000 miles.

The supporters of the market economy cite this as a shining example of the achievements of free enterprise. In reality the railway bosses received huge state subsidies. Twelve million acres of government land along the railway's right of way were given outright to the Union Pacific Railway, which, in addition, received a government loan of $27 million in US bonds. Union Pacific, which set out with no funds at all, then entered into an agreement with a small financial entity in Pennsylvania called Crédit Mobilier, to build the railway. One of the directors of Crédit Mobilier was a member of Congress, Oake Ames, who sold stock in the company to his fellow congressmen. The Congressional investigation later discovered that the bank, its stockholders and friends had obtained a profit of $23 million on an initial investment of less than a million.

It is also worth noting that the USA, which today (theoretically at least) stands for "free trade" was originally firmly committed to protectionism and tariffs. Indeed, this was an important element in the conflict between the capitalists of the North and the slaveholding South. The Tariff Act of 1870, which pretended to be a step in the direction of tariff reduction, in fact raised tariffs steeply on things like steel rails that were of fundamental importance to the Northern industrialists. The manufacturers of the North and East, sheltering behind high tariff barriers, were making vast fortunes in easy, unearned profits at the expense of the South and West.

Up to 1860 the government of the United States was largely in the hands of the landowners of the South. From 1865 the Northern capitalist oligarchs pushed them aside and took over the power. Cornelius "Commodore" Vanderbilt, whose rapacious greed was equalled only by his crudeness and ignorance, was the richest man in America. The attitude of these men was shown by his words: "Law! What do I care about law? Hain't I got the power?" Yes, the Vanderbilts and their like had the power, and they still have it. W.E. Woodward provides us with a good account of this capitalist adventurer:

> He was considered a great constructive genius and a pattern for poor boys. But there was in him no constructiveness of any kind. He waited for the other fellow to do all the preliminary work, and when the industry—steamships, railroads, or whatever it was—had turned the corner and was about to be a big thing, then Cornelius Vanderbilt proceeded to crowd out the originators and inventors and get control of the property by methods which would fill an ordinary cardsharp with envy. He was a financial gangster with many lesser gangsters working for him. When he died the reverend gentleman who officiated at his funeral said that "riches and honors had been heaped on Vanderbilt, that he might devote all his ability to the cause of humanity and seek to lay up treasures in heaven."
>
> The net worth of the treasures he laid up in heaven is unknown, but the value of his worldly assets was large. He left about one hundred million dollars (Woodward, 607–8).

The American ruling class has always surrounded itself in the "rags to riches" myth, made popular in Horatio Alger's penny novels. In fact, it has its origins in crime, swindling, and downright robbery. The present rulers of America are descended from a real rogue's gallery of speculators and crooks, such as the pious Daniel Drew, who was a deacon of the church on Sundays and a common stock market swindler the rest of the week. He began his career as a cattle drover who sold cows to the butcher by weight and just before they got to market fed them salt and gave them large quantities of water to drink to increase their weight.

Drew saw no contradiction between this kind of activity and religion. Religion has its place in the church and the home, he said, but not in business. He took this principle to its logical conclusion when he unloaded a pile of worthless stock on the unsuspecting members of his congregation. But that was done on a weekday, so it was presumably OK. When he died he left a fortune to Drew Theological Seminary, an institution that trains preachers—presumably in the same moral principles.

Under the Grant presidency, gangsters like these were allowed to rule unchecked by any controls. The administration was in their pocket, and Grant himself was corrupted by big business, although not as much as other members of his entourage:

> Since the War Grant had played the part of little Jack Horner with much gusto. In his particular corner the plums were numerous. He accepted valuable presents from anybody and everybody. The gifts ran from horses to houses. A group of "fifty solid men" of Boston gave him a library which had cost seventy-five thousand-dollars. Alexander Stewart, a wealthy department store proprietor of New York, sent Mrs. Grant a thousand-dollar shawl, which was gratefully accepted. Whisky distillers contributed cases of their product, and there were donations of furniture, paintings, choice hams, boxes of sausages, and a vast collection of elaborate toys for the general's youngest son (Woodward., 605).

The Grant administration was the first to reveal the real content of bourgeois democracy in the USA. The government was firmly wedded to big business and served it faithfully, while the new class of capitalist robber barons showed their gratitude by generously filling the pockets of the politicians. And all of them regarded the state and its treasury as a gigantic pork barrel from which it was legitimate to help oneself.

The salary of the president was raised from $25,000 to $50,000 a year—a fortune in those days. Senators and representatives also did quite well, their stipends being boosted from $5,000 to $7,500 a year. But unfortunately Congress got too greedy. It proposed to make the measure retroactive for two years. This outstanding piece of legislation became known as the *Back Pay Grab*. It caused a public uproar almost as furious as the Union Pacific bribery case. In the end the Grant presidency sank under a heap of financial scandals. The president's private secretary adviser and friend, Babcock, had received valuable presents and money from the leaders of the Whisky Ring, which he had used to finance Grant's election campaign. There were many other such cases. Grant wrote: "Let no guilty men escape." But they nearly all did and have been escaping ever since. The clique of super wealthy oil barons who control the Bush administration today behave no differently to the crooks and swindlers of the Grant administration. Only the quantities involved are infinitely larger.

Inequality

*It matters not one iota what political party is in power or what president holds
the reins of office. We are not politicians or public thinkers; we are the rich; we
own America; we got it, God knows how, but we intend to keep it if we can by
throwing all the tremendous weight of our support, our influence, our money,
our political connections, our purchased senators, our hungry Congressmen,
our public-speaking demagogues into the scale against any legislature, any
political platform, any presidential campaign that threatens the integrity of
our estate.*—Frederick Townsend Martin, *The Passing of the Idle Rich*

Progress in the last decades of the 19th century was tremendous, but the
fruits of progress were not equally enjoyed by all. The growth of the economic
might of the USA signified a simultaneous growth in the power of big business. By 1904 the Standard Oil Company controlled over 86 percent of the
refined illuminating oil of the country. By 1890, gigantic corporations were in
control of each great industry. The Aluminium Company produced 100 percent of the output of virgin aluminium in the United States. The Ford Motor
Company and the General Motors Corporation together produced three out
of every four cars. The Bell Telephone Company owned four out of every five
telephones in the United States. The Singer Sewing Machine Company made
at least three out of every four sewing machines sold in the United States. And
so on.

The huge polarization between labor and capital, between rich and poor,
was the real basis on which the class struggle developed on the soil of the
United States. In the old days the differences between rich and poor were so
small that a man like de Tocqueville could regard them as insignificant. But
for the last hundred years or more the gulf between rich and poor, between
haves and haves not, has widened into an abyss. The bosses were utterly in-
different to the conditions of their workers. These so-called Christians were
all ardent believers in *laissez-faire* and "Social Darwinism." John D. Rockefeller
is reported to have said: "the growth of a large business is merely a survival
of the fittest." For millions of Americans, living and working conditions were
very bad, and the hope of escaping from a lifetime of poverty virtually nonexistent. As late as the year 1900, the United States had the highest job-related
fatality rate of any industrialized nation in the world. Most industrial workers
worked a 10-hour day (12 hours in the steel industry), yet earned from 20 to
40 percent less than the minimum deemed necessary for a decent life. The
situation was only worse for children, whose numbers in the work force doubled between 1870 and 1900.

Under these conditions socialist ideas were beginning to get an echo in the USA. In 1892 the People's Party noted in its platform:

> The fruits of the toil of millions are boldly stolen to build up colossal wealth for a few . . .
>
> Wealth belongs to him who creates it, and every dollar taken from industry without an equivalent is robbery. If any will not work, neither shall he eat . . .
>
> We believe that the time has come when the railroad corporations will either own the people or the people must own the railroads . . . Transportation being a means of exchange and a public necessity, the government should own and operate the railroads in the interests of the people . . .
>
> The telegraph and telephone, like the post office system, being a necessity for the transmission of news, should be owned and operated by the government in the interest of the people . . .

Karl Marx pointed out that without organization the working class is only raw material for exploitation. The American workers began to organize quite early on. The roots of the labor movement were already well established in the 19th century. William Sylvis, an early trade union activist, founded the Iron Molders' Union, and helped found the National Labor Union, which he wanted to affiliate to the International Workingmen's Association—the body in which Marx played the leading role. He was far ahead of his day on issues of black workers and women—he wanted them in the unions—against considerable opposition. This great advocate of working-class unity, cutting across all artificial lines, died in great poverty at age 41.

The attempts of working people to defend themselves against rapacious employers were met with extreme brutality. As one contemporary labor leader wrote: "a great deal of bitterness was evinced against trade-union organizations, and men were blacklisted to an extent hardly ever equalled." In response the workers formed a clandestine union—The Noble Order of the Knights of Labor—founded in 1869. Originally a secret society organized by Philadelphia garment workers, it was open to all workers, including African Americans, women, and farmers. The Knights grew slowly until they succeeded in defeating the great railroad baron, Jay Gould, in the strike of 1885. Within a year they added 500,000 workers to their membership.

The Knights of Labor had a very advanced program that called for the eight-hour day, equal pay for equal work for women, the abolition of convict and child labor, the public ownership of utilities, and the establishment of cooperatives. The terrible conditions and brutality of the bosses sometimes provoked a violent response. The "Molly Maguires" were a secret society of Irish immigrant coal miners who fought for better working conditions in the coalfields of northeastern Pennsylvania. Called murderers and framed, 14 of their leaders were imprisoned and ten of them were hanged in 1876.

In reply to the labor movement the bosses sent in their shock troops, the Pinkerton Detective Agency—those hated private cops of the monopolists, scabs, strike breakers, hired guns, and murderers—to fight the workers. The bosses also had at their disposal the forces of the state. Workers were imprisoned, beaten up, and killed for the "crime" of fighting for their rights. This state repression was carried out on behalf of private interests, in particular Lehigh Valley Railroad founder Asa Packer, as well as Franklin Gowen of Philadelphia and Reading Railroad, and the coal company bosses who wanted to crush the fledgling labor organizations.

The Workers' Uprising of 1877

> *The power of money has become supreme over everything. It has secured for the class who controls it all the special privileges and special legislation which it needs to secure its complete and absolute domination ... This power must be kept in check. It must be broken or it will utterly crush the people* (*The New York Sun*, quoted in Philip S. Foner, *The Great Labor Uprising of 1877*).

In 1876, as the nation prepared to celebrate a hundred years of American Independence, an economic depression (or panic, as it was then known) gripped the country. Millions had been thrown out of work. In New York one quarter of the workforce was unemployed. The already meager wages of the workers were cut. The police attacked meetings of the unemployed, mercilessly beating up men, women, and children.

This was the period of the most violent labor conflicts in the history of the United States. The first of these occurred with the Great Rail Strike of 1877, when rail workers across the nation went out on strike in response to a 10-percent pay cut. A contemporary labor paper called the Great Strike the beginning of a Second American Revolution. *The Journal of the Brotherhood of Locomotive Engineers* asked in April 1873:

> Are not railway employees in this year of grace, 1873, enduring a tyranny compared with which British taxation in colonial days was as nothing, and of which the crack of the slave whip is only a fair type?

Attempts to break the strike led to a full scale working-class uprising in several cities: Baltimore, Maryland; Chicago, Illinois; Pittsburgh, Pennsylvania; Buffalo, New York; and San Francisco, California. At several locations the military was called in to crush the uprising workers. Many workers were killed and wounded. The first victim of this repression was shot on July 17 by the militia in Martinsburg, West Virginia, and died a few days later of his wounds. But the workers were not intimidated and the strike continued to spread like wildfire along the main railroad lines. On July 20, a clash between strikers and militia at the Camden depot in Baltimore left eleven unarmed people dead and many more wounded. President Hayes called in three companies of regular soldiers to deal with the subsequent protests.

In Pittsburgh the militia fraternized with the workers, obliging the authorities to call in the First Division of the National Guard from Philadelphia. These "heroes" shot into an unarmed crowd of men, women, and children, killing ten people and wounding another eleven. A report in the *Pittsburgh Post* described the scene of carnage:

> Women and children rushed frantically about, some seeking safety, others calling for friends and relatives. Strong men halted with fear, and trembling with excitement, rushed madly to and fro, tramping upon the killed and wounded as well as upon those who had dropped to mother earth to escape injury and death (Quoted in Foner, 63).

The workers responded by burning the property of the railroad. Everywhere there was the same insurrectionary spirit. The situation in Baltimore was so serious that the marines were called in to guard the railroad company's buildings and equipment with artillery. Six companies of the Fourth National Guard arrived in Reading, Pennsylvania, where they shot into a crowd, killing eleven more. Everywhere the authorities responded to the strike with great brutality, beating up strikers and demonstrators. But still the strike spread.

On July 25 there was a monster demonstration in St. Louis, including many black workers, closing down businesses, and carrying out a general strike. The women of the working class played a prominent role, fighting shoulder to shoulder with their men, as the following account from the *Chicago Inter-Ocean* shows:

> Women with babes in arms joined the enraged female rioters. The streets were fluttering with calico of all shades and shapes. Hundreds were bareheaded, their dishevelled locks streaming in the wind. Many were shoeless. Some were young, scarcely women in age, and not at all in appearances. Dresses were tucked up around the waist, revealing large underthings. Open busts were common as a barber's chair. Brawny, sunburnt arms brandished clubs. Knotty hands held rocks and sticks and wooden blocks. Female yells, shrill as a curfew's cry, filled the air. The swarthy features of the Bohemian women were more horrible to look at in that scene than their men in the Halsted Street riots. The unsexed mob of female incendiaries rushed to the fence and yards of Goss Phillips' Manufacturing company. The consternation which this attack created extended to Twenty-second Street, at that

hour very quiet. A crowd of men gathered on Fisk Street to witness this curious repetition of the scenes of the Paris commune. The fence surrounding the yard gave way, and was carried off by the petticoated plunderers in their unbridled rage. There was fear for a while that the Amazonian army would continue their depredations. Word was dispatched to the Himmon Street Station, and a force of officers under Lieutenant Vesey pushed down to the corner of the contest. The women hissed as they saw the blue coats march along. Some of the less valorous took to their heels . . . Others stood their ground.

A shower of missiles greeted the boys as they came smiling along left front into line. One woman pitched a couple of blocks at the heads of the officers, and then moved on to attend to her family duties. The men were weak in the strength and forcefulness of their language compared to these female wretches. Profanity the most foul rolled easily off their tongues with horrid glibness. Expressions were made use of that brought the blood mantling to the cheek of the worst-hardened men in the crowds of spectators. It was awful (Quoted in Foner, 154–5).

The police showed no sign of sex discrimination. They beat up the women with the same enthusiasm as they beat up the men.

One significant element in this great strike that was close to an insurrection was the active participation of the Workers' Party of the United States, an anticipation of the great party of American labor, which one day must emerge and lead the working class to victory. The Workers' Party played a most active role in the strike, issuing leaflets and proclamations and providing practical guidance to the strikers. At a rally organized by the WPUS, one of the speakers, an Englishman named John E. Cope, a former member of the International Workingmen's Association, spoke in favor of the nationalization of the railroads:

> In his speech, Cope insisted that the workingmen were not going to destroy the railroads. Rather, the railroads were going to become national property for the benefit of the people, and the working class would not destroy its own property. If the railroad corporations starved their workers, he went on, it was as if they murdered them, and whoever murdered a man should be hung. Yet under the existing system, these "murderers" were honored: "A man who stole a single rail is called a thief, while he who stole a railway is a gentleman." Cope concluded by warning the workers to be prepared to meet the military once the authorities called them in to crush their strike (Foner, 167).

The strikers were accused in the press of being communists (the Paris Commune just six years earlier had terrified the ruling class of America). Someone signing himself "a red-hot striker" replied:

You challenge me to compare "the Communist and the Railway." The way to do it is, first to see what is the idea of both, what each of them demands. Now, I say—and I challenge you, or any other fellow like you, to show I'm not right—I say the "Commune" *represents the cause of the poor in this: that its object is to give every human born into this world a chance to live; live long, and die well.* And I say of the "Railway," it *represents the few rich who don't want everybody to have a chance for a decent living, but intend to grind out of the rest of the world all the wealth possible for their own special benefit.* I say this, and don't fear you can show the contrary. The difference is, the one is struggling to make it possible for all the world to get on; the other is doing its damnedest to make it impossible for anybody to get on, save the few rich it represents. Let the public judge which side is most worthy—as it will judge in good time, and don't you forget it (Quoted in Foner, 211).

Marx followed the unfolding of the Great Strike with tremendous interest. Writing to his friend and comrade Friedrich Engels, he called it "the first uprising against the oligarchy of capital which had developed since the Civil War." He predicted that, although it would inevitably be suppressed, it "could very well be the point of origin for the creation of a serious workers' party in the United States" (Letter to Engels, July 24, 1877).

Marx's prediction proved to be premature. The spectacular upswing of the productive forces in the United States was sufficient to give capitalism a new lease of life and blunt the political consciousness of the masses for far longer than Marx or anyone else could have anticipated. But the need to create a class-independent mass party of labor in the USA remains as correct and necessary today as then. Sooner or later the American working class, through the experience of struggle, will come to the same conclusion.

The Chicago Martyrs and May Day

The bosses met the workers' movement with extreme violence. The list of the martyrs of American Labor is endless, the most celebrated being the Chicago martyrs of 1886—as a result of which the American working class gave May Day to the rest of the world. It is ironic that in the USA, "Labor Day" is now held at the beginning of September, far from the more significant date of May 1. It is generally seen as a last three-day weekend of summer with lots of grilling and beer drinking. The union marches in major cities have been emasculated in order to reduce the importance of May Day by moving it to September and making it a "fun" weekend. In this way, the ruling class in the USA does everything possible to make the working class forget its own history and traditions.

On May 1, 1886, Albert Parsons (his wife Lucy was a tireless activist who campaigned to have him pardoned), the head of the Chicago Knights of Labor, led a demonstration of 80,000 people through the city's streets in support of the eight-hour day. In the next few days they were joined nationwide by 350,000 workers who went on strike at 1,200 factories, including 70,000 in Chicago. On May 4, August Spies, Parsons, and Samuel Fielden were speaking at a rally of 2,500 people held to protest the police massacre when 180 police officers arrived, led by the Chicago police chief. While he was calling for the meeting to disperse, a bomb exploded, killing one policeman. The police retaliated, killing seven of their own men in the crossfire, plus four others; almost two hundred were wounded. The identity of the bomb thrower remains unknown.

Of course another Red Scare was invoked ("Communism in Chicago!") when all the workers were fighting for was the eight-hour day. On June 21, 1886, eight labor leaders, including Spies, Fielden, and Parsons went on trial, charged with responsibility for the bombing. The trial was rife with lies and contradictions, and the state prosecutor appealed to the jury: "Convict these men, make an example of them, hang them, and you save our institutions."

Even though only two were present at the time of the bombing (Parsons had gone to a nearby tavern), seven were sentenced to die, one to fifteen years imprisonment. The Chicago bar condemned the trial, and several years later Governor John P. Altgeld pardoned all eight, releasing the three survivors (two of them had had their sentences reduced from hanging to life imprisonment). Unfortunately, the events surrounding the execution of the Haymarket martyrs fueled the stereotype of radical activists as alien and violent, thereby contributing to ongoing repression. On November 11, 1886, four anarchist leaders were hanged; Louis Lingg had committed suicide hours before. Two hundred thousand people took part in the funeral procession, either lining the streets or marching behind the hearses.

As the crisis of capitalism deepens, workers need to arm themselves with a program that can answer their needs and aspirations. In doing so they need to reclaim May Day's tradition of struggle. May Day itself was born out of struggle. The fight for the 8-hour working day in the United States in the 1880s was the issue that gave birth to May Day as International Labor Day. In 1884 the Convention of the Federation of Organized Trades raised a resolution that was to act as a beacon to the whole working class: "that eight hours shall constitute a legal day's labor from and after 1st May 1886." This call was taken up by the labor movement with the creation of Eight Hour Leagues, which wrung significant concessions out of the bosses, and led to the doubling of trade union membership.

Shortly after the Chicago tragedy of May 1886, which became known thereafter as International Workers' Day, workers representatives set up the Second (Socialist) International in 1889, under the banner of workers' internationalism. A key resolution of the Congress was that on every May Day workers in every country would strike and demonstrate for the 8-hour day. On May 1, 1890, workers struck all over Europe, with 100,000 demonstrating in Barcelona, 120,000 in Stockholm, and 8,000 in Warsaw, while thousands stayed at home in Austria and Hungary where demonstrations were banned. Strikes spread throughout Italy and France. Ten workers were shot dead in Northern France. In the words of the Austrian Social Democratic leader, Adler, "Entire layers of the working class with which we would otherwise have made no contact, have been shaken out of their lethargy."

In Britain and Germany, huge demonstrations were held on the Sunday following May Day. The importance of these developments was not lost on Friedrich Engels, the lifelong comrade of Karl Marx, who had lived through the long period of quiescence in the British labor movement after the great Chartists days of the 1840s. He wrote enthusiastically about May Day: "more than 100,000 in a column, on 4th May 1890, the English working class joined up in the great international army, its long winter sleep broken at last. The grandchildren of the old Chartists are entering the line of battle." *Yet again, a great tradition of international labor was "made in the USA."*

Craft Unionism

The rise of American capitalism as a world power in the last decades of the 19th century was marked by a sharp upturn of the productive forces, booming industry, and high profits that permitted certain concessions to the upper layer of the working class in the skilled trades. This "labor aristocracy" formed the basis of the kind of "craft unionism" typified by the AFL.

In 1881, six prominent unions, the printers, iron and steel workers, moulders, cigar-makers, carpenters, and glass workers met together with other groups to launch the Federation of Organized Trades and Labor Unions (FOTLU), led by Samuel Gompers and Adolph Strasser. With only 45,000 members, it was initially weak and overshadowed by the Knights of Labor. But on the basis of the booming economy, the tendency towards class collaborationism gathered ground. In the 1880s the tendency of "practical trade unionism" or "pure and simple unionism" gained ground at the expense of the Knights of Labor who, by 1890, had only 100,000 members.

The strength of the AFL—as it later became—was primarily in the crafts already named. It began with a membership of around 138,000 in 1886 and slowly doubled that number in the next twelve years. Gompers and his ilk represented what one might call the aristocracy of labor. By appealing to craft prejudices with their narrower outlook, they succeeded in turning the labor movement away from the socialist views of earlier labor leaders. In this sense it represented a big step back as compared to the Knights of Labor.

Lenin explained that apolitical trade unionism is bourgeois trade unionism. The idea that the unions must be nonpolitical inevitably leads to them falling under the domination of one or other of the bosses' parties. This assertion has been proved by the history of the American trade union movement from this time onwards. Samuel Gompers, a real bosses' man, was elected first president and held onto the position until his death in 1924.

The rise of this so-called trade unionism "pure and simple" was no accident, but flowed from the material conditions at that time. In the exceptionally privileged position of US capitalism, which was already beginning to challenge Britain's position as the main industrial power by the beginning of the 20th century, concessions could be given to buy off the labor aristocracy. A similar situation led to the national-reformist degeneration of the labor and Social Democratic organizations in Britain, France, and Germany in the years before 1914. From 1900 to 1904, the membership of the AFL went from half a million to a million and a half, and then to two million on the eve of the First World War. During and immediately following the war, membership again increased rapidly to more than four million in 1920. During this period, an estimated 70 to 80 percent of all unionized workers in the USA were in the AFL.

However, the organizational and numerical strengthening of the unions was accompanied by a process of bureaucratic degeneration at the top. In this period the basis was laid for the policies of class collaboration and non-political, that is for "yellow" trade unionism that has characterized the leadership of the AFL ever since. Leaders like Gompers and Meany accommodated themselves to capitalism, preaching the unity of interest between capital and labor—which is like preaching the unity of interest between horse and rider. Meanwhile, the vast majority of American workers remained unorganized, unrepresented, and oppressed.

Moreover, the class collaborationist views of the AFL leaders were not at all shared by the bosses, who viewed the growth of trade unionism with alarm. Caroll Dougherty writes in his book *Labor Problems in American Industry*:

> Most of the powerful ones [employers], believing that unionism was growing too strong and fearing further encroachments on their control of industry, decided to break off relations, and the years from 1912 to World War I, were characterized by a definitely increasing antiunionism . . .

Scientific management and "efficiency" systems were introduced in many plants, much to the discomfiture of many skilled craft unions. A variety of union-smashing tactics were adopted by employers. Vigilante groups and citizens' committees were fostered to resist unionization activities. Court decisions upheld as a rule most of the employers' antiunion practices. In the face of these new difficulties, the membership of the AFL at first fell off a little and then resumed growth at a much slower rate than before 1902.

This is the eternal contradiction of reformist politics in general—that it produces results that are the exact opposite to those intended. The compromising attitude of the labor leaders always leads to a hardening of attitudes on the part of the employers: *weakness invites aggression.* This is shown by the record of that period—and the same applies today.

In spite of the class collaboration of Gompers and Co., the class struggle reached a fever pitch. In 1892 the bitter Homestead strike by the Amalgamated Association of Iron, Steel, and Tin Workers at the Carnegie steel mills in Homestead PA, resulted in the death of several strikers and Pinkerton guards. A group of 300 Pinkerton detectives the company had hired to break the strike by the Amalgamated Association of Iron, Steel, and Tin Workers were fired upon and ten were killed. Unions were not let back into the plant until 1937. The workers were sacked from most of the mills in the Pennsylvania area.

Two years later a strike of the American Railway Union led by Eugene V. Debs against the Pullman Company was defeated by the use of injunctions and federal troops sent into the Chicago area. The National Guard was called in as a result to crush the striking workers; nonunion workers were hired and the strike was broken. Debs and others were imprisoned for violating the injunctions, and the union was defeated.

Then, as now, workers could not rely on the law to come to their aid. The bosses could buy expensive lawyers and bend the law to their will. The following example is quite typical. Wage cuts at the Pullman Palace Car Company just outside Chicago led to a strike, which, with the support of the American Railway Union, soon brought the nation's railway industry to a halt. As usual, as soon as labor began to fight for its rights, the federal government stepped in on the side of capital. US Attorney General Richard Olney, himself a former lawyer for the railroad industry, deputized over 3,000 men in an attempt to keep the rails open. This was followed by a federal court injunction against "union interference" with the trains.

The IWW

In the stormy years before and after the First World War, the labor movement in the USA was alive and vibrant. This was a period of giants—people like Eugene Debs, the "grand old man" of US labor. Born in Terre Haute, Indiana, Debs left home at 14 to work in the railroad shops. As a locomotive fireman, he became an early advocate of industrial unionism, and was elected president of the American Railway Union in 1893. His involvement in the Pullman Strike led to a six-month prison term in 1895. In 1898 he helped found the US Socialist Party; he would run as its presidential candidate five times in the period from 1900 to 1920. In 1905 he helped found the Industrial Workers of the World. Debs was charged with sedition in 1918 after denouncing the 1917 Espionage Act; he conducted his last presidential campaign from prison, winning 915,000 votes, before being released by presidential order in 1921.

During the early 1900s, mass production industries had expanded rapidly. Most of the workers in these industries lacked union representation. The AFL opposed unionizing these largely unskilled or semiskilled workers, arguing that such attempts would fail. This view was challenged—successfully—by one of the most extraordinary militant union movements ever seen in any country. The Industrial Workers of the World (IWW)—also known by their nickname, "the Wobblies"—would prove to be the most radical and militant movement in the nation's labor history.

Formed from an amalgam of unions fighting for better conditions in the West's mining industry, the IWW gained particular prominence from the Colorado mine clashes of 1903 and the singularly brutal fashion in which they were put down. In 1905 a handful of the nation's most radical political and labor figures met in Chicago. Featuring Big Bill Haywood of the Western Federation of Miners and Eugene V. Debs of the Socialist Party, the group aimed to ignite a grassroots fire that would sweep the nation and pull down an evil and unjust system, brick by brick.

The IWW engaged in militant action in the years before the war. Led by larger-than-life figures like Joe Hill and Big Bill Haywood, the "Wobblies" succeeded in organizing layers of the working class that had never been organized. They were free from all routinism, reformist prejudices, and craft narrowness, and approached the class struggle with enthusiasm and verve. Fresh from his acquittal on murder charges in Idaho, Bill Haywood soon became a driving force for the IWW. Convinced that the Western Federation of Miners was not the answer, Haywood wanted the IWW to represent all workers in one big union—and to bring that union into a head-on clash with the centers of power in America.

The ideas of the IWW were a peculiar and colorful mixture of anarcho-syndicalism and Marxism. At its founding convention in 1905, it adopted a preamble that was a stirring statement of the class struggle:

> The working class and the employing class have nothing in common. There can be no peace so long as hunger and want are found among millions of working people and the few, who make up the employing class, have all the good things.
>
> Between these two classes a struggle must go on until all the toilers come together on the political, as well as the industrial, field, and take and hold that which they produce by their labor, through an economic organization of the working class without affiliation with any political party.

The IWW declared war on the kind of narrow craft unionism represented by the AFL:

> The rapid gathering of wealth and the centering of the management of industries into fewer and fewer hands make the trade unions unable to cope with the ever-growing power of the employing class, because the trade unions foster a state of things which allows one set of workers to be pitted against another set of workers in the same industry, thereby helping defeat one another in the wage wars.

The answer of the IWW was to fight for the principle of industrial unionism under their famous slogan "One Big Union." In combating craft narrowness and fighting to organize all workers in one union, they were undoubtedly on the right lines, and although their policies were distorted by some anarcho-syndicalist prejudices, they led the way with militant class politics. In 1908 they approved another preamble, which ended with a call for the abolition of capitalism:

> Instead of the conservative motto "A fair day's pay for a fair day's work," we must inscribe on our banner the revolutionary watchword, "Abolition of the wage system."
>
> It is the historic mission of the working class to do away with capitalism. The army of production must be organized, not only for the everyday struggle with capitalists, but also to carry on production when capitalism shall have been overthrown. By organizing industrially we are forming the structure of the new society within the old.

In reality, the organizations of the labor movement in the USA and every other country are just that: *the embryo of the new society that has taken shape and is slowly maturing in the womb of the old.* That is why the capitalists have historically shown such bitter hostility to the unions and try to destroy, by one means or another, any attempt of the workers to organize in defense of their class interests. The IWW, uniting in its ranks the most advanced, resolute, and revolutionary elements of the American working class, led a series of militant strikes before the First World War, in the teeth of the most ferocious repression by the employers and their state.

By openly calling for class warfare, the Wobblies gained many adherents. Among other mass actions, they organized a brilliantly successful strike by textile workers in Lawrence, Massachusetts, in 1912. Their militant actions in the midst of World War I, however, provided the excuse for a government crackdown in 1917, which virtually destroyed the IWW. Some of the leaders later joined the young American Communist Party. The IWW degenerated into a small sect.

The reason for this was only partly state repression. It had a sectarian attitude to the AFL, which represented the big majority of the American workers. This conduct tended to separate the most militant and revolutionary workers from the mass, dooming them to impotence. In the end, the left wing of the union movement emerged through a big split in the AFL with the founding of the CIO.

Joe Hill

> *Tomorrow I expect to take a trip to the planet Mars and, if so, will immediately commence to organize the Mars canal workers into the IWW and we will learn to sing the good old songs so loud that the learned star-gazers on earth will once and for all get positive proof that the planet Mars is really inhabited . . . I have nothing to say for myself only that I have always tried to make this earth a little better for the great producing class, and I can pass off into the great unknown with the pleasure of knowing that I have never in my life double-crossed a man, woman, or child.*—Joe Hill to editor Ben Williams, *Solidarity*, October 9, 1915

On November 19, 1915, a 33 year-old Wobbly songwriter was executed by a firing squad in the prison yard of the Utah State Penitentiary, framed on a murder charge. Thus ended the life of one of the most extraordinary figures of the history of American labor—Joe Hill.

Joe was born in Gavle, Sweden, on October 7 1879, and, like so many of his compatriots, emigrated to the Lower East Side Bowery section of New York City via Ellis Island in 1902. Joe Hill, also known as Joseph Hillstrom and Joel Hagglund, was an American labor songwriter and martyr of the working class. His naive idealism about American society was soon shattered by the harsh conditions and exploitation of immigrant workers that he witnessed. He became an itinerant laborer, working in mines, the lumber industry, and as a longshoreman. He also developed skills as a hobo, traveling on freight trains and living off the land.

Joe joined the IWW around the year 1910 and became the "Wobbly bard," showing tremendous ability as a poet and songwriter. He was the author of dozens of Wobbly songs, which were printed on song cards and published in the *Industrial Worker*, *Solidarity* and in the IWW's little red songbook. These songs were based on his personal experience of the lives of the ordinary working people of his day. His most famous songs, including *Rebel Girl*, *The Preacher and the Slave*, and *Casey Jones*, became world famous and were used in labor organizing drives and in rallies supporting strikes.

The Wobblies used many varied weapons in their fight against capital, including art, poetry, and music. These songs, with their air of cheerful proletarian defiance, were not written only for amusement. *They were weapons of struggle.* One of the participants in the Lawrence strike recalled:

> It is the first strike I ever saw which sang. I shall never forget the curious lift, the strange sudden fire of the mingled nationalities at the strike meetings when they broke into the universal language of song. And not only at the meetings did they sing, but in the soup houses and in the streets. I saw one group of women strikers who were peeling potatoes at a relief station suddenly break into the swing of the *Internationale*. They have a whole book of sings fitted to familiar tunes—*The Eight Hour Song, The Banners of Labor, Workers, Shall the Masters Rule Us?* But the favorite was the *Internationale* (Ray Stannard Baker, "The Revolutionary Strike", in *The American Magazine*, May, 1912).

The IWW also used that most devastating proletarian weapon, particularly important in the United States: humor. This is a good example:

> On one occasion a non-union man entered a butcher's shop to purchase a calf's head. As the butcher was about to wrap it up for him the customer noticed the union shop card.
>
> "Say, is that a union calf's head?" he asked.
>
> "Yes, sir," answered the butcher.
>
> "Well, I'm not a union man and I don't want union meat," said the customer.
>
> "I can make it nonunion," said the meat man, picking it up and retiring to the back room. He returned in a few minutes and laid the head on the counter with the remark, "It's alright now."
>
> "What did you do to make it nonunion?" asked the prospective buyer.
>
> "I just took the brains out of it."

Joe Hill arrived in Utah in 1913 and found employment in the Park City mines while becoming acquainted with the Swedish community in Murray, Utah. In 1914 he was accused of the murder of a Salt Lake City storeowner, John A. Morrison, and convicted on circumstantial evidence. There ensued an international battle to prevent his execution by the State of Utah. What exactly happened can never be ascertained. But it is certain that the business interests of the West, especially the copper bosses of Utah, had conspired to eliminate him.

The bosses used all manner of dirty methods against the labor movement but were always careful to cover their tracks. The climate of opinion in the West and in Utah was decidedly hostile to the IWW and to Joe Hill and he could never get a fair trial. Under today's laws, Joe Hill would not have been executed on the evidence presented at his trial. President Woodrow Wilson intervened twice in an attempt to prevent the execution, but Hill was executed at the Utah State Prison in Sugar House, Utah, on November 19, 1915.

Joe Hill has become a folk hero and labor martyr, a symbol of the American revolutionary tradition and the fight to defend the working class and the poor and downtrodden sections of society. One of his final statements, "Don't mourn, organize!" has become a labor-rallying cry. There can be few more moving human documents in world literature than Joe Hill's Last Will, written while he was awaiting execution in the condemned cell:

> My will is easy to decide,
> For there is nothing to decide.
> My kin don't need to fuss and moan—
> Moss does not cling to a rolling stone.
>
> My body?—Oh!—If I could choose,
> I would to ashes it reduce,
> And let the merry breezes blow
> My dust to where some flowers grow.
>
> Perhaps some fading flower then
> Would come to life and bloom again.
> This is my last and final will.
> Good luck to all of you.
>
> Joe Hill.

There have been many attempts to portray Joe Hill's life in different media over the years: biographies, novels, songs, plays, and movies have been written about him. *I Dreamed I Saw Joe Hill Last Night* by Alfred Hayes and Earl Robinson has become an American folk song of enduring quality. Today the songs of Joe Hill, the Wobbly bard, class fighter and martyr of the American labor movement, are known, loved, and sung around the world.

Literature and Revolution

Joe Hill showed how music and poetry could be powerful weapons in the class struggle. His example was followed by others, including the great Woody Guthrie. The beloved "dust bowl" and "hobo" folksinger established a new genre of radical folk song that marries the best traditions of the songs of the American West with revolutionary class politics. Spokesperson of the working class, one of greatest American songwriters of any genre, and a continued influence on musicians today, especially singers and songwriters like Bob Dylan and Pete Seeger. Although most Americans know the song *This Land Is Your Land*, few know that it is a socialist song. As the song says—"*this land was made for you and me*"!

It is a shame that many young Americans today are unaware that there was a great American tradition of left-wing writers, starting with Jack London who was a committed and active socialist. Jack London, at his peak, was the highest paid and the most popular of all living writers. He is best known as author of wildlife novels *Call of the Wild* and *White Fang*, which remain popular with young readers. But how many have ever read his inspiring essays such as *War of the Classes*, *Revolution*, and *How I Became a Socialist*? One of the most interesting is the autobiographical sketch called *What Life Means to Me*:

> So I went back to the working class, in which I had been born and where I belonged. I care no longer to climb. The imposing edifice of society above my head holds no delights for me. It is the foundation of the edifice that interests me. There I am content to labor, crowbar in hand, shoulder to shoulder with intellectuals, idealists, and class-conscious workingmen, getting a solid pry now and again and setting the whole edifice rocking. Some day, when we get a few more hands and crowbars to work, we'll topple it over, along with all its rotten life and unburied dead. Its monstrous selfishness and sodden materialism. Then we'll cleanse the cellar and build a new habitation for mankind, in which there will be no parlor floor, in which all the rooms will be bright and airy, and where the air that is breathed will be clean, noble, and alive.
>
> Such is my outlook. I look forward to a time when man shall progress upon something worthier and higher than his stomach, when there will be an incentive to impel men to action other than the incentive of today, which is the incentive of stomach. I retain my belief in the nobility and excellence of the human. I believe that spiritual sweetness and unselfishness will conquer the gross gluttony of today. And last of all, my faith is in the working class. As some Frenchman has said, "The stairway of time is ever echoing with the wooden shoe going up, the polished boot descending."

One of Jack London's most remarkable works is his novel *The Iron Heel,* which both Lenin and Trotsky admired. In it he predicts the rise of fascism and depicts the heroic struggle of the American workers for socialism—long before the Russian Revolution and the rise of Hitler proved how eerily accurate he was. Trotsky states in his introduction:

> In reading it, one does not believe his own eyes: it is precisely the picture of fascism, of its economy, of its government technique, its political psychology! The fact is incontestable: in 1907 Jack London already foresaw and described the fascist regime as the inevitable result of the defeat of the proletarian revolution. Whatever may be the single "errors" of the novel—and they exist—we cannot help inclining before the powerful intuition of the revolutionary artist.

There were many other great American socialist novels. Upton Sinclair's novel *The Jungle* is a vivid exposure of conditions in the stockyards and slaughterhouses of America, ending with an uncompromisingly socialist message, its root-and-branch condemnation of capitalism that still reads well today, and its depiction of the appalling conditions of the workers in the slaughterhouses.

Sinclair's novel appeared as early as 1906, when it caused a major scandal in America. Ever since the Cuban War, when thousands of American soldiers died as a result of the rotten meat supplied to the army by the Chicago meat packers, the industry had been the target of public suspicion. Sinclair himself had got a job in a large Chicago meatpacking firm and obtained first-hand information about the appalling conditions of the workers. As a result his novel comes close to the best work of Emile Zola. The characters in it are mostly workers in packing plants like the one Sinclair worked in:

> There was no heat upon the killing beds; the men might exactly as well have worked out of doors all winter. For that matter, there was very little heat anywhere in the building, except in the cooking rooms and such places—and it was the men who worked in these who ran the most risk of all because whenever they had to pass to another room they had to go through ice-cold corridors, and sometimes with nothing on above the waist except a sleeveless undershirt. On the killing beds you were apt to be covered with blood, and it would freeze solid; if you leaned against a pillar, you would freeze to that, and if you put your hand upon the blade of your knife, you would run a chance of leaving your skin on it. The men would tie up their feet in newspapers and old sacks, and these would be soaked in blood and frozen, and the soaked again, and so on, until by night-time a man would be walking on great lumps the size of the feet of an elephant. Now and then, when the bosses were not looking, you would see them plunging their feet and ankles into the steaming hot carcass of the steer, or darting across the room to the hot-water

jets. The cruelest thing of all was that nearly all of them—all of those who used knives—were unable to wear gloves, and their arms would be white with frost and the hands would grow numb, and then, of course, there would be accidents. Also the air would be full of steam, from the hot water and the hot blood, so that you could not see five feet before you; and then, with men rushing about at the speed they kept up on the killing beds and with butcher's knives, like razors, in their hands—well, it was to be counted as a wonder that there were not more men slaughtered than cattle.

The Jungle became a best seller in a week. It sold hundreds of thousands of copies. The sales of canned meat plummeted. A board of investigation was set up that substantiated all of Sinclair's assertions. Legislation was put before Congress to control the industry. The owners tried to kill it but it was passed. Even the stupidest congressman must have realized that failure to act would have led to a collapse of the sales of American canned meat abroad. Almost a hundred years later, however, they are up to the same tricks, putting profits before people.

The powerful US food and agriculture lobby—which, despite its hostility to socialism and state control, gets huge subsidies from the US government—is currently trying to force reluctant European consumers to eat genetically modified food. This is just the tip of a very large and ugly iceberg that potentially menaces the health of the entire planet. We look forward to the appearance of a new Upton Sinclair who will be capable of exposing the scandals of adulteration perpetrated by the modern food monopolies that will undoubtedly make the activities of the Chicago meat packers in 1906 look like child's play.

CHAPTER VI

IMPERIALISM

The end of the 19th century saw the birth of imperialism. Germany, France, Britain, and Belgium struggled to gain possession of markets, territory, raw materials, and spheres of influence. This policy led to the establishment of colonies and empires in Africa, Asia, and the Middle East. In the Pacific, Japan's development followed a similar pattern, following the Western lead in industrialization and militarism, enabling it to gain a foothold or "sphere of influence" in China. As Germany emerged as a great power after victory in the Franco-Prussian War, which completed the process of German unification, so the US would emerge as a great power after the victory of the North in the Civil War.

The United States, as the youngest member of the capitalist club, entered late into the scramble for markets and colonies. As a result, it found itself at a disadvantage with respect to the older imperialist nations of Europe. The Panic of 1893 exacerbated the already fierce competition over markets in the growing "spheres of influence" of the United States, which tended to overlap with Britain's, especially in the Pacific and South America. Like all newly industrializing great powers, the US adopted protectionism, seized a colonial empire of its own (the Spanish-American War of 1898), and built up a powerful navy (the "Great White Fleet"). Following the example of Germany, the United States tried to solve the depression by the adoption of protective tariff protection with the passage of the McKinley Tariff of 1890.

The nascent trend of American imperialism found its voice in a new generation of US politicians, such as Henry Cabot Lodge, William McKinley, and Theodore Roosevelt, all of whom advocated a more aggressive foreign policy as a means of pulling the United States out of the depression of the second Grover Cleveland administration.

In addition to the strictly economic content of imperialism, it also fulfilled an important social and political role. Europe in this period witnessed the re-emergence of far more militant working-class organization and mass strikes. The existing social order felt threatened by the growth of the trade unions and Social Democratic parties. A period of increasing unemployment and deflated prices for manufactured goods gave an additional impulse to imperial expansion.

Very soon after it had thrown off the yoke of British and European imperialism and established itself as a young and vigorous capitalist power, the USA began to flex its muscles and assert its power, developing territorial designs on its neighbors, especially Mexico. This was expressed in the Monroe Doctrine, which, as early as 1823, proclaimed that the American continent was closed to European colonization, that America was for the Americans, and that any attempt on the part of Spain or any other European state to reconquer the South American republics would be considered "a manifestation of unfriendly disposition towards the United States."

On this subject W.E. Woodward writes:

> ... the South American republics were not grateful then and are not grateful now. On the contrary, they hate us heartily on account of the Monroe Doctrine, as they assume that the doctrine is our indirect way of asserting an overlordship over the countries to the south of us (Woodward, 358).

Whatever may have been the original intention, there can be no doubt that that has been precisely the result.

Under the pretext of reaffirming the Monroe Doctrine, US imperialism in reality extended it beyond all recognition through the Roosevelt Corollary of 1904. In practice, this was taken to mean that the USA claimed the exclusive right to "lead" the entire American continent—North and South. Under McKinley's Republican administration, the USA aimed to restore prosperity and obtain new markets through the "Open Door" policy. The meaning of this was already demonstrated in the US-Cuban War.

Spain was the weakest of all the European imperialist states, and its last remaining possession in the New World, Cuba, was an obvious target. In 1895 the people of Cuba rose in revolution against their Spanish colonial masters. The Madrid government sent 200,000 soldiers but were unable to put down the uprising. The Cubans made use of guerrilla war, avoiding pitched battles and resorting to hit and run tactics—just like the Iraqis at the present time. The Spanish imperialists resorted to brutal repression. All suspected rebels were rounded up and placed in concentration camps, where many died of disease and starvation. These events were followed with great interest in the United States, and not only from humanitarian motives. American citizens had about $50 million worth of Cuban property, including sugar and tobacco plantations and iron mines. American property was being destroyed.

A vociferous campaign began in the USA in favor of "going to Cuba and sorting out the whole damn mess." This was an early expression of the pent-up chauvinism that was pushing America to assert its power on the world stage. President McKinley was not sympathetic to the imperialists and attempted to keep the USA out of war. But he was under increasing pressure from the imperialists who made sure that every Spanish atrocity, real or imaginary, was splashed all over the front pages of American newspapers in what was called "yellow journalism."

We know from more recent experience how easy it is to whip up pro-war feelings by using the mass media to create hate figures and manipulate public opinion—as George W. Bush and his administration did very effectively after 9/11. It was even easier at that time because the American public had no experience of foreign wars. In such a situation, some incident is always needed to spark off war hysteria. In this case it was provided by the notorious *Maine* incident. The US war party had a very vocal leader in the person of Theodore ("Teddy") Roosevelt, who imagined that the USA should act on the world stage in the same way as General Custer leading the Seventh Cavalry into battle against the "injuns." He declared that President McKinley had "no more backbone than a chocolate éclair." All the war party needed was that useful little incident. They got it on February 15, 1898, when the *Maine* was blown up in Havana harbor.

Late in January 1898, the US government sent the battleship *Maine* to Havana on what was supposed to be a "good will" mission. In fact, "good will" had nothing to do with it. The *Maine* had been sent to protect US property and citizens in Cuba. Despite this act of blatant interference, the Madrid government swallowed hard, maintained a diplomatic silence, and publicly accepted the "good will" fairy story. It could hardly do anything else!

To this day nobody knows what happened. It may be that the *Maine* was blown up by Spanish loyalists, indignant at the affront to their government. But it is also possible that it was the work of Cuban rebels, intending to provoke a US military intervention against Spain. It is even possible that the ship's magazine may have blown up through some kind of accident or spontaneous combustion. Certainly the official report on the incident was inconclusive. But it really made no difference. All this has quite a modern ring about it. After

9/11, the right wing clique in the White House found the perfect excuse for carrying into practice the plans for the invasion of Iraq that they had already prepared long before. The destruction of the Twin Towers was the perfect excuse for this, although it is well known that Iraq had nothing whatever to do with it. Once the war machine starts to roll, like the Juggernauts of ancient India, it crushes everything in its path.

Is it not remarkable how every war is always humanitarian and pacific in intent, no matter how many lives are lost? Chauvinistic and anti-foreigner feeling is whipped up and all kinds of false moralizing arguments are put forward to dress up an act of aggression under the banner of the noblest and most humanitarian sentiments. But behind the scenes the most sordid self-interest is at work. Listen to Senator Thurston of Nebraska: "War with Spain," he said, "would increase the business and earnings of every American railroad, it would increase the output of every American factory, it would stimulate every branch of industry and domestic commerce." In other words, war was just another department of big business, or, as old Clausewitz might have said *"the continuation of business by other means."*

Faced with pressure of such intensity, McKinley took the honorable way out and joined the war party. In his speech to Congress, the president was economical with the truth. He did not inform Congress that Spain had agreed to accept all the terms imposed by Washington for reform in Cuba. He doubtless understood that a "splendid little war" would not do his prospects for reelection any harm. He would have been right, except that his presidential aspirations were cut short by an assassin's bullet.

On April 19, Congress declared war on Spain. The US Navy moved in with gusto, although it was based on the other side of the world in Asia. Admiral Dewey entered Manila where the Spanish fleet was anchored and reduced it to scrap iron in the space of five hours. US land forces backed by Filipino insurgents defeated the Spanish. But later the same insurgents were fighting the US forces. Not for the last time, one imperialist power had simply replaced another.

From the American point of view the Spanish War was a brilliant success. Casualties on the US side were few. The US Navy lost fewer than 20 men, having destroyed the entire Spanish fleet. The total fatalities of the US army in Cuba were 5,462. Of these, 379 were killed in action. The rest died from disease and bad food sold to the army by unscrupulous Chicago meat companies and accepted without question by stupid or corrupt military managers.

The Seizure of Panama

It was the "splendid little war" in Cuba that brought fame to Teddy Roosevelt, the man who discovered the art of public relations, photo opportunities, and political marketing. He commanded a division known as the "Rough Riders" made up, supposedly, of cowboys from "out West," whose barnstorming tactics were excellent material for the front pages back home. War correspondence has never been the same since. The face of TR is the face of the American bourgeoisie in its expansionist phase: crude, vigorous, self-confident, greedy, and uncultured. He enriched the English-American language with picturesque words like "*muckraker,*" "*mollycoddle,*" "*big stick,*" "*undesirable citizen,*" and other gems.

Here was a plain, ordinary American millionaire, proud of his lack of culture, a man who hated the kind of educated, highfalutin' language of politicians, or "*weasel words,*" as he called them. His main interest in life was shooting lions and tigers, and especially being photographed in the performance of this manly activity. His moral views were slightly more progressive than those of Attila the Hun. He opposed birth control as "willful sterility" and "more abasing, more destructive than ordinary vice." He also condemned divorce. His taste in literature was as refined as those of the class he represented. He denounced Tolstoy's *Kreutzer Sonata* as "filthy and obscene."

George W. Bush may trace his political line of descent back to Teddy Roosevelt. But there is an important difference. When the USA invaded Cuba and occupied Philippines, capitalism was still on its ascending curve. It easily dominated countries that lagged behind historically and economically. But now we are in an entirely different historical period. Capitalism on a world scale has long since outlived its historical usefulness. Its progressive role is played out. That is why it is faced with crises, wars, instability, and terrorism everywhere.

The decline of capitalism can be seen by comparing the invasion of Cuba with the invasion of Iraq. Even the comparison between the persons of Bush and Roosevelt reveals all the symptoms of decline. They have many things in common: reactionary politics, provincial narrowness, and cultural philistinism. But Theodore Roosevelt possessed the élan, the drive, and the raw pioneer energy of the American capitalist class in the period of its expansion. In his rhetoric there was a certain defiant style, and he showed personal courage in spite of the theatricalities. Yes, the man was a gangster, but he was a gangster with style. This was a reflection of the boundless self-confidence of rising American capitalism thrusting its way to world domination.

George Bush has all the negative features of his illustrious predecessor without any of his virtues. A mean-spirited provincial, this cowardly and hypocritical second-rater from the Bible Belt perfectly personifies the nature and intellect of the class he represents: the monopoly capitalists in the age of capitalism's senility. Here is no great idea, no broad horizon, no audacious rhetoric, only vicious intrigues combined with shameless bullying covered with a thin veneer of religious hypocrisy. Insofar as Roosevelt gave any thought to the Almighty, it was to thank Him for the invention of the machine gun. And despite his aversion for Tolstoy, at least he was capable of putting together a coherent sentence when he wanted to.

The truth is that for the USA the Cuban war was a small war, though not for Spain, for which it began a period of national humiliation and soul-searching that eventually had revolutionary consequences. For America, on the contrary, it marked the beginning of a long career of imperialist expansion and a fatal involvement in world affairs. The war was supposed to have been fought for Cuban independence from Spanish tyranny. But at the Paris Peace Conference the USA demanded the control over Puerto Rico and the Philippines. The Spanish were in no position to argue. As a cover for their actions the USA paid Spain $20 million for the Philippines, and as we know, fair exchange is no robbery. The opinion of the people living on the islands was not asked.

There is a Russian proverb: appetite comes with eating, and the appetite of the new member of the imperialist club was insatiable. Theodore Roosevelt was determined that the United States should control the passage from the Atlantic to Pacific oceans. This was a vital objective both militarily and economically, a major step in the USA's march towards world domination. Admittedly there was a small snag: *Panama was part of Colombia, a sovereign nation.* However, such trifles have never been known to deter imperialists, from Teddy Roosevelt to George W. Bush.

Roosevelt proceeded to negotiate with the Colombians to obtain the necessary permission to control the all-important canal. In early 1903 the Hay-Herran Treaty was signed by both nations, but the Colombian Senate failed to ratify the treaty. Not deterred, Roosevelt got into contact with Panamanian rebels (as George Bush got in touch with the Northern Alliance in Afghanistan and later the Iraqi Kurds and Shiites) and gave them to understand that if they revolted the US Navy would assist their cause for independence. Panama proceeded to proclaim its independence on November 3, 1903, and the *USS Nashville* in local waters impeded any interference from Colombia—a classic case of gunboat diplomacy.

When the fighting began Roosevelt ordered US battleships stationed off of Panama's coast for "training exercises." Fearing war with the United States, the Colombians avoided any serious opposition to the uprising. As we know, one good turn deserves another. The "independent" Panamanians returned the favor to Roosevelt by generously handing over to the United States control of the Panama Canal Zone on February 23, 1904, for the quite modest amount of $10 million. All in all, a very nice little business deal!

The Philippine-American War

The ambitions of US imperialism went far beyond the New World. The successful outcome of the war with Spain led to bigger things. Although US capital investments within the Philippines and Puerto Rico were relatively small, nevertheless these colonies were strategic outposts for expanding trade with Asia, particularly China and Latin America. The United States suppressed an armed independence movement in the Philippines in the first decade of its occupation. During the ensuing (and largely forgotten) Philippine-American War, 4,234 US soldiers were killed, and thousands more were wounded. Philippine military deaths were estimated at roughly 20,000. Filipino civilian deaths are unknown, but some estimates place them as high as one million.

US attacks into the countryside often included "scorched earth" campaigns where entire villages were burned and destroyed, torture (the "water cure"), and the concentration of civilians into "protected zones." As a result many Philippine civilians perished of disease and famine. All these methods were later repeated and developed in Vietnam, where civilians were forced into so-called fortified villages. The depersonalization of colonial peoples as a justification for treating them as animals, to be tortured and killed without a second thought—all were put into practice in the Philippine-American War, and even earlier in the genocidal wars against the Native American peoples.

As in Vietnam and Iraq, reports of the execution of US soldiers taken prisoner by the Filipinos was used to justify disproportionate reprisals by American forces. Many US officers and soldiers called the war a "*nigger killing business*." In the same way, the Vietnamese were described as "*gooks*" and the people of Iraq are depicted as *bloodthirsty terrorists*. Racism is always the inevitable concomitant of imperialism.

The forcible interference of one nation in the internal affairs of another is conveniently justified on the grounds of alleged racial and cultural superiority. This is supposed to give "our" people the right to decide what another people is supposed to believe and how they should organize their internal government and laws. During the US occupation of the Philippines, English was declared the official language, although the languages of the Philippine people were Spanish, Visayan, Tagalog, Ilokano, and other native languages. Six hundred American teachers were imported aboard the *USS Thomas*. The people of the Philippines were compelled to accept the language, culture, and religion of the conquerors, whether they wanted it or not. In 1914, Dean C. Worcester, US Secretary of the Interior for the Philippines (1901–13), described "the regime of civilization and improvement which started with American occupation and resulted in developing naked savages into cultivated and educated men." In 2004, the Iraqi people are being treated in exactly the same way; only the politicians do not speak so honestly.

The United States and World War One

The USA's entry into World War I (the "War to End All Wars") in 1917 marked a qualitative new stage in American history. The whole logic of America's position in the two decades prior to 1914 rendered American intervention inevitable. The enormous and growing economic strength of the USA and its resulting military power made a clash with the older imperialist powers of Europe a certainty. That is why during the 20th century the US was involved in two world wars. However, when World War I began in 1914, the United States at first firmly protested neutrality—and none more loudly than the president, Woodrow Wilson. He was a strange figure in history. Wilson was neither a socialist nor a radical but a man of rigid views who tried to reconcile imperialism with democracy and pacifism. This was approximately like trying to reconcile a man-eating tiger with the principles of vegetarianism. No wonder Wilson died a bitter and disappointed man.

To imagine that the USA could keep out of the war in Europe, given America's important and growing role in world affairs, was utopian. The logic of events was pushing her into the war. All that was required was the usual incident to justify intervention. This was provided when early in 1917 Germany resumed its policy of unrestricted submarine warfare. The *RMS Lusitania*, a British ship carrying many American passengers, was sunk by German submarines. The *Lusitania*, like the *Maine*, Pearl Harbor, and the Gulf of Tonkin incident later, served as a convenient excuse to justify intervention in a European war, in a way that was to turn the USA into the de facto arbiter of the destiny of Europe—and hence the world. This created the necessary public indignation and led to a final break of relations with the Central Powers. President Wilson requested that the United States Congress declare war, which it did on April 6, 1917.

All sides in this war claimed that they had entered it with the purest and most Christian and civilized reasons. But, as in all other imperialist wars, this was only for the gallery. That goes just as much for the "idealist" Wilson as for Lloyd George and Clemenceau. The British and French insisted that the United States emphasize sending infantry to reinforce the line. They needed more cannon fodder to replace the millions who had been already led like sheep to the slaughter since the summer of 1914. The United States Army and the National Guard had already been mobilized in 1916 to pursue the Mexican "bandit" Pancho Villa, which helped speed up the mobilization. However, it would be some time before the United States forces would be able to contribute significant manpower to the Western and Italian fronts.

With American help, Britain, France, and Italy won the war. The latter naturally (from an imperialist point of view) took their revenge on the defeated and imposed savage economic penalties on Germany in the Treaty of Versailles. Wilson gained a short-lived popularity by proposing his famous Fourteen Points, which proposed a democratic peace without annexations or crippling indemnities, as well as self-determination for all peoples, etc., etc. As a list of good intentions it was admirable. But as a program for the postwar world it was useless. The British and French leaders, Lloyd George and Clemenceau, thought Wilson was mad. But they needed America's money and soldiers, and so they bit their tongues. Lloyd George was the wilier and more cunning of the two. He loudly demanded small concessions on matters of no importance, in order later to abandon them in exchange for getting his way on all the important questions later.

The style of French President George Clemenceau was of a different type, although the substance was the same. As W.E. Woodward correctly states:

> Clemenceau spoke English well. He was annoyed by Wilson's abstractions and ideals, and by his dissertations on the inalienable rights of mankind. His only comment on Wilson's essays was frequently an expressive, obscene and unprintable English word, which has been expunged from the record.
>
> Clemenceau did not want to be considered a gentleman; he looked upon all that as a lot of flummery and a waste of time. He made it perfectly plain that he was not in sympathy with the Fourteen Points, except those which gave something substantial to France (Woodward, 794).

The conduct of Lloyd George and Clemenceau has rightly earned them the reputation of callous brigands. But there was a definite logic behind their conduct. It was largely determined by the relations between Europe and America. The Allies owed a large amount of money to the USA and they intended to squeeze it out of Germany. Despite all President Woodrow Wilson's calls for reasonable terms, *the Versailles Treaty amounted to a decision to plunder Germany.*

A New World Power

I spent 33 years in the Marines. Most of my time being a high-classed muscle man for big business, for Wall Street and the bankers. In short, I was a racketeer for capitalism. I helped purify Nicaragua for the international banking house of Brown Brothers in 1909–12. I helped make Mexico and especially Tampico safe for American oil interests in 1914. I brought light to the Dominican Republic for American sugar interests in 1916. I helped make Haiti and Cuba a decent place for the National City Bank boys to collect revenue in. I helped in the rape of half a dozen Central American republics for the benefit of Wall Street . . .
—Smedley D. Butler (1881–1940), Major General (US Marine Corps)

Somebody once said to Lenin "war is terrible," to which he replied: "Yes, terribly profitable." In 1922, the US government created the Nye Committee to investigate the reasons the United States got involved in the war. The committee reported that between 1915 and April 1917, the US loaned Germany 27 million dollars ($27,000,000). In the same period, the US loaned Britain and its allies 2.3 billion dollars ($2,300,000,000), or about 85 times as much. They concluded that the US entered the war because it was in its commercial interest for Britain not to lose. In other words, the decision to enter the war was *the result of a simple business calculation.*

The human balance of the First World War was as follows: Allied soldiers killed: 5,497,600; Central Powers soldiers killed: 3,382,500; civilians killed: 6,493,000. However, the economic balance of the war was quite satisfactory. The American firm J.P. Morgan and Co. bought approximately three billion dollars' worth of goods during the war on behalf of the Allies, and made a profit of thirty million dollars from this source. In addition they made a great deal more from the sale of Allied War Bonds in the USA.

The world war turned the USA into the most powerful nation on earth. As the world's creditor, it was in a position to put Europe on hunger rations. The Allies were in debt to America to the tune of $10,350,000,000. Italy owed $2,000,000,000 and was given 62 years to pay up at an interest rate of four-tenths of one percent. The French owed twice as much and were to pay it back at an interest of 1.6 percent. Great Britain had the biggest debt of all: $4,600,000,000, to be amortized in a similar period at 3.3 percent.

Since Europe was ruined, these debts could not realistically be paid. The ruling class in Britain and other countries passed the bill to the working class in the form of savage wage cuts that led to a sharp upswing in the class struggle. In order to pay their bills, the French and British ruling classes exerted brutal pressure on the defeated Germans. They intended to pay the United States out of reparation funds squeezed from the German people. But bleeding, shattered, starving Germany could not pay.

Within one year the German payments stopped. The Dawes Commission looked into the situation and decided to reduce the amount paid to a more "lenient" sum: $500,000,000 in gold, payable by 1925, followed by an increasing amount thereafter. As a guarantee of payment, Germany's railroads, controlled revenues, and large-scale industries were placed under international control. The author of this plan, Charles G. Dawes, was given a Nobel Prize in 1925, but the plan collapsed immediately.

In 1928 Germany ceased to make any payments. Another committee of experts was formed under Owen D. Young. It proposed that Germany liquidate its debts in 59 years. During the first 37 years the annual payments were to be $512,500,000; after that, "only" $391,250,000. The total amount was twenty-seven and a half billions. The only problem that the authors overlooked was that it is not possible to squeeze blood from a stone.

In 1931, President Hoover had to face the facts and announced a moratorium on all foreign debts owed to the US government. The economic impact of the reparations mandated by the treaty caused chaos and misery on an unprecedented scale. These conditions ultimately led to the rise of Adolf Hitler who seized power in Germany in 1933. The United States Senate did not ratify the Treaty of Versailles; instead, the United States signed separate peace treaties with Germany and her allies. But the power of the USA was enormously reinforced by its intervention in the war.

By 1934 all the foreign debtors, except Finland, had ceased to make payments of either principal or interest. From 1920 to 1932 the total payments on the consolidated principal amounted to $583,000,000. All these payments were made in gold or its equivalent in international exchange. In this way, the United States accumulated the biggest stock of gold ever held by a national treasury in the whole of human history. Other nations were forced off the gold standard as a result of this huge drain. This opened the door to a chain of competitive devaluations that seriously aggravated the Great Depression of the 1930s.

The Russian Revolution

In March 1917, demonstrations in Petrograd culminated in the overthrow of Tsar Nicholas II. The workers and soldiers organized themselves in soviets—democratically elected action committees. The appointment of the Provisional Government, dominated by bourgeois liberals and politicians of the old regime, solved nothing. Power was really in the hands of the workers and the Petrograd Soviet. This confused and chaotic situation of dual power could not last. The bourgeois Provisional Government could neither end the war, nor solve any other of the pressing problems of the Russian workers and peasants. As a result, discontentment grew and the government became more and more unpopular.

Inside the soviets, the Bolshevik Party, led by Vladimir Ilyich Lenin and Leon Trotsky, began to gain an echo. By the autumn of 1917 they had won an overwhelming majority in the soviets and were in a position to take power. The triumph of the Bolsheviks in November (October, according to the old pre-revolutionary calendar) was a turning point in world history. Here, for the first time—if we exclude that glorious episode that was the Paris Commune—working people succeeded in overthrowing the old oppressive order and at least beginning the socialist transformation of society.

It is true that the revolution later suffered a process of bureaucratic degeneration, as the result of being isolated under conditions of extreme backwardness. But at least the Russian workers showed that a socialist revolution was possible. As Rosa Luxemburg said: "They alone dared." The Bolshevik Revolution lighted a beacon that inspired hope in the hearts of millions of downtrodden and exploited people everywhere. Its echoes were heard far across the Atlantic in the United States.

If you ever visit Moscow and take a stroll around the Kremlin walls, you will find among the tombs of famous Russian revolutionaries the graves of two outstanding Americans—"Big" Bill Haywood and John Reed, the celebrated American writer and journalist who was the central character of the movie *Reds*. John Reed was active in the American labor and socialist movement before the First World War and is best remembered for his marvelous book about the Russian Revolution, *Ten Days that Shook the World*, which Lenin himself described as a most truthful account of the October Revolution. After Trotsky's monumental *History of the Russian Revolution* it is the best book one could read about this subject. Not only is this a great and truthful work of historical journalism, it is a remarkable human document in which every line is vibrant with the excitement of the moment:

> It is still fashionable, after a whole year of the Soviet Government, to speak of the Bolshevik insurrection as an "adventure." Adventure it was, and one of the most marvellous mankind ever embarked upon, sweeping into history at the head of the toiling masses, and staking everything on their vast and simple desires. Already the machinery had been set up by which the land of the great estates could be distributed among the peasants. The Factory-Shop Committees and the Trade Unions were there to put into operation workers' control of industry. In every village, town, city, district and province there were Soviets of Workers', Soldiers' and Peasants' Deputies, prepared to assume the task of local administration.

> No matter what one thinks of Bolshevism, it is undeniable that the Russian Revolution is one of the great events of human history, and the rise of the Bolsheviki a phenomenon of world-wide importance. Just as historians search the records for the minutest details of the story of the Paris Commune, so they will want to know what happened in Petrograd in November, 1917, the spirit which animated the people, and how the leaders looked, talked and acted. It is with this in view that I have written this book.
>
> In the struggle my sympathies were not neutral. But in telling the story of those great days I have tried to see events with the eye of a conscientious reporter, interested in setting down the truth (*Ten Days that Shook the World*, preface).

What a refreshing change from the kind of book that now floods onto the market every day, written by allegedly "objective" and "scholarly" authors whose only intention is to blacken the name of the Russian Revolution, to bury it under a heap of lies and calumnies and thereby to convince the new generation that revolution is a very bad thing. What concerns these "impartial" hypocrites, of course, is not so much what happened in Russia almost a century ago, but what might happen in America tomorrow.

The modern American who wishes to understand the Russian Revolution could do no better than to read this marvellous book. John Reed was by no means an exception. Many Americans were inspired by the Russian Revolution at the time. And despite what happened subsequently, it remains a source of infinite inspiration and hope for the human race. Future generations of Americans will look back with infinite gratitude and affection to people like John Reed who were prepared to face slander, isolation, persecution, and worse to defend the cause of socialism and justice.

White Terror in the USA

John Dos Passos's *USA* is yet another socialist American literary masterpiece. It comprises three novels—*The 42nd Parallel*, *1919*, and *The Big Money*. The second of these novels expresses with extraordinary vividness the nature and atmosphere of the period that followed the Russian Revolution. It is an extraordinary work, written in a highly original form, combining newspaper headlines and telegraphic episodes with real-life and fictional stories. Although in later life dos Passos went to the right, he wrote a book that really gives a flavor of the times.

The notorious Versailles Treaty that set the seal on Germany's defeat in 1919 was put together by the USA, Britain, and France. As an example of cynical power politics and imperialist robbery, it is perhaps without parallel. With the sureness of touch of a master artist, dos Passos conveys the essence of the wheeling and dealing of the great imperialist powers and the sheer hypocrisy of the leaders of the "civilized Christian world":

> Clemenceau,
> Lloyd George,
> Woodrow Wilson.
> Three old men shuffling the pack,
> dealing out the cards:
> Rhineland, Danzig, the Polish Corridor, the Ruhr, self-determination of
> small nations, the Saar, League of Nations, mandates, the Mespot, Freedom
> of the Seas, Transjordania, Shantung, Fiume, and the Island of Yap:
> machinegun fire and arson
> starvation, lice, cholera, typhus;
> oil was trumps. . . .

On June 28 the Treaty of Versailles was ready and Wilson had to go back home to explain to the politicians, who'd been ganging up on him meanwhile in the Senate and House, and to sober public opinion and to his father's God how he'd let himself be trimmed and how far he'd made the world safe for democracy and the New Freedom.

Whether it is Germany in 1919 or Iraq in 2004, the diplomatic representatives of the great powers never admit that their activities are dictated by crude economic interests (*oil was—and is—trumps*). Their motivations are always pure and noble ("*making the world safe for democracy*"). And just as the monstrous Treaty of Versailles, which was supposed to make the world safe for peace, made the world a lot more unsafe and guaranteed the Second World War, so the present wars waged by the USA in Afghanistan and Iraq to "make the world a safer place" only render it far more unstable, unsafe, and dangerous than before. George W. Bush also believes fervently in the God of his fathers, to whom he prays while ordering the bombing of Iraqi cities and inflicting machine-gun fire, arson, starvation, and disease on millions of people. Meanwhile, behind all the rhetoric, oil is still trumps.

The description of the class struggle in the USA in the stormy years after the First World War in Dos Passos's book is outstanding in its raw and uncompromising realism. These were the years when the bosses and the government, fearing the effect of the Russian revolution on the American working class resorted to the methods of lynch law and mob rule to crush the labor movement. The year 1919, which gives Dos Passos's book its name, was a high point in the class struggle in the USA. The war, as we have seen, was a time when the bosses were making easy profits. The coming of peace was marked by more difficult conditions. The party was over for the capitalists.

As in other countries, the American bosses tried to pass the bill for post-war readjustments to the workers. As a result, an epidemic of strikes and labor disputes broke out, involving, at one time or another, 4,160,000 workers. In April 1922, there was the first coal mining strike in American history in which both the bituminous and anthracite coalfields were involved. More than half a million miners struck against sweeping reductions in wages. The strike lasted four months and ended in victory for the miners.

The repression against the labor movement had begun during the war when many were sent to prison, including socialist veteran Eugene Debs, now an old man. His only offense was that he had opposed the war. This gentle old man of American socialism was sentenced to ten years in a federal penitentiary. After the war, that fine Christian humanitarian, Woodrow Wilson, out of spite, refused to pardon him. President Harding finally released him, after he had spent three years in prison.

Congress passed draconic espionage and sedition laws. The postmaster general was given autocratic powers of censorship over written or printed matter sent through the mail. Socialist publications like the *Milwaukee Leader* and *The Masses* were excluded from the mail—a measure intended to bankrupt them. As if that was not enough, Congressman Victor L. Berger, the editor of the *Leader*, was given a twenty-year prison sentence. All these measures were in direct violation of the First Amendment of the Constitution, which guarantees all American citizens freedom of speech and of the press. More than fifteen hundred people were dragged before the courts for disloyal utterances.

State repression reached a feverish peak after the war. Terrified of the events in Russia, and fearful that revolution would spread to the United States, the ruling class unleashed a white terror against the American labor movement. When the AFL unions, which had grown to a membership of five million by 1920, organized a wave of strikes to combat the postwar inflation, corporate leaders denounced them as "radicals, connected with Bolshevism, aided by Hun money." Given the record of the moderate AFL leadership, this was ironic. But as always the ruling class was not afraid of the leaders of the unions but of the masses that were behind them.

A wave of violence was unleashed against the strikers, of whom twenty were killed. The strikes were defeated. Thousands of spies were hired to infiltrate the unions and identify labor leaders who were fired and blacklisted right across the USA. The bosses attempted to destroy the unions by forcing the workers to sign "yellow dog" contracts, promising not to join unions. It is an indication of how far back we have been thrown that such contracts still exist in the US at the beginning of the 21st Century. And this is regarded as acceptable in a supposedly democratic country! A mood of hysteria was created that fed the flames of lynch law. *The Washington Post* reported approvingly that when an irate citizen shot someone who had criticized a patriotic pageant, "the crowd burst into cheering and hand clapping" (Carroll and Noble, 331).

In Indiana it took a jury just two minutes to acquit another patriotic citizen who killed a man for saying "to hell with the United States." In Connecticut a salesman for a clothing company was sentenced to prison for calling Lenin "one of the brainiest men in the world." As usual, the most violent expressions of hate were reserved for the religiously minded. Billy Sunday, the nation's most powerful evangelists, said: "If I had my way with those ornery, wild-eyed socialists, I would stand them before a firing squad" (Carroll and Noble, 331). Senator McKellar of Tennessee was much more moderate. He merely advocated the establishment of a penal colony on Guam for political prisoners. The senator was a man ahead of his times. It took another 85 years for his ideal to be realized by another great democrat and patriot, George W. Bush. However, some of his contemporaries had a good crack at it.

The Attorney General, A. Mitchell Palmer, set in motion widespread raids, breaking into private homes and union halls without even the pretence of a warrant. On Palmer's initiative, a special antiradical division was set up under a young officer by the name of J. Edgar Hoover. Thousands of suspected radicals were arrested, held without bail, denied access to lawyers, and often brutally beaten after being marched in chains through the streets. Most were later released. But not all were so lucky. In Massachusetts two anarchists, Nicola Sacco and Bartolomeo Vanzetti, were convicted on a murder charge. The trial was clearly politically motivated. Judge Thayer, who presided, declared that he wanted to get "those anarchist bastards." Despite a huge international campaign to save them, Sacco and Vancetti were executed—two more martyrs to the cause of American labor. They were not the only ones.

In his book *1919*, John Dos Passos recounts the story of the brutal lynching of war veteran and Wobbly Wesley Everest in one of the most moving episodes of the work:

> Armistice Day was raw and cold; the mist rolled in from Puget Sound and dripped from the dark boughs of the spruces and the shiny storefronts of the town. Warren O. Grimm commanded the Centralia section of the parade. The ex-soldiers were in their uniforms. When the parade passed by the union hall without halting, the loggers inside breathed easier, but on the way back the parade halted in front of the hall. Somebody whistled through his fingers. Somebody yelled, "Let's go . . . at 'em boys." They ran towards

the wobbly hall. Three men crashed through the door. A rifle spoke. Rifles cracked on the hills back of the town, roared in the back of the hall.

Grimm and an ex-soldier were hit.

The parade broke in disorder, but the men with rifles formed again and rushed the hall. They found a few unarmed men hiding in an old icebox, a boy in the stairs with his arms over his head.

Wesley Everest shot the magazine of his rifle out, dropped it and ran for the woods. As he ran he broke through the crowd in the back of the hall, held them off with a blue automatic, scaled a fence, doubled down an alley and through the back street. The mob followed. They dropped the coils of rope they had with them to lynch Britt Smith the IWW secretary. It was Wesley Everest's drawing them off that Kept them from lynching Britt Smith right there.

Stopping once or twice to hold the mob off with some scattered shots, Wesley Everest ran for the river, started to wade across, up to his waist in water he stopped and turned.

Wesley Everest turned to face the mob with a funny quiet smile on his face. He'd lost his hat and his hair dripped with water and sweat. They started to rush him.

"Stand back," he shouted, "if there's bulls [police] in the crowd I'll submit to arrest."

The mob was at him. He shot from the hip four times, then his gun jammed. He tugged at the trigger, and taking cool aim shot the foremost of them dead. It was Dale Hubbard, another ex-soldier, nephew of one of the big lumbermen of Centralia.

Then he threw his empty gun away and fought with his hands. The mob had him. A man bashed his teeth in with the butt of a shotgun. Somebody brought a rope and they started to hang him. A woman elbowed through the crowd and pulled the rope off his neck.

"You haven't the guts to hang a man in the daytime" was what Wesley Everest said.

They took him to the jail and threw him on the floor. Meanwhile they were putting the other loggers through the third degree.

That night the city lights were turned off. A mob smashed in the outer door of the jail. "Don't shoot, boys, here's your man," said the guard. Wesley Everest met them on his feet, "Tell the boys I did my best," he whispered to the men in the other cells.

They took him off in a limousine to the Chehalis River Bridge. As Wesley Everest lay stunned in the bottom of the car, a Centralia businessman cut his penis and testicles off with a razor. Wesley Everest gave a great scream of pain. Somebody has remembered that after a while he whispered, 'For God's sake, men, shoot me . . . don't let me suffer like this. Then they hanged him from the bridge in the glare headlights.

Having described this bloody lynching in merciless detail, Dos Passos reverts to a cold and crushing irony:

The coroner at his inquest thought it was a great joke. He reported that Wesley Everest had broken out of jail and run to the Chehalis River Bridge and tied a rope around his neck and jumped off, finding the rope too short he'd climbed and fastened on a longer one, had jumped off again, broke his neck and shot himself full of holes.

They jammed the mangled wreckage into a packing box and buried it.

Nobody knows where they buried the body of Wesley Everest, but the six loggers they caught they buried in Walla Walla Penitentiary.

CHAPTER VII

THE GREAT DEPRESSION

"Happy Days Are Here Again"

The American Plan; automotive prosperity seeping down
From above; it turned out there were strings to it.
But that five dollars a day
paid to good, clean American workmen
who didn't drink or smoke cigarettes or read or think,
and who didn't commit adultery
and whose wives didn't take in boarders,
made America once more the Yukon of the sweated
workers of the world;
made all the tin lizzies and the automotive age, and
incidentally,
made Henry Ford the automobilieer, the admirer of Edison,
the birdlover,
the great American of his time.
—John Dos Passos, *The Big Money*

The so-called "Golden Twenties" witnessed a boom that was very similar to the boom of the 1990s through which we have just passed. Production soared to dizzy heights, the stock exchange still higher. President Coolidge believed fervently in the supreme wisdom of the market and its invisible hand. The business of government was to do nothing, to allow business a free hand and all would be well. For a time it seemed to work. No attempt was made to control speculation, which soared to the sky and beyond. Big fortunes were made, and as long as the money kept rolling in, why ask awkward questions? The same mood of what we now know as *"irrational exuberance"* has existed in every boom in capitalism from the Dutch tulip speculation of the 17th century to the new technology boom of the 1990s. And they all end the same way.

In the boom of the 1920s the illusion was created that wealth could be plucked out of thin air. In the stock exchange, money seemed to beget money in a miraculous and mysterious process. As a matter of fact, the boom of the 1920s, like any other boom under capitalism, was based on the super-exploitation of the working class. Between 1925 and 1929, the number of manufacturing establishments in the USA increased from 183,000 to 206,000 and the value of their output rose from $60 billion to $68 billion.

J.K. Galbraith comments:

> The Federal Reserve index of industrial production which had averaged only 67 in 1921 (1923–25 = 100) had risen to 110 by July 1928, and it reached 126 in June 1929. In 1926, 4,301,000 automobiles were produced. Three years later, in 1929, production had increased by over a million to 5,358,000, a figure which compares very decently with the 5,700,000 new car registrations of the opulent year of 1953. Business earnings were rising rapidly, and it was a good time to be in business (J.K. Galbraith, *The Great Crash 1929*, 31).

This is the real secret of the boom of the 1920s—the extraction of bigger and bigger amounts of surplus value from the sweat and nervous strain of the workers. Workers in the mass production industries—steel, auto, rubber, textiles, oil, chemicals, etc.,—were unorganized, atomized, and at the mercy of the employers. They were deprived of all rights and open to the most vicious kind of exploitation. Anyone who stood up for the workers' rights ran the risk of being accused of being a Communist, a Red, or a Bolshevik. Harry M. Daugherty, head of the Justice Department in the corruption-ridden Harding administration, was put on trial on charges of conspiracy to defraud the federal government. Incredibly, he blamed his downfall on a Red plot: "I was the first public official that was thrown to the wolves by the Red borers of America." In his book *The Inside Story of the Harding Tragedy*, Daugherty wrote:

> I believed then, as I firmly believe now, that Soviet Russia is the enemy of mankind. That unless the forces of civilization stamp out this nest of vipers who have enslaved a hundred and sixty million human beings, our social system as well as our form of government will perish from the poison that is being poured into our vitals.

There is a surprising degree of unanimity on this question that extends right across the spectrum of opinion in the community of red-blooded, freedom-loving American entrepreneurs. The following is another good example from an impeccable source:

We must keep America whole and safe and unspoiled. We must keep the worker away from Red literature and Red ruses; we must see that his mind remains healthy.

This ringing endorsement of the free market economy was the work of Al Capone, the notorious gangster, while awaiting trial. But Mr. Capone's touching faith in the market economy was misplaced. Even when he was speaking, America had already entered the Great Depression of the 1930s.

There is always a speculative element in every boom. Demand increases, the market expands, credit is needed for new investment, banks lend money as if there were no tomorrow. Prices rise in step with demand, and wages follow. Real estate prices soar along with the stock markets. Industrial production reaches dizzying heights and there is the beginning of what is now called overinvestment, but which is more properly termed overproduction. The whole thing is reaching its limits, but nobody knows or cares. Paradoxically, it is precisely at the apex of a boom, when it is on the point of collapsing, that the illusion is strongest that the boom will last forever, and that the boom-slump cycle is a thing of the past. Then comes the collapse. In the language of Marxist dialectics, everything turns into its opposite: all the factors that created the upswing now push the whole thing downwards. Cause becomes effect and effect cause. The result is a slump.

Marx explains that the ultimate cause of every real capitalist crisis is overproduction. The automobile tire industry in the USA had expanded far more than the demand for tires. Shoe factories had a productive capacity about twice the shoe-purchasing requirements of the country. Two-thirds of the potential capacity of the flour industry was not needed. It would have been possible to close about 40 percent of the U.S. steel industry and nobody (except the sacked workers) would have noticed the difference. And so on. When the stock market finally collapsed in October 1929, it was not, as is generally assumed, the cause of the Great Depression, but only a symptom of the underlying problems of the real economy, and a warning of worse to come.

The Great Crash—Then and Now

On December 4 1928, President Coolidge delivered his State of the Union speech to the nation. In it we read the following:

No Congress of the United States ever assembled, on surveying the state of the Union, has met with a more pleasing prospect than that which appears at the present time. In the domestic field there is tranquillity and contentment . . . and the highest record of years of prosperity. In the foreign field there is peace, the goodwill which comes from mutual understanding . . .

He told the legislators that they and the country might:

> regard the present with satisfaction and anticipate the future with opti-
> mism." And breaking sharply with the most ancient of our political conven-
> tions, he omitted to attribute this well-being to the excellence of the admin-
> istration which he headed. "The main source of these unexampled blessings
> lies in the integrity and character of the American people.

As late as March 1929, when Hoover took over the presidency, he was still
singing the same song:

> We are a happy people—the statistics prove it. We have more cars, more
> bathtubs, oil furnaces, silk stockings, bank accounts, than any other people
> on earth.

Then in October 1929 the stock market collapsed. Industrial production fell
by 50 percent and national income fell from $82 billion to $40 billion in just
four years. Unemployment soared from two million in 1928 to three million
in 1929, four million in 1930, seven million in 1931, twelve million in 1932
and 15 million in 1933.

The optimistic speeches of America's leaders on the eve of the collapse
have been frequently quoted as proof of the stupidity and short sightedness
of Coolidge, Hoover, and their contemporaries who failed to foresee the Great
Crash of 1929 or to take measures to prevent it. The comforting assumptions
are that a) slumps are produced by the stupidity or mistakes of governments
and leaders, and that b) our present governments and leaders are much
cleverer than Coolidge and will not make the same mistakes again. Unfortunately, both assumptions are false. The history of the past 200 years should
be enough to convince any reasonable person that the boom-slump cycle is
something inherent to the capitalist system and not an accident caused by
clumsy behavior. As sure as night follows day, a period of boom will be followed by a slump. Only the timing, duration, and depth of the slump is unpre-
dictable. But slumps under capitalism cannot be avoided.

It is true that the capitalists have evolved a number of mechanisms for
postponing a slump, but the problem is that usually the very act of postponing it makes it all the more severe when it finally arrives. Chief among these
mechanisms is credit, which, as Marx explained long ago, is a way by which
the market ("demand") is extended beyond its natural limits. This can work
for a time, but only at the cost of increased levels of indebtedness. This means
that the market is expanded today at the cost of undermining it tomorrow.
The central problem is not abolished but aggravated in the long run.

The idea has often been repeated that "we have learned from history"
and that therefore a repeat of 1929 is not possible. This is an excessively

optimistic view of things. Hegel was much more realistic when he wrote that anyone who studies history can only conclude that nobody has ever learned anything from it. He said that precisely because the same situations continually repeat themselves in history in general, and, we might add, in economic history in particular. There are many striking similarities between the boom of the second half of the 1920s and the boom of the second half of the 1990s. Then too the economists and politicians assured us that the boom-slump cycle had been vanquished forever. Marx had been consigned once and for all to the dustbin of history. Once again, they were all merrily plunging into a speculative orgy that drove the stock markets to unprecedented heights. Then came the fall.

It is true that so far, the fall has not been as steep as in 1929. Indeed it has been one of the mildest on record. But the story is not yet ended. The boom of the 1990s, like the boom of the 1920s, was based on a speculative bubble of vast proportions. That bubble has not yet been entirely burst. In fact, they are currently busy reflating it. The astronomical levels reached by the housing market internationally is a symptom of this fact. It bears an uncanny resemblance to the property boom in the 1920s, the bursting of which was one of the things that led to the collapse of 1929. Alan Greenspan long ago referred to the "irrational exuberance" of the boom of the 1990s. But he is doing nothing to restrain this exuberance, which poses a serious threat to the future prospects of both the U.S. and world economy. The longer the bubble is allowed to inflate, the more painful the final reckoning will be. This is what J.K. Galbraith has to say on this subject:

> A bubble can easily be punctured. But to incise it with a needle so that it subsides gradually is a task of no small delicacy. Among those who sensed what was happening in early 1929, there was some hope but no confidence that the boom could be made to subside. The real choice was between an immediate and deliberately engineered collapse and a more serious disaster later on. Someone would certainly be blamed for the ultimate collapse when it came. There was no question whatever as to who would be blamed should the boom be deliberately deflated (For nearly a decade the Federal Reserve authorities had been denying their responsibility for the deflation of 1920–21.) The eventual disaster also had the inestimable advantage of allowing a few more days, weeks, or months of life. One may doubt if at any time in early 1929 the problem was ever framed in terms of quite such stark alternatives. But however disguised or evaded, these were the choices which haunted every serious conference on what to do about the market (J.K. Galbraith, 52).

These lines could have been written yesterday. They are a graphic warning of just how little the economists and politicians have learned from the past, and just how little they can control the boom-slump cycle. Contrary to the received wisdom, a repeat of 1929 at some stage is not at all ruled out. In fact, it is implicit in the whole situation.

The New Deal

The stock market crash in 1929 and the ensuing economic slump punctured the dream of never-ending prosperity and pushed millions into poverty. Construction and housing stagnated after 1929, joining declines in the agriculture, mining, and petroleum industries. Overproduction dragged down prices and profits. Wages did not rise fast enough to enable consumers to purchase all the new homes and home products offered for sale. Foreign trade was constrained by growing protectionism in the industrialized world. The stock market crash led to a collapse of consumer confidence and led to a crisis of the financial institutions. Investment slumped. The economy sank into a severe depression, referred to by Americans as the "Great Depression." This was characterized by high levels of unemployment, negligible investment, and falling prices and wages. Millions of Americans were out of work and living precariously on public or private charity. When Russia invited Americans to apply for six thousand skilled jobs in 1931 it received a hundred thousand applications. Millions of Americans were reduced to penury. A survey in New York City in 1932 concluded that 20 percent of the children were suffering from malnutrition.

A report in a Chicago newspaper graphically describes the conditions:

> Around the truck which was unloading garbage and other refuse, were about thirty-five men, women, and children. As soon as the truck pulled away from the pile, all of them started digging with sticks, some with their hands, grabbing bits of food and vegetables.

John Steinbeck was the author of novels depicting the lives and struggles of ordinary working Americans during the Great Depression—*The Grapes of Wrath*, *Cannery Row*, *Of Mice and Men*. *The Grapes of Wrath* was published in 1939, when America had still not emerged from the Great Depression and millions were living in dire poverty. Steinbeck's poignant description of the conditions of the hungry and downtrodden, and their struggle to maintain human dignity, won him the Pulitzer in 1940.

In this novel Steinbeck vividly describes the ruthlessness of the big corporations that sent in the bulldozers to demolish the smallholdings and cabins that represented so much hope and so many years of labor. Men, women, and children were evicted overnight and transformed from small farmers into propertyless vagrants. The most remarkable thing about this novel is that it does not seem to be a description of the masses written from without. The author has succeeded in getting under the skin of the "Okies," and expressing, in their own words and language the innermost thoughts, feelings, and aspirations of the people. Here, for example, is how they see the police:

> "What'd the deputy say?" Huston asked.
> Well, the deputy got mad. An' he says: "You goddamn reds is all the time stirrin' up trouble," he says. "You better come along with me." So he takes this little guy in, an' they give him sixty days in jail for vagrancy.
> "How'd they do that if he had a job?" asked Timothy Wallace.
> The tubby man laughed. "You know better'n that," he said. "You know a vagrant is anybody a cop don't like. An' that's why they hate this here camp. No cops can get in. This here's United States, not California."

Tom Joad expressed the voice of the underdog:

> They're a-workin' away at our spirits. They're a tryin' to make us cringe an' crawl like a whipped bitch. They tryin' to break us. Why, Jesus Christ, Ma, they comes a time when the on'y way a fella can keep his decency is by takin' a sock at a cop. They're workin' on our decency.

In a situation where millions were going hungry, Hoover decided that relief was exclusively a matter for the local and state authorities. This worthy representative of big business, a millionaire himself, was concerned lest federal relief should corrupt the American character and undermine the spirit of free enterprise. For Hoover and the establishment there was no problem: the market would sort things out in the long run. But as the English economist John Maynard Keynes pointed out, in the long run we are all dead.

There was a sharp increase of political ferment and discontent among the workers of America. At that time many of the strategists of capital feared a socialist uprising in the USA. In order to prevent revolution from below, as so often happened in history, the more farseeing sector of the U.S. ruling class decided to launch a program of reforms from above. In this way the idea of the New Deal was born. The Democratic President Franklin D. Roosevelt was elected in 1932. He implemented a number of programs to relieve the plight of the poor and unemployed. Over the past twenty years, historians have emphasized the "revolutionary" legislation of the Roosevelt administration. However, at the time, he was bitterly attacked by conservative businessmen as a revolutionary and a communist.

F.D. Roosevelt was no radical, but the son of a wealthy patrician family and a relative of Theodore Roosevelt. Actually, he was attempting to combat the spread of communism in the USA and save the capitalist system from revolution. He probably saved the American ruling class from the threat of social revolution, which was closer then than at any other time in American history. But the establishment was too stupid to realize this. They distrusted Roosevelt and heaped abuse on him as a covert socialist and a dangerous radical. Roosevelt protested that this was a misunderstanding—and he was right. "I am fighting Communism, Huey Longism, Coughlinism, Townsendism," he declared. "I want to save our system: the Capitalist system." The difference is that he was a more competent defender of capitalism than his opponents. Roosevelt was smart enough to see that Hoover's policies would undermine capitalism in the USA quicker than anything else.

In the middle of a terrible agricultural crisis, Hoover had the brilliant idea of asking the farmers to reduce their crops, a piece of advice that rivals Marie Antoinette's "let them eat cake." Roosevelt correctly said that it was a "cruel joke" to advise the "farmers to allow 20 percent of their wheat to lie idle, to plough up every third row of cotton and shoot every tenth dairy cow." In order to defend the fundamentals of capitalism, Roosevelt was prepared to be flexible. In an emergency, he was prepared to resort to deficit financing to keep the level of unemployment within certain limits. But this policy has its limits. If it is continued for a long time it will have inflationary consequences. Therefore, as soon as there were signs of a modest economic recovery, Roosevelt cut back on state expenditure. This produced a sharp recession in 1937 and unemployment again doubled from five to ten million and remained high until the outbreak of war.

A whole mythology has grown up about the New Deal. Those who believe that capitalism can be reformed in such a way that it can avoid slumps and achieve social justice point to it as proof of their assertions. But in practice, Roosevelt's policies had at best only a marginal effect in pulling the U.S. economy out of the slump. The recovery, when it finally came, was not due to the New Deal but to the Second World War. The lowest point of the Great Depression was in 1933, but the U.S. economy showed very little improvement through the end of the decade, and remained grim until it was dramatically reshaped through America's arms program and participation in the Second World War, which had an even bigger effect than the previous one in stimulating the U.S. economy.

The CIO and the Sit-In Strikes

Following the Great Crash of 1929, the bosses launched on program of savage wage cuts. The AFL responded by announcing "no-strike" deals. This was supposed to be the result of a "gentleman's agreement" between the unions and the bosses. But in practice the unions conceded everything, the bosses nothing. From 1922 to 1929 the number of labor disputes diminished year after year. In 1929 there were only 903 labor disputes involving 203,000 workers. On September 1, 1929, noting with satisfaction that the number of strikes in the USA had gone down from 3,789 in 1916 to 629 in 1928, AFL President William Green asserted that "collective bargaining is coming to be accepted more and more as a preventative of labor disputes."

Weakness invites aggression. In June-July 1930, 60 corporations and industries announced wage cuts, and the AFL did nothing about it. The result was a rapid decline in union membership. In 1929 only one in five industrial workers belonged to a union in the USA. Of those who did, nearly half were either building or transport workers. By 1931 the AFL was losing 7,000 members a week, and from a high of 4,029,000 in 1920, fell to 2,127,000 in 1933. This is a fitting epitaph on the supposedly "realistic" policies of "unionism pure and simple."

These were years of violent class struggle in the USA. As Art Preis recalled in his book *Labor's Giant Step*: "Almost all picket lines were crushed with bloody violence by police, deputies, troops and armed professional strike-breakers." The mass demonstrations of unemployed workers organized by the Communist Party were broken up violently by the police, with many jailed, wounded, or killed. On March 7, 1932, a demonstration of unemployed demanding work at the Ford Rouge Plant was dispersed with machine guns, leaving four dead and many wounded. On the direct orders of President Hoover, General Douglas MacArthur, riding a white horse at the head of his troops, attacked a demonstration of 25,000 unemployed war veterans and their families with tear gas, gunfire, and bayonets. Such "incidents" were common throughout the 1930s—including under Roosevelt's "New Deal." In 1937, for example, ten people were killed and 80 wounded in a Memorial Day clash between police and members of the Steel Workers Organizing Committee at a plant of the Republican Steel Co. in South Chicago.

Several AFL unions established the Committee for Industrial Organization (CIO) to organize the unorganized industries. This organization effort had great success in the rubber, steel, and automobile industries. The internal dispute over organizing these industries continued and, in 1938, the AFL expelled the unions, which formed their own federation, calling itself the Congress of Industrial Organizations. John L. Lewis of the United Mine Workers became the organization's first president. The formation of the CIO was labor's giant step. Overnight the unorganized were organized. It is not generally realized that the Trotskyists—especially in Minneapolis—helped lead the big Teamsters strikes, which led to the formation of the CIO. People like Farrell

Dobbs played a key role, all the more extraordinary given that he had voted Republican in the most recent elections. As a result of the experience of the class struggle he went straight from Republicanism to revolution. This little detail shows how fast moods can change.

Most people believe that it was the French workers who invented the method of factory occupations during the 1930s. Not so! The American workers in the early 1930s developed a powerful movement known in the USA as *the sit-down strikes*. It involved employees going to their workplaces and then refusing to work. That is a factory occupation in all but name. The first successful sit-down strike happened in Flint, Michigan in 1937 when the United Auto Workers at a GM factory stopped production. This controversial method proved effective, yet controversial among management and some labor leaders. In the first large sit-down strike the United Rubber Workers (CIO) won recognition from the Goodyear Tire and Rubber Co. But not every strike ended in victory. The five week long "Little Steel" strike was broken when Inland Steel workers returned to work without even having won union recognition.

The militancy of the CIO had dramatic results. It quickly reversed the decline in union membership and led to the organization of new layers who showed great energy and élan. Very soon the CIO had gained two million new members. The mass factory occupations were illegal, but the workers newly awakened to the struggle were determined to fight for their rights. One worker recalled the tremendous spirit of class solidarity:

"It was like we was soldiers, holding the fort. It was like war. The guys became my buddies." And it was war: class war. The big corporations like General Motors and Ford spent millions of dollars a year on spies and private police to fight the strikers. But the workers' organization, class consciousness, and discipline defeated the bosses and their hired gunmen.

CHAPTER VIII

WORLD WAR II

America and the Second World War

Marx explained long ago that capitalism develops as a world economic system. Today nobody can doubt the correctness of this statement. In 1935 Roosevelt stated: "Foreign markets must be regained if America's producers are to rebuild a full and enduring domestic prosperity for our people." That is the reason why the USA was compelled to participate in the world, despite the objections of the isolationists.

Since the First World War, America's position as the most powerful and wealthy imperialist power had been clear to all. So when in 1939 a new conflict broke out between the old imperialist powers of Europe, it was only a matter of time before the USA would have to be involved. After some early ambiguity, Roosevelt came down decisively in favor of using America's colossal military, industrial, and economic power to enhance its position as the leading capitalist nation on earth.

Paradoxically, until the 1930s, the main antagonism on a world scale was between the rising power of the USA and the old imperial master of the planet, Great Britain. Trotsky had even posed the possibility of war between the two if the USA insisted on boosting its naval strength to the point of challenging Britain's dominance of the seas. In the end, however, it was the threat to American commercial interests posed by Japan and Germany that decided the issue. In particular, the clash of interests of the USA and Japan in Asia and the Pacific was decisive. Japan was challenging the Open Door policy of the United States in China, and Germany was making a similar challenge in Europe.

Even more threatening was the expansion of Japanese and German interests in Latin America.

Roosevelt attempted to modify the Neutrality Acts in order to prepare for war, but was thwarted at every step by the powerful isolationist lobby. However, the outbreak of war in Europe gave him an excuse to embark on a major program of rearmament with the approval of a budget of $18 billion in 1940. By September Congress was ready to approve the first peacetime conscription act. All that was missing was the necessary incident that could ignite a mood of mass indignation leading to a declaration of war. At the time of the election of 1940, the polls indicated that the majority of the US public was still opposed to intervention. Roosevelt played along with the general mood: "I have said this before, but I shall say it again and again. Your boys are not going to be sent into any foreign wars."

No sooner had he been reelected, however, Roosevelt took steps to involve America in the war. He persuaded Congress to approve a Lend-Lease Act to send arms and supplies to Britain. He ordered the navy to attack German submarines that interfered with the shipment of these supplies. He announced on the radio: "America has been attacked by German rattlesnakes of the seas." These were concrete steps in the direction of war.

The decisive turning point was the Japanese attack on Pearl Harbor on December 7, 1941. This was precisely the incident that Roosevelt needed. In fact, it is perfectly obvious that he brought it about deliberately. For the whole of the previous year, Roosevelt and his Secretary of State, Cordell Hull, had refused to sell crucial resources, notably oil and steel, to Japan. This embargo convinced the war party in Tokyo that war with the United States was inevitable. The war party demanded immediate action to secure the economic supplies denied to them by the USA. This led inexorably to the attack on Pearl Harbor. US intelligence had cracked the Japanese secret codes and therefore knew about the Japanese plans. Roosevelt and Hull were also well aware of the consequences of their embargo and their refusal to negotiate. The American fleet at Pearl Harbor was an obvious target. Yet strangely, when the Japanese attacked, the American commanders were completely unprepared.

Pearl Harbor was the excuse Roosevelt was looking for. He demanded that Congress recognize that a state of war existed with Japan, and who could argue? Yet as late as 1945, 80 percent of Americans consulted in a poll considered that Roosevelt had violated his 1940 pledge to keep America out of the war. Pearl Harbor was worth more than ten divisions to Roosevelt.

Russia and the War

The policies and tactics of the British and American ruling classes in the Second World War were not at all dictated by a love of democracy or hatred of fascism, as the official propaganda wants us to believe, but by class interests. When Hitler invaded the USSR in 1941, the British ruling class calculated that the Soviet Union would be defeated by Germany, but that in the process Germany would be so enfeebled that it would be possible to step in and kill two birds with one stone. It is likely that the strategists in Washington were thinking on more or less similar lines. But like Hitler, the British and US ruling circles had miscalculated. Instead of being defeated by Nazi Germany, the Soviet Union fought back and inflicted a decisive defeat on Hitler's armies.

The defenders of capitalism can never admit the real reason for this extraordinary victory, but it is a self-evident fact: the existence of a nationalized planned economy gave the USSR an enormous advantage in the war. Despite the criminal policies of Stalin, which nearly brought about the collapse of the USSR at the beginning of the war, the Soviet Union was able to swiftly recover and rebuild its industrial and military capacity. The truth is that the war against Hitler in Europe was fought mainly by the USSR and the Red Army. For most of the war the British and Americans were mere spectators. Following the invasion of the Soviet Union in the summer of 1941, Moscow repeatedly demanded the opening of a second front against Germany. But Churchill was in no hurry to oblige them. The reason for this was not so much military as political.

The Soviet working class was fighting to defend what remained of the gains of the October Revolution. Despite the monstrous crimes of Stalin and the bureaucracy, the nationalized planned economy represented an enormous historic conquest. Compared with the barbarism of fascism—the distilled essence of imperialism and monopoly capitalism, these were things worth fighting and dying for. The working people of the USSR did both on the most appalling scale.

In 1943 alone, the USSR produced 130,000 pieces of artillery, 24,000 tanks and self-propelled guns, 29,900 combat aircraft. The Nazis, with all the huge resources of Europe behind them, also stepped up production, turning out 73,000 pieces of artillery, 10,700 tanks and assault guns, and 19,300 combat aircraft (See V. Sipols, *The Road to a Great Victory*, 132). These figures speak for themselves. *The USSR, by mobilizing the immense power of a planned economy, managed to outproduce and outgun the mighty Wehrmacht.* That is the secret of its success.

To some extent the same was true of the United States. The need to mobilize all the productive forces of the USA for the war effort made it necessary to introduce at least some measures of central control and planning. This was, of course, not socialism but "state capitalism." Roosevelt appointed a War Resources Board with a prominent representative of big business at its head, Edward Stettinius of US Steel. His ideal was not a workers' democracy but an economy run by a handful of big corporations operating without price competition within the parameters of objectives laid down by the state: a kind of "managed capitalism."

It goes without saying that a genuine planned economy is not possible under capitalism. Nevertheless, we are entitled to ask the following question to the defenders of market economics and free enterprise: if the capitalist system is so superior, when America (and Britain) had its back to the wall, when economic efficiency and production were a matter of life and death, did your government simply rely on the laws of the free market? *It did not. It introduced elements of central planning, state control and even nationalization. Why? The answer is very clear: because this gave better results!*

And we are entitled to ask another, even more interesting question: if a semi–planned economy could give such good results in time of war, why cannot a genuine socialist planned economy, combined with democratic control and administration by the workers themselves, not give even better results in time of peace?

The Turn of the Tide

The real turning point of the war was the Soviet counteroffensive in 1942, culminating in the Battle of Stalingrad and later in the even more decisive Battle of Kursk. After a ferocious battle lasting one week, the German resistance collapsed. To the fury of Hitler, who had ordered the Sixth Army to "fight to the death," General Paulus surrendered to the Soviet army. Even Churchill, that rabid anti-Communist, was compelled to admit that the Red Army had "torn the guts out of the German army" at Stalingrad.

Throughout the war, the Russians were demanding that the Allies open a second front against Germany in Europe. This was resisted particularly by Churchill. Churchill wanted to confine the Allies' war to the Mediterranean, partly with an eye on the Suez Canal and the route to British India, and partly because he was contemplating an invasion of the Balkans to block the Red Army's advance there. In other words, his calculations were based exclusively on the strategic interests of British imperialism and the need to defend the British Empire. In addition, Churchill had still not entirely given up the hope that Russia and Germany would exhaust themselves, creating a stalemate in the east.

The conflicts between Churchill and Roosevelt on the question of D-Day were of a political and not a military character. The interests of US imperialism and British imperialism were entirely contradictory in this respect. Washington, while formally the ally of London, was all the time aiming to use the war to weaken the position of Britain in the world and particularly to break its stranglehold on India and Africa. At the same time it was concerned to halt the advance of the Red Army and gain control over a weakened Europe after the war. That explains the haste of the Americans to open the second front in Europe and Churchill's lack of enthusiasm for it. Harry Hopkins, Roosevelt's main diplomatic representative, complained that Churchill's delaying tactics had "lengthened the timing of the war."

In the end, Churchill's calculations backfired. The Red Army defeated the Wehrmacht and embarked on the most spectacular advance in military history. They took control of Eastern Europe and held onto it. The landlords and capitalists of Poland, Hungary, and the other countries of the region had collaborated with the Nazis, and fled together with them.

Trotsky once said that to kill a tiger one requires a shotgun, but to kill a flea, a thumbnail is sufficient. The Stalinists liquidated capitalism in Eastern Europe but they did not introduce socialism. These regimes began where the Russian Revolution ended—as bureaucratically deformed workers' states. The expropriation of the capitalists and landlords was undoubtedly a progressive task, but it was carried out bureaucratically, from above, without the democratic participation of and control by the working class.

The regimes that emerged from this were a bureaucratic and totalitarian caricature of socialism. Unlike the Russian workers' state established by the Bolsheviks in 1917, they offered no attraction to the workers of Western Europe. With the exception of Czechoslovakia, the bourgeoisie of Eastern Europe had been very weak before the war. The US imperialists attempted to strengthen the bourgeois elements and gain control of Eastern Europe by offering them Marshall Aid. Stalin understood the maneuvre and gave the order. The Stalinists took power by expelling the bourgeois elements from the coalitions and nationalizing the means of production.

Origins of the Cold War

President Roosevelt died on April 12, 1945, and was replaced by Vice President Truman. Many people have assumed that Roosevelt was less anti-Communist than his successor. But this is not the case. The reason why Roosevelt did not want an immediate clash with Moscow was that it did not suit the interests of American imperialism to break with Moscow *at that point in time*. In addition to the considerations already mentioned, the Americans had another reason for not sharing Churchill's enthusiasm for a "crusade against Bolshevism"—or, at least, the timing. The Americans' main preoccupation was the war in the Pacific, where they were still locked in a life-or-death struggle with Japanese imperialism.

The problem was that the USSR had a huge army in the heart of Europe. Only the possession of nuclear weapons gave the USA a potential advantage, since the USSR did not yet have the atom bomb. But the bomb had not yet been tested, and there was no guarantee that it would work. The Americans tested the first atom bomb on June 16, 1945, at the very time the wartime Allies were meeting in Berlin to discuss the postwar situation.

Truman and Churchill were informed that the test had been successful and wasted no time in letting Stalin know all about it. They hoped to use the threat of nuclear devastation to tip the balance of the negotiations in their favor. Some have maintained that the Cold War did not begin until 1947, but in fact it began immediately after the surrender of Japan, and was prepared even before that. D.F. Fleming states: "President Truman was ready to begin it before he had been in office two weeks" (D.F. Fleming, *The Cold War and its Origins, 1917–1960, Vol. 1*, 268).

The possession of the atom bomb gave Truman a sense of superiority, which he did not feel the need to hide. James F. Burns, director of the US war mobilization department, assured Truman that possession of the atom bomb would put the USA in a position "to dictate our own terms at the end of the war" (Harry S. Truman, *Memoirs, Vol. 1, Year of Destiny*, New York, 87).

As usual, Churchill was the first to foment an anticommunist crusade. This rabid reactionary and warmonger did everything in his power to push the Americans into a conflict with Russia. Describing his mood at this time, General Allen Brooke, the Chief of the British Imperial General Staff, noted in his diary that "*he was always seeing himself capable of eliminating all the Russian centers of industry and population*" (Arthur Bryant, *Triumph in the West, 1943–1946*, London, 1959. 478). But the British working class had had enough of Churchill. They had had enough of war, too, and certainly had no desire to engage in a new war, least of all against the Soviet Union. In the 1945 general election they kicked Churchill and the Conservatives out of power and voted massively for a Labour government.

In any case, Britain was already reduced to the role of a secondary power, a mere satellite of the USA—a role that has continued to the present day. The Americans did not pay much attention to Churchill's raving because they still had unfinished business in the Pacific. They needed the help of the Soviet Union to defeat Japan, and therefore were not in a hurry to bring about a premature confrontation with the Russians in Europe. That could wait until Japan had surrendered.

The Defeat of Japan

All the peoples paid a terrible price for the war. Britain's casualties totalled 370,000, the USA, 300,000. But the Soviet Union lost a staggering 27 million—about half of all the casualties of the Second World War. According to one estimate, even before the Normandy landings, 90 percent of all young men between the ages of 18 and 21 in the Soviet Union had already been killed. These chilling figures accurately express the real situation. They show that the people of the Soviet Union suffered a disproportionate number of casualties, because the main front in Europe was the Eastern front.

Western historians, motivated rather by political considerations than historical truth, have systematically minimized the role of the Soviet Union in the Second World War. This systematic campaign of distortion has increased a hundred-fold since the fall of the Berlin Wall. The defenders of capitalism are not willing to acknowledge the achievements of the nationalized planned economy in the USSR. They cannot admit that the spectacular military victory over Hitler's Germany was due precisely to this.

In order to belittle the role of the USSR in the war, they exaggerate the importance of things like American Lend-Lease to the Soviet Union. This falsification is easy to answer. The fact is that the Red Army had halted the German advance and begun to counterattack by the end of 1941 in the Battle of Moscow—before any supplies had reached the USSR from the USA, Britain, or Canada.

These supplies came mainly in the period 1943–45, that is, at a period when the Soviet economy was already producing more military hardware than the German war machine. They accounted only for a fraction of Soviet war production: two percent of artillery, ten percent of tanks, and twelve percent of aircraft. In no sense can this be considered decisive to the Soviet war effort as a whole. Its importance was marginal.

The real reasons for the marvellous achievements of the Soviet Union in the Second World War was something the Western historians are never prepared to admit—*firstly, the superiority of a nationalized economy and central planning, and secondly, the determination of the Soviet working class to defend what remained of the conquests of the October Revolution against fascism and imperialism.*

This was no thanks to Stalin and the bureaucracy, who had placed the USSR in extreme danger by their criminal and irresponsible policy before the war, but in spite of them. The Soviet workers, despite all the crimes of Stalin and the bureaucracy, rallied to the defense of the USSR and fought like tigers. This was what ultimately guaranteed victory.

The role of the USSR in the defeat of Japan has always been overlooked. Actually, it was quite a significant one. Americas war in the Pacific had resolved itself into a bloody slogging match to wrest control of one coral atoll after another from Japanese control. What is never mentioned is that the Japanese had a powerful land army in Manchuria, the Kwantung Army. Its total strength was up to a million men. It had 1,215 tanks, 6,640 guns and mortars, and 1,907 combat aircraft.

This formidable fighting force was faced by 1,185,000 Soviet troops stationed in the Soviet Far East. These were reinforced with additional forces after the surrender of Germany, and when the offensive began on August 9 totalled 1,747,000 troops, 5,250 tanks and self-propelled guns, 29,835 guns and mortars, and 5,171 combat aircraft. In a campaign lasting just six days the Red Army smashed the Japanese forces and advanced through Manchuria with lightning speed. The Soviet forces entered Korea and the South Sakhalin and Kurile Islands and were in striking distance of Japan itself.

On August 6, Truman ordered the US Air Force to drop an atom bomb on Hiroshima. Three days later, the very day the Soviet army began its offensive, they dropped a second bomb on Nagasaki. They did this despite the fact that these were civilian cities with no military value and the Japanese were already defeated and suing for peace. The fact is that these atom bombs were intended as a warning to the USSR not to continue the Red Army's advance, otherwise they could have occupied Japan. The use of the atom bomb was a political act. It was intended to show Stalin that the USA now possessed a terrible new weapon of mass destruction and was prepared to use it against civilian populations. There was an implicit threat: what we have done to Hiroshima and Nagasaki we can do to Moscow and Leningrad.

Once Japan had surrendered, Washington's attitude to Moscow changed immediately. The whole shape of the postwar world was now determined. The world would be dominated by two great giants: mighty US imperialism on the one hand and mighty Russian Stalinism on the other. They represented two fundamentally opposed socio-economic systems with antagonistic interests. A titanic struggle between them was inevitable.

The American imperialists now felt themselves masters of the world. They had suffered relatively little from the war. Their productive base was intact, whereas most of Europe's industry lay in a heap of smoldering rubble. Two-thirds of all the available gold in the world was in Fort Knox. The USA had a huge army and a monopoly of nuclear weapons. They could impose their conditions on the rest of the world. Only the Soviet Union stood in their way. The arrogance of American power was put into words by the managing director of *The New York Times*, Neil MacNeil, who wrote that

> both the United States and the world need peace based on American principles—a *Pax Americana* . . . We should accept an American peace. We should accept nothing less (Neil MacNeil, *An American Peace*, New York, 1944, 264).

The Postwar Economic Upswing

The period after the Second World War was completely different to the period that followed the First World War. After 1945 there was a remarkable up-swing of the productive forces in the USA and internationally. What were the basic reasons for the developments of the post–Second World War economy? In 1938, Leon Trotsky had predicted that the war would end with a revolutionary wave. In fact, there were a whole series of revolutionary explosions after 1943, in Italy, France, Greece, and even Denmark. Unfortunately, the Stalinists and the social democrats, in Britain and Western Europe succeeded in diverting this revolutionary movement into safe reformist channels, and the revolutionary potential was wasted. This created the *political* climate for a recovery of capitalism.

The effects of the war, in the destruction of consumer and capital goods, created a big market (war has effects similar to, but deeper than, a slump in the destruction of capital). These effects, according to United Nations statisticians, only disappeared in 1958. Moreover, during the war a whole series of new avenues of investment were opened up as a by-product of arms production—plastics, aluminum, rockets, electronics, atomic energy and its by-products.

The growth of these new industries provided the basis for an enormous increase in productive investment after the war. The increasing output of the newer industries—chemicals, artificial fibers, synthetic rubber, plastics, rapid rise in light metals, aluminum, magnesium, electric household equipment, natural gas, and electric energy, together with the building activity caused by postwar reconstruction, provided the basis for a huge boom.

However, a key role was played by the USA. America had emerged virtually unscathed from the war, while her main competitors—Britain, France,

Germany, Japan—were either severely damaged or completely shattered. Two-thirds of the world's gold was in the vaults of Fort Knox. The USA was therefore able to dictate terms to the rest of the Western world. The Bretton Woods agreement established the dollar as the world currency, which further assisted the growth of world trade.

The war had created enormous amounts of fictitious capital, created by the armaments expenditure, which amount to 10 percent of the national income in Britain and America. But in a situation of a gigantic upswing of the productive forces, nobody was worried about the danger of inflation. On the contrary, everybody wanted to get hold of dollars (the pound sterling was now reduced to a secondary currency, reflecting the decline of Britain as a world power). The dollar was considered to be "as good as gold."

Fear of revolution and "Communism" compelled Washington to intervene decisively to save the European capitalists. The Marshall Plan and other economic aid played a key role in assisting the recovery of Western Europe. This in turn provided new markets for the mighty productive capacity of the USA. The increasing trade, especially in capital goods and engineering products, between the capitalist countries, consequent on the increased economic investment, in its turn acted as a spur. State intervention also played a role in stimulating economic activity, especially in countries like Britain where the postwar Labour government carried out a policy of nationalization and reforms.

A new world order was gradually taking shape. The old empires ruled by Britain, France, Holland, and Belgium had been shaken to their foundations by the war and the Japanese conquests in Asia. One by one, the old colonial masters were being driven out by national liberation movements. This provided new opportunities for US imperialism to muscle in on the new markets in Asia, Africa, and the Middle East, elbowing their European rivals to one side.

The new market for capital and engineering products gave the local bourgeoisie the opportunity to develop industry on a greater scale than ever before. All these factors interacted on one another. The increased demand for raw materials, through the development of industry in the metropolitan countries in its turn, reacted on the undeveloped countries and vice-versa. All these factors explain the increase in production since the war. But the decisive factor was the increased scope for capital investment, which is the main engine of capitalist development.

America After 1945

For all these reasons, after the Second World War, America experienced a period of tremendous and sustained economic growth that set its stamp on her entire development. It shaped the consciousness of its people in a decisive way. For decades, American capitalism seemed to be "delivering the goods." The economy was growing rapidly and the recessions were so shallow and fleeting that they were barely noticed. Living standards were increasing. There was an abundance of things like refrigerators, televisions, telephones, and cars that made people feel prosperous.

The feeling that "we have never had it so good" was reinforced by what Americans could see in the rest of the world. Whenever anybody complained, the defenders of the established order could point triumphantly to Stalinist Russia, that monstrous bureaucratic and totalitarian caricature of socialism, and say: "You want socialism? That's socialism for you—dictatorship and the rule of an autocratic bureaucracy! You will be slaves of the state. Is that what you want?" And even the most critical American worker would shake his or her head and conclude that the devil they knew was probably a lot better than the one they didn't.

In case they were not completely convinced, however, a little coercion could be brought to bear. It was not as severe as the white terror that followed the First World War. That was not necessary, given the full employment and rising living standards. But during what was known as the Cold War, state repression was unleashed in quite a ruthless manner. It was known as the McCarthy Era.

On February 9, 1950, Senator Joseph R. McCarthy of Wisconsin claimed that there were no fewer than two hundred Communists in the State Department. This outrageous allegation unleashed a witch hunt against everyone who was even slightly "tainted" with left wing, progressive, or even vaguely democratic opinions in public life. The hysteria that accompanied this campaign closely resembled the kind of pathological collective hysteria of the notorious Salem witch trials of the 17th century. This comparison was made explicit in Arthur Miller's famous play *The Crucible*.

In fact, the witch-hunting of the American Left had commenced a couple of years earlier. After 1945 the American ruling class lived in dread of Communism and revolution, and launched a "Reds under the bed" campaign, using the House Un-American Activities Committee (HUAC) to grill suspects. Prominent among the interrogators was an ambitious young Republican congressman, Richard Milhous Nixon (later dubbed "Tricky Dicky"), who was out to make a name for himself as a notorious red-baiter. He subsequently became president, only to be removed for crooked practices following the Watergate scandal.

The power behind the scenes of these witch hunts was FBI chief and ultra-reactionary J. Edgar Hoover, who for years ran a state within the state, acting as a law unto himself, scorning all the principles of democratic government, and imitating the conduct of the Mafia that he was supposed to be fighting. This paragon of public virtue said in March 1947: "Communism, in reality, is not a political party. It reveals a condition akin to a disease that spreads like an epidemic and like an epidemic a quarantine is necessary to keep it from infecting this nation" (Quoted in Jeremy Isaacs and Taylor Downing, *Cold War*, 109).

Since his death, Hoover has been exposed as a corrupt gangster who used extortion and blackmail to exert unconstitutional control over elected politicians while he extolled the virtues of American democracy, and secretly led a luxurious and degenerate lifestyle while he delivered lectures on the need for puritanical morals. These were the kind of heroes who led the crusade against Communism in the USA.

Obsessed with his hatred of Communism and radicals, Hoover ordered his agents to use illegal means: wiretaps, break-ins, phone intercepts, and bugging of private homes to get incriminating evidence. Neighbors were encouraged to spy on neighbors; parents were asked to spy on their children, and children on their parents. When defense lawyers exposed these illegal practices and used this to get cases thrown out, Hoover launched an attack on the National Lawyers' Guild, which he accused of being a Communist front (!).

One of the first great achievements of the witch hunt was to send to the electric chair a young electrical engineer, Julius Rosenberg, and his wife Ethel. They were charged with passing atomic secrets to the Soviet Union. The evidence against Rosenberg came largely from his brother-in-law, David Greenglass, who had been part of a wartime spy network. Though interrogated by the FBI, Julius Rosenberg refused to give information or name any other agents. So the FBI arrested his wife, Ethel, although she was clearly not a spy, in order to break her husband. It did not work. He remained silent.

Rosenberg was found guilty of passing secrets to the Russians. Spying in wartime is punishable by death, but when Rosenberg passed secrets to Russia, it was an ally of the USA. But despite pleas for clemency, among others from Albert Einstein and Pope Pius XII, both Julius and Ethel Rosenberg were sent to the electric chair. What is interesting is the conduct of the judicial system in this case. The judges were clearly intimidated to the point where they did not dare defy the general hysteria. Arthur Kinoy, the Rosenberg's lawyer, reports the words of one such judge:

> Judge Frank looked at us and he said something that we have never, never forgotten. He said, "If I were as young as you are, I would be sitting there saying the same things you're saying, arguing the same points you're arguing, making the same argument that these planned executions are invalid. But when you are as old as I am, you will understand why I cannot do it." And he stands up, turns his back to us, and walks away, and we were devastated. We began to sense something which in later years we understood so clearly. That was that Jerome Frank, as the leading liberal judge, was terrorized himself and frightened by the atmosphere of fear in the country. That if he as a liberal would do something to save Julius and Ethel Rosenberg's life, he would be charged as a commie (Quoted in Isaacs and Downing, 113).

The tentacles of the witch hunters extended into every branch of public life. Given the importance of the film industry in American life, Hollywood became a key target. Hoover established an extensive network of spies and informers, chief among whom was a second-rate actor in B-movies called Ronald Reagan. Based in Los Angeles, Reagan was president of the Screen Actors Guild. He used his position to pass on information about his colleagues to Hoover. This was the start of a promising political career that ended in the White House. When he died recently, there was a flood of laudatory obituaries, praising the former president for his great intellect and ability and attributing to him the posthumous title of "the man who defeated Communism."

Although he could be accused of many things (bad acting, lack of principles, cowardice, dishonesty, ignorance, provincial narrow-mindedness, disloyalty towards friends and colleagues, etc.), no serious person could ever accuse Ronald Reagan of possessing either *intellect* or *ability*. As a matter of historical record, the USSR (which, in the period under consideration, had very little in common with communism) collapsed because of its internal contradictions, and this had nothing to do with the intellect or abilities of Ronald Reagan.

In 1951, HUAC launched an all-out offensive against Hollywood. Prominent actors and film directors were grilled by HUAC, in scenes reminiscent of the Inquisition. The only way to escape from this torture was to incriminate others. Some brave souls refused. The great German composer Hans Eisler, who had fled to America from Nazi persecution and wrote distinguished film scores, when he was accused of being the "Marx of the music world," answered that he was flattered by the comparison, and was deported for his courage.

However, others were not so courageous. The bosses of the big Hollywood studios pledged not to employ anybody who had ever been a Communist or had refused under oath to declare that they had never been a Communist. Many of the big names in Hollywood decided that discretion was the better part of valor and collaborated in the dirty name of denouncing their fellow actors. Elia Kazan, the famous director who introduced Marlon Brando to the cinema, named eleven former Communists to HUAC. Jerome Robbins, the successful Broadway and Hollywood choreographer, also cooperated with the Inquisition, as did Sterling Hayden. But the man who broke the record for denunciation was screenwriter Martin Berkeley, who named no fewer than 162 Hollywood artists as Communists, past or present.

The consequences for those so-named were dire. They would be sacked and never work again in any studio in Hollywood or any other part of the USA. They would immediately lose their livelihood and reputation and be treated as outcasts and pariahs. About 250 Hollywood personalities were blacklisted in this way in the early 1950s. Some just disappeared. Others went into exile. A few continued to work under assumed names, like Dalton Trumbo, author of *Johnny Got His Gun*, who caused the whole industry considerable embarrassment when he actually won an Oscar in 1956 for a screenplay written under the name of Robert Rich. One group of blacklisted filmmakers and actors made the marvellous film *Salt of the Earth*, brilliantly depicting the class struggle in the silver mines of New Mexico.

Among the victims of McCarthyism were some of the most talented directors, writers, and performers in America. Some did not work again till the 1960s. The great black singer Paul Robeson was savagely persecuted. The legendary Charles Chaplin, although British by birth and nationality, had lived in the USA for over 30 years. He had learned while in England that he would be denounced as a Communist and decided to live the rest of his life outside the USA. He did not return to the USA until 1972 and then only briefly to accept a special Academy Award. American culture was the real loser.

The place of talented people was taken by hacks who were prepared to write third-rate trash like *I was a Communist for the FBI*, which won an Oscar for the best documentary (this shows how much an Oscar is really worth). Other gems of the period included *My Son John*, which depicts a nice young American boy who, unknown to his parents, becomes a Communist; and *I Married a Communist*, which depicts a nice American girl who married one; *Evil Epidemic*, in honor of J. Edgar Hoover, and so on.

The health of the American cinema industry was in good hands. The Motion Picture Alliance for the Preservation of American Ideals was presided by good old John Wayne. This fearless, clean-living cowboy of the silver screen was always speaking lines like "a man's gotta do what a man's gotta do." In this case what a man like John Wayne had to do was to betray his friends and colleagues and throw them to the wolves. This did not require much courage but definitely did one's career no harm.

Other heroes of the same kind were Clark Gable ("*Frankly, my dear, I don't give a damn*"), Gary Cooper, and John Ford, who were all on the executive committee of the Motion Picture Alliance for the Preservation of American Ideals. The presence of the last two named is perhaps ironical, since the celebrated film *High Noon*, starring Gary Cooper and directed by John Ford, has been widely interpreted as a criticism of McCarthyism in the guise of a Western.

The witch-hunters then turned their unwelcome attentions to American education. The worthy senator from Wisconsin discovered that American colleges and universities were hotbeds of Red subversion. Formally, there was no blacklist as in Hollywood, but in practice anyone involved in political activity of the "wrong sort" would not easily get a job in academia. J. Edgar Hoover, whose educational qualifications were somewhat comparable to those of Conan the Barbarian, complained that American schools were in the hands of "*Reducators.*" The latter were "*tearing down respect for agencies of government, belittling tradition and moral customs and . . . creating doubts in the validity of the American way of life.*"

The ruling class let these mad dogs off the leash to snap and snarl to their heart's content. It was useful to have such people intimidate the left. But the real establishment had no intention of handing power to the mad dogs. In the end, McCarthy overreached himself when he began to interfere with the most sensitive part of the state, the armed forces. In a series of sensational television interviews in 1954, McCarthy accused the US Army of being infiltrated by Communists. That was too much. Having made use of the Senator's services, the establishment unceremoniously ditched him. The Senate voted to condemn him for bringing it into disrepute. He was politically a dead man.

The Unions After 1945

Many European leftists regard Americans as hopelessly reactionary. This view demonstrates a lamentable ignorance of American history. I hope that this short study will serve at least partially to correct the error. Americans are neither more nor less revolutionary than anybody else. What is true, as Marx pointed out long ago, is that social being determines consciousness. For several decades after 1945, for the special reasons that we have outlined above, capitalism entered into a phase of upswing. It was the greatest economic fireworks display in history. The main beneficiary was the USA. The living standards of most Americans increased (some more than others, it is true). This was the material basis for a major psychological change. The idea was widely accepted that capitalism was "delivering the goods." Workers are generally very practical people, and pragmatism has sunk deeper roots in America than any other country. "If it ain't broke, don't fix it" is a wise old American saying.

Under these conditions the old revolutionary traditions of US labor, old traditions that went back to the Knights of Labor, passing through the Labor Uprising of 1877, the Chicago Martyrs, the Wobblies, and the class struggles of the 1920s and 1930s, receded from the collective consciousness and were largely forgotten. The new generation knew little of them. In that sense, the knot of history was broken. There is no automatic mechanism whereby the traditions of the working class, the lessons of past victories and defeats can be transmitted from one generation to another. The only mechanism that can fulfill this role is the revolutionary party. The absence of a Marxist revolutionary party with deep roots in the working class in America is a serious problem. It means that the class can only learn through its own experience: this is a slow and painful process that can take decades. This is a situation that must be remedied in the coming period.

Although politically speaking the American workers are not as educated as their European counterparts and lack a class party through which to express their interests and aspirations, even in a distorted and incomplete manner, this by no means signifies that they lack class consciousness. What they lack in political organization they have made up for in terms of industrial organization and militancy. On the industrial front the American workers have had a tradition that is second to none. It is true that, as in Europe, the American unions are under attack and the control of a bureaucracy that does its best to suffocate the militancy of the rank and file. The capitalist class does its best to corrupt and bribe the union tops. Through the bureaucracy of the unions, the influence of bourgeois ideology, class collaboration, and so on, can percolate down into the working class. In particular, the leaders of the big unions are linked to the Democrats, just as the British union leaders were linked to the Liberals in the 19th century. But this situation was the logical consequence of the long years of economic upswing and prosperity. It did not survive in Britain, and will not survive the new period of storm and stress into which we are now heading in the United States.

The traditions of the CIO in its early years are something that the new generation of young Americans should take time out to study. They were reflected very poorly in the big Hollywood movie *Hoffa*, and much better in the earlier and lesser-known film called *FIST*—the only decent film Sylvester Stallone ever made. The main thing to see is that this is not ancient history. The class struggle did not cease in the 1930s but has continued, with ebbs and flows, ever since. The American workers have always had a good union tradition, and as a matter of fact, the number of strikes actually increased in the years after the Second World War. From 1936 through 1955, there was a staggering total of 78,798 strikes in the United States, involving 42,366,000 strikers. The breakdown was as follows:

Years	Number of Strikes	Number of Strikers
1923–32	9,658	3,952,000
1936–45	35,519	15,856,000
1946–55	43,279	26,510,000

In order to curb union militancy, the bosses and the government introduced the anti-union Taft-Hartley Act in 1947. Yet in 1949 there were major strikes in the coal and steel industries; 1952 was a year of coal and steel strikes; and 1959, the year of the 116-day steel strike, the largest strike of all-time in the United States as measured by total workdays on strike.

Big business and its state were, and remain, bitterly hostile to trade unionism. Although unions are no longer illegal, the state does not hesitate to invoke anti-union legislation whenever it suits the bosses to do so. The national emergency machinery provided under the Taft-Hartley Act for the investigation of disputes threatening to "imperil national health or safety" was invoked by the president in 23 situations from the time of its enactment in 1947 through 1963—and is still called upon today.

This is not ancient history. Taft-Hartley is alive and well, and still used for busting unions in the USA. President Ronald Reagan fired most of the nation's air traffic controllers for striking illegally and ordered their union, the Professional Air Traffic Controllers Association, decertified. 13,000 air traffic controllers defied the return-to-work order. Subsequently 400,000 unionists participated in the largest labor rally in American history, which was held in Washington in protest against the policies of the Reagan administration. More recently still, George W. Bush used Taft-Hartley against the longshoremen of the ILWU.

In addition, there are other laws that are regularly invoked by the legal establishment to prevent the workers from using their legitimate right to strike. In the war between labor and capital, the state is not impartial now any more than it was in the past! The fight for union rights against unjust anti-union laws is a burning need for the American working class. This fact also shows the utter futility of trying to separate trade unionism from politics.

If anyone believes the class struggle is dead in the USA, I advise him or her to look at experience of strikes such as that of the miners in 1989. In April of that year the United Mine Workers (UMW) called a strike against the Pittston Coal Group for unfair labor practices. These miners had worked 14 months without a contract before the UMW called the strike. Among the practices cited by UMW were the discontinuing of medical benefits for pensioners, widows, and the disabled; refusal to contribute to a benefit trust established in 1950 for miners who retired before 1974; and refusing to bargain in good faith. Miners in Virginia, Kentucky, and West Virginia struck against Pittston.

The miners and their families engaged in an inspiring civil disobedience campaign against the company. In the time-honored tradition of the American bosses, the strike was met with calculated violence, as state troopers were called out to arrest striking miners. The miners fought back courageously with dynamite. Despite the enormous importance of this strike, the "free press" of the USA made practically no mention of it, preferring to give a great deal of coverage to another miners' strike—*in Russia!*

The movement of the American working class to fight for its own interests continues—as the recent disputes at UPS and on the West Coast docks shows very clearly. If there have not been more strikes and if the living standards and conditions of the workers have not kept pace with the huger increase in profits, it was due to a failure of the leadership of the unions, not the workers. In recent years the trade unions have hit difficulties as a result of this. As in other countries, the unions in the United States have become heavily bureaucratized and the leaders were out of touch with the problems of ordinary workers.

The rundown of heavy industries in the North and East—the traditional base of unionism—has led to a fall in membership. Yet the leadership proved incapable of responding to the challenge posed by big business to the union movement. With the development of new industries in the South and West, millions of workers in the United States are now unorganized. The task of organizing them into unions is perhaps the most pressing need at the present time. In order to solve this problem, the unions must go back to their roots, to the militant traditions of the CIO when they organized the unorganized in the stormy years of the 1930s. When that happens, we shall discover that those formerly inert and "backward" layers will be among the most militant and revolutionary in the whole union movement.

The unions have always been the basic organizations of the class. They are on the front line in the defense of the most basic rights of the working class.

Without the day-to-day struggle for advance under capitalism, the socialist transformation of society would be utopian. Therefore, the struggle to transform the unions, to democratize them at all levels and make them genuinely responsive to the wishes and aspirations of working people, to turn them into genuine organs of struggle, is a prior condition for the fight for a socialist America, in which the unions will play the role that was envisaged for them by the pioneers of labor—as the basic organizations for running the economy in an industrial democracy.

CHAPTER IX

THE COLONIAL REVOLUTION

Vietnam

The war in Vietnam, which completely transformed the situation in the USA, did not begin in a planned way. The USA was sucked into it almost by accident. It began with a covert operation, the sending of officers and "advisers" to prop up an unpopular and corrupt government against its own people. This is the usual style of US imperialism! The regime of Ngo Dinh Diem was guilty of vicious repression in South Vietnam. Buddhist monks burned themselves alive in protest. Finally, Diem was assassinated by his own generals.

Three weeks later, the president of the USA suffered the same fate. Kennedy was succeeded by his vice president, Lyndon B. Johnson, who immediately announced that he was "not going to lose Vietnam." "Win the war!" was his clear instruction. But despite all its tremendous wealth and military firepower, the USA did not win the war. On the contrary, Vietnam was the first war America ever lost. Korea was a draw. But in the steamy jungles and swamps of Vietnam, the Americans suffered a bitter defeat at the hands of a barefoot army.

In order to step up its military activities in Vietnam, (as usual) an incident was required. This was (as usual) manufactured in the so-called Gulf of Tonkin incident. It was alleged that a US warship, the *Maddox*, had been fired upon by North Vietnamese naval vessels in the Gulf of Tonkin. For years it was believed that the US Navy had been the target of unprovoked "Communist aggression." That was completely untrue. Even at the time, the captain of the *Maddox* admitted that none of his crew had made "actual visual sightings" of North Vietnamese naval vessels, and not one sailor either on the *Maddox* or the *Turner Joy* had actually heard North Vietnamese gunfire. The opening of the Hanoi archives has proven conclusively that the North Vietnamese did not fire on the American ships, which were actually inside Vietnamese territorial waters at the time. Yet the American public was persuaded to back a foreign war on the basis of false information—and not for the last time, as we know.

The very next day, Lyndon Johnson ordered the bombing of North Vietnamese naval bases and an oil depot. It was the start of a huge campaign of bombing that caused havoc in Vietnam, killing a large number of civilians and destroying its industry and infrastructure. On television, President Johnson declared:

> Repeated acts of violence against the armed forces of the United States must be met not only with alert defense but with positive reply. That reply is being given as I speak to you tonight (Quoted in Isaacs and Downing, 216).

There was not a word of truth in any of this. Johnson and co. had decided to send US troops to Vietnam and that was that. In the same way, George W. Bush and his friends decided long before 9/11 to invade Iraq and lied through their teeth about the alleged weapons of mass destruction that were supposed to pose a deadly threat to American security to sell it to the public.

In the years that followed, high explosives, napalm, and cluster bombs rained down on Vietnam. The US Air Force dropped toxic chemicals, including the notorious agent orange on forests, allegedly to kill the vegetation and deny shelter to the Vietnamese guerrillas. A total of 18 million gallons of herbicide were dropped. Even today US servicemen are dying from the effects of just handling these toxic agents, especially cancer. One shudders to think of the effects they had on the Vietnamese men, women, and children on whom they were dropped. Tests have shown that the South Vietnamese have levels of dioxin three times higher than those in US citizens. It will take many years to flush these toxins out of the fragile ecosystem. This was chemical warfare pursued with a vengeance!

In all, the US dropped more tons of explosives on Vietnam than were dropped by all sides in the Second World War. After bombing one village to rubble, one US officer was quoted as saying: "We had to destroy the town in order to save it." They are still "destroying towns in order to save them" today. Ask the inhabitants of Fallujah. And the tactic of dropping tons of poisonous chemicals still continues in Colombia, where herbicides are being used in the so-called war against drugs. The damage to people, vegetation, and wild life will be the same as in Vietnam. But nobody talks about that.

The name of this particular operation was "Rolling Thunder." There must be somebody in the Pentagon, some frustrated poet, whose sole function is to think up picturesque names for such acts of barbarity. Lately we had "Operation Shock and Awe." It is a pity such talented people were not around at the time of the fall of the Roman Empire, or Attila the Hun might have called his activities "Operation Sweetness and Light." No matter what the name was, it did not succeed. Once an entire people stands up and says "no!" to a foreign invader, no amount of troops, guns, bombs, or chemical agents will make any difference, as George W. Bush will learn to his cost in Iraq. The Vietnamese continued to resist. More and more US troops had to be sent in, and more and more body bags were being flown home.

At first the US authorities simply hid the facts of the growing escalation from the American public. They continued to lie and deceive with the active assistance of what is known in some quarters as the free press. But as Abe Lincoln pointed out, you can fool some of the people all the time, and all of the people some of the time, but you cannot fool all of the people all of the time. Slowly, by degrees, and not all at the same time, the people of the United States became aware of what the true situation was.

The suffering of the Vietnamese population will never be fully known. Apart from the huge number killed and maimed, the war caused many other human casualties. The relentless bombing, shelling, and defoliation drove tens of thousands of peasants from the countryside to the outskirts of the big cities where they lived in humiliating poverty. The traditional structures of Vietnamese village life were shattered. Young girls became prostitutes for the US soldiers.

A drug culture flourished, which later fed back into the cities of the USA, with devastating results. In 1971 the Pentagon calculated that nearly 30 percent of the US troops in Vietnam had taken heroin or opium, while smoking marijuana was commonplace. Attempts to stamp out the drug trade met with the opposition of the South Vietnamese puppet regime, which was heavily involved in it. That was an indication of the rottenness of the regime the USA was trying to prop up.

By the end of 1967 the US was spending $20 billion a year on the Vietnam War, which contributed massively to a balance of payments deficit of $7 billion. By the end of 1968, the number of US troops in Vietnam was over 500,000. Towards the end of the war, the US troops in Vietnam were completely demoralized. They understood the situation, that they were fighting an unwinnable war. The Vietnamese were fighting a just war of national liberation, while the US army was a hated army of foreign occupation. In any army there is an element of killers and sadists, and in such a situation atrocities and brutality against civilians became routine. Eventually, these horrors became known at home, with the massacre at My Lai among the most infamous. The supposed moral justification for the war was blasted to pieces—just as in Iraq today.

In January 1968, President Johnson announced that the USA was winning the war. This was immediately blown apart by the Tet offensive. The Vietnamese mounted simultaneous attacks in more than a hundred cities. In Saigon a sapper unit even managed to penetrate the US embassy compound. These events were shown all over America on the television screens to a shocked public. This cruelly exposed the fact that for all its military might, the USA had not succeeded. The war finished Johnson's political career. Richard Nixon, the Republican candidate, defeated L.B.J.'s Vice President Hubert Humphrey in the presidential elections of November 1968.

The Anti-Vietnam War Movement

While these dramatic events were unfolding, on the other side of the world, France was facing revolution. In May 1968 the French working class staged the biggest revolutionary general strike in history. Ten million workers occupied the factories, while the students demonstrated on the streets of Paris, built barricades, and fought with the police. The general mood of radicalization naturally affected the youth first. The youth of America was mobilizing for civil rights and against the Vietnam War. Already in October 1967 antiwar protesters organized a huge march. For the first time since 1930 the Federal government called in armed troops to defend the capital. The kids tried to fraternize with the troops, but that night the troops attacked the demonstrators, kicking and clubbing them with extreme violence. One eyewitness spoke of "troops and marshals advancing, cracking heads, bashing skulls."

This was a good lesson in the realities of bourgeois state power. Engels and Lenin explained that the state in the last analysis is "armed bodies of men." Its whole purpose is to keep the majority under control by means of organized violence or the threat of violence. The rest is just show. The pent-up tensions of American society, which exposed deep, unresolved contradictions, were about to erupt in a most violent way. Dramatic events were being prepared. The broad sweep of the civil rights movement had shaken America from top to bottom. The assassination of black leader Martin Luther King sparked-off mass rioting in a hundred cities. There were more than 20,000 arrests and fifty deaths. 75,000 troops were called out to keep order. King's death meant that the leadership of the black movement passed to more radical elements. The Black Panthers, who embraced Marxism and advocated the united struggle of the black and white poor, were organizing military training in the ghetto of Oakland, California. People were calling openly for revolution. The assassination of Robert Kennedy underlined the general mood of violence and social tension.

A million students and faculty members were boycotting classes in protest at the war. Things came to a head with the Democratic Party convention in Chicago, where the party was to choose its presidential candidate. Mayor Richard J. Daley announced, "As long as I am mayor, there will be law and order on the streets." He gave the Chicago police the order to shoot to kill. When thousands of demonstrators descended on the city, they were brutally attacked by the police. The demonstrators were infiltrated by 200 plainclothes policemen. Demonstrators, newsmen, and passers-by were all clubbed and beaten. So much tear gas was thrown that it entered the ventilation system of the hotel where Humphrey was giving his acceptance speech, with predictable results. He commented bitterly: "Chicago was a catastrophe. My wife and I went home heartbroken, broken and beaten." Some of the demonstrators went home rather more broken and beaten than Mr. Humphrey.

'A Nation on the Edge of Chaos'

The election of Richard Nixon signified the continuation of the war. It also signified the continuation of the antiwar movement. Nixon authorized the extension of the war into Cambodia, where the US Air Force staged an even more vicious bombing campaign than in Vietnam. The massive destruction and loss of life caused by this bombing was the real explanation for the fanatical hatred of the Americans and their Cambodian allies that motivated the later brutal conduct of the Khmer Rouge, ending in the "Killing Fields," and a new period of chaos, death, and bloodshed.

The student protests against the war led to the shooting of students at Kent State and Jackson State Universities. This poured gas on the fire. Five hundred universities closed in protest. *"Four Dead in Ohio,"* sang the rock group Crosby, Stills, Nash, and Young. There was a general outcry. Meanwhile, an increasingly paranoid president authorized wiretaps, surveillance, and "surreptitious entry"—a euphemism for burglary—against the leaders of the antiwar movement. This was the slippery slope that led the Nixon administration to Watergate.

Nixon was reelected, just as George W. Bush was reelected. But his troubles had only just begun. He tried to force Hanoi to come to terms by stepping up the bombing of the North. For twelve days over Christmas, the North was battered by wave after wave of B-52 bombers. Still, Nixon spoke of "peace with honor." The people of Vietnam still faced two more gruelling years of war, but in reality the will to fight on the part of the Southern army and the US troops in Vietnam had collapsed. In early 1975 the North launched another offensive, leading to the fall of the cities of Hue and Da Nang. First there was military rout, then political collapse. The American stooge Thieu fled. Within days the Vietnamese Liberation Army entered Saigon. The world was witness to the incredible scenes of panic as the last remaining American personnel had to scramble into helicopters from the roof of the embassy building in Saigon.

The Vietnam War was not only the greatest military defeat in American history. It had a profound effect on American society. The truth is that US imperialism was defeated, not in the swamps and jungles of Vietnam, but in the cities, campuses, and streets of the USA From a military point of view, there was no reason why the USA should not have won the war—in time. But the colossal drain of the war had a revolutionary effect on American society. In fact, if a revolutionary party had existed in the USA at that time, it would have been on the brink of a social revolution. This is not an exaggeration. A presidential commission set up to investigate the shootings in Ohio concluded:

> The crisis has its roots in a division of American society as deep as any since the Civil War. A nation driven to use the weapons of war upon its youth is a nation on the edge of chaos.

The word "*chaos*" must here be understood as a synonym for *revolution*.

The explosive mood of discontent was not confined to the students, as has often been maintained. The student youth is always a sensitive barometer reflecting deep moods of discontent in the bowels of society. The wind always blows through the tops of the trees first. A radicalization of the students is an anticipation of a later revolutionary movement in society as a whole. That was true of the first Russian revolution, which commenced with student agitation against the war with Japan and ended with the revolution of 1905. The student demonstrations in Paris in May 1968 did not cause the general strike, as many have believed. It merely acted as the catalyst for moods of discontent that had been accumulating silently over a long period of time. In the same way, the student agitation in the USA was the expression of a general mood of dissatisfaction and discontent, which had not yet surfaced but which was being prepared.

It is no accident that the movement of the black Americans reached its most explosive point at the same time, and found its expression in the Black Panthers, the most conscious, courageous and consistently revolutionary of all the tendencies in the black community (along with Malcolm X before his death). They were seen as a particularly dangerous threat by the establishment because they had moved beyond black nationalism towards Marxism and were advocating the revolutionary unity of black and white workers—an absolutely correct policy. For this they were deliberately targeted by the state and systematically exterminated.

But the greatest danger to the state came from within the state. The US troops in Vietnam were not only completely demoralized by this time. They were in a state of open revolt. There were many cases of mutiny, and also of the killing of officers by their own troops. A new verb entered into the English language at this time: "fragging." This is derived from "fragmentation grenade." A soldier would pass the officer's mess or quarters and casually lob a grenade in, killing and wounding those inside. *The fact is that the US government had to withdraw the troops from Vietnam, or else face a general revolt.* One American general, commenting on the state of the US troops in Vietnam, said that there was only one possible historical analogy, and that was the morale of the Petrograd garrison in 1917. That is correct. If there had been an American equivalent of the Bolshevik Party, which would have had cells in the army, the analogy could have been carried to its logical and successful conclusion.

Intervention in Latin America

For more than a century, the USA regarded Latin America and the Caribbean as its own back yard. In 1954, the CIA organized the overthrow of the democratically elected government of President Jacobo Arbenz Guzman in Guatemala. Arbenz was a reformist leader who had intervened in labor disputes between workers and the US-owned United Fruit Company. The latter had considerable influence in Washington, where one of its directors had been US Secretary of State, John Foster Dulles. His brother, Allen Dulles, by a fortunate coincidence, was head of the CIA. By an even more fortunate coincidence, the latter was a former member of the company's board of trustees.

With a little friendly encouragement from United Fruit, the Eisenhower administration approved a secret plan to depose Arbenz, now dubbed "Red Jacobo." In fact, Arbenz was never a Communist, although he had been supported in the election by the Left Parties in Guatemala. But Arbenz was carrying out a land reform. He had nationalized 400,000 acres of uncultivated private land, much of it belonging to United Fruit. That was sufficient for Washington. The US ambassador wrote to John Foster Dulles: "If the President is not a Communist, he will do until one comes along" (Quoted in Isaacs and Downing, 185).

In June 1954, an army of Guatemalan anti-Communist exiles, armed and trained by the CIA, crossed the frontier. Prior to this, the CIA had subverted the officers of the Guatemalan army, who defected to the rebels. Arbenz was forced into exile and a right-wing US puppet, Colonel Castillo Armas, was installed in power. His junta immediately reversed the land reform and evicted 500,000 peasants from the land they had occupied.

A nightmare began for the people of Guatemala, which has lasted to the present day. The junta unleashed a white terror, killing hundreds of left-wingers, union leaders, and peasants. The Eisenhower administration, however, was euphoric. Guatemala was considered to be pacified. Central America was safe for United Fruit. But this was an overly optimistic assessment. Guatemala and the whole of Central America was plunged into instability. Castillo Armas was murdered by unknown assassins three years later. Guatemala suffered years of civil war, resulting in genocidal slaughter.

The Guatemalan incident shows just how far the government of the USA is controlled by the big corporations like United Fruit and just how far the foreign policy of the USA is dictated by big business interests. There is an uncanny resemblance between these events and the events leading to the invasions of Afghanistan and Iraq, and the ongoing US intrigues within Venezuela.

The USA and Cuba

In 1898 the USA invaded Cuba, allegedly to free it from Spanish rule. But, as the people of Iraq have discovered, such "liberators" tend to hang around for a long time after the "liberation." In the decades after driving out the Spaniards, Cuba was virtually bought up by American companies. Unlike Puerto Rico, the island could not be directly annexed, since this was ruled out under an amendment signed by the USA at the time of Cuba's "independence." But there was nothing to prevent US businessmen from buying up most of the land and industry. In this way, Cuba's so-called independence became a fiction. US business ruled there with the collusion of corrupt puppet governments like that of the dictator Fulgencio Batista y Zaldivar, who ruled the island directly or indirectly for 25 years until he was overthrown by the Cuban Revolution in 1959.

Fidel Castro organized a guerrilla struggle against Batista's increasingly unpopular and corrupt regime. After two years his government collapsed like a house of cards. A general strike by the workers of Havana dealt the regime the final death blow. On January 8, 1959, Castro led his guerrilla forces into Havana, after Batista had fled to Miami. At that time, his program went no further than democracy and land reform. It did not include proposals to nationalize US property. Moscow adopted a cautious attitude. The Cuban "Communists" had supported the dictator Batista.

The initial program of the Cuban Revolution was therefore not socialist but national-democratic. But all history shows that under modern conditions the national-democratic program cannot be carried out under capitalism. Either the revolution is prepared to go beyond the limits of capitalism, or it is doomed. The Cuban Revolution is a classical case. The US companies in Cuba tried to sabotage Castro's land reform, just as United Fruit had done in Guatemala. In response, Castro leaned on Moscow for support. The Russians signed a trade agreement with Cuba and Washington responded by imposing an economic blockade and stopped buying Cuban sugar. This was a blatant act of aggression against a sovereign state. Since sugar was Cuba's main export, it would have meant the swift strangulation of its economy.

When the Soviet Union agreed to buy Cuban sugar, Washington responded by refusing to sell petroleum products to Cuba. This was really an act of economic war. The Cubans replied by nationalizing US businesses. Almost overnight, capitalism was abolished in Cuba. Eisenhower reacted by approving yet another covert program of action by the CIA, on the lines of the one that successfully destabilized the Arbenz government. But this time the result was very different.

The CIA trained a force of anti-Castro Cuban guerrillas in the jungles of Guatemala. Eisenhower also endorsed a plan for an amphibious landing by these forces, backed by the CIA, which they hoped would lead to a nationwide uprising against Castro. These plans, hatched by Eisenhower and Allen Dulles, were passed on to the new president, John Kennedy, on the day before his inauguration in January 1961. He was apparently surprised by the scale of the operation but supported it anyway.

Despite the attempts to present Kennedy as a progressive president, he acted no differently than his predecessors. He kept the plans for the invasion secret and lied about them in public. Three days before the invasion was due to start, he told a press conference: there would not be "under any conditions an intervention in Cuba by United States armed forces." But privately he told his aides:

> The minute I land one marine, we're in this thing up to our necks . . . I'm not going to risk an American Hungary (Quoted in Isaacs and Downing, 189).

The reference to Hungary is instructive. In October 1956 there was a popular uprising in Hungary, which was put down by the Russians with extreme violence. Kennedy's words reveal the real situation and intentions of the US imperialists in Cuba. They understood that, like in Hungary, they would be faced with the opposition of the majority of the population, and that, like in Hungary, they would have to wade through a sea of blood to obtain their objectives. They were quite prepared to do this.

The only problem is that they were defeated. The reactionary rabble that landed was immediately routed by Castro's forces. The Bay of Pigs episode was one of the most humiliating defeats suffered by US imperialism in its history. After only three days of fighting, the remaining counterrevolutionary forces surrendered. More than a hundred of these bandits had been killed. Only fourteen were picked up by the US Navy.

US imperialism has never forgiven Cuba for this humiliation. It has maintained its criminal blockade. Although this has failed in its objective, it has caused a lot of suffering for the people of Cuba. The CIA has carried on a policy of terrorism against Cuba for decades, including numerous plans to assassinate Fidel Castro. But the Cuban Revolution remains a source of hope and inspiration to the oppressed and downtrodden peoples of Central and South America and the Caribbean.

From Chile to Nicaragua

In 1970 the Socialist Salvador Allende was elected in Chile. Once again the CIA began a campaign of destabilization, backing the right wing in its attempts to overthrow a democratically elected reformist president. On September 11, 1973, they finally succeeded, by using the services of General Augusto Pinochet to overthrow the government. Allende was either murdered or committed suicide. In the bloody dictatorship that followed, thousands of people were arrested, savagely tortured, murdered, or were simply "disappeared"— all with the complicity of the CIA and Washington.

A similar story unfolded later in Nicaragua, where a left-wing guerrilla movement overthrew the dictatorship of General Anastasio Somoza. The Somoza family had ruled Nicaragua, the largest country in Central America, for decades. They had enriched themselves by plundering the country's wealth mercilessly with the wholehearted backing of the USA. Franklin D. Roosevelt once commented about the founder of this dynasty of scoundrels: "*I know he's a son of a bitch, but he's our son of a bitch.*"

In 1979, there was a national uprising against this rotten and corrupt dictatorship. After a bloody civil war costing nearly 50,000 lives, the Somoza regime was overthrown. As in Cuba, a general strike in Managua put paid to the dictatorship. Somoza fled to Paraguay, where he was later murdered. The Sandinista government began a program of agrarian reform, as in Cuba. But unlike Cuba they failed to expropriate the capitalists. This was a mistake that cost them dearly.

It is not possible to make half a revolution. The Nicaraguan capitalists organized a campaign of sabotage directed against the government with the active support of Washington. But this was only the tip of the iceberg. In November 1981 the US National Security Council authorized substantial funds to assist the extreme right-wing counterrevolutionary insurgency of the Contras. With CIA arms, funds, and training, a small counterrevolutionary army grew from a few hundred in 1981 to about 15,000 in the mid-1980s.

The stated objective of the NSC was "to eliminate Cuban/Soviet influence in the region" and, in the longer term, to "build politically stable governments able to stand such influences." Heavy pressure was put on the Sandinista government: the US Navy patrolled Nicaragua's coast, US aircraft violated its air space, and the US Army staged maneuvres in Honduras just over the border. As a result of this combined internal and external pressure, in the end the Sandinista government fell and was replaced with a bourgeois government more to Washington's liking.

In El Salvador, another dictatorial regime was faced with a guerrilla war that had lasted for many years. President Reagan increased the US military aid to the ruling junta from $36 million to $197 million in 1984. The junta used the most savage methods to defeat the opposition, sending death squads into the villages to torture and murder any peasants suspected of sympathies with the guerrillas. Tens of thousands of people were killed or just went "missing." Almost one in five of the population fled abroad to escape.

In El Salvador US imperialism preferred a bloody right-wing dictatorship to the victory of a popular insurrection. Likewise in Argentina, when the brutal military junta seized power in 1976, Washington supported the generals and had excellent relations with the dictatorship until it invaded the Falkland Islands, provoking a clash with British imperialism, the USA's main European ally. With extreme reluctance, Reagan was forced to support Thatcher against his old friend Galtieri. But this decision was made purely for political convenience, not out of hatred for dictatorship and love of democracy.

Now Washington is faced with a new problem: the Venezuelan Revolution. The people of Venezuela, after decades of oppression and exploitation at the hands of a corrupt and degenerate oligarchy of landlords, bankers, and capitalists backed by US imperialism, have begun to shake off the old despotism and move to take control of their own lives and destinies. As in Cuba, this revolutionary movement poses a mortal threat to US imperialism because of the example it gives to millions of workers and peasants in Latin America.

With monotonous predictability, Washington has organized a plan to destabilize the democratically elected government of Hugo Chavez. It has backed a coup, which failed, then a bosses' lockout thinly disguised as a "general strike," which also failed. Finally, it backed a recall referendum, which also failed. Chavez has won every election or referendum in the last six years with big majorities, yet the lie machine in Washington continues to churn out the legend that he is a "dictator."

In their hostility to the Venezuelan Revolution, there was no difference between Bush and Kerry in the 2004 presidential elections. If anything, Kerry's statements on Venezuela were more aggressive than those of Bush. This fact only serves to underline the extremely reactionary nature of US policy in Latin America. US imperialism is the declared enemy of democracy and progress throughout the entire continent. Everywhere and at all times it has allied itself with the forces of reaction, the oligarchies, the thieves, the cutthroats, the torturers, and the dictators, against the people.

Dynamite in the Foundations

On the eve of the Second World War, Leon Trotsky made a very perceptive prediction. He predicted that US imperialism would emerge victorious from the war and would become the decisive force in the planet. But he added that it would have dynamite built into its foundations. Decades later this remarkable prediction has come true. America has inherited the role of world policeman that was once held by Britain. But Britain had that position in a different period, when capitalism was in its phase of historical ascent. At that time Britain could make considerable profits out of its imperial possessions, despite the overheads involved in maintaining direct military-bureaucratic rule. But now all that has changed.

The USA has taken over the mantle of British imperialism at a time when the capitalist system is in decline. There is a general crisis, reflected in turbulence everywhere. Wars, uprisings, and terrorism are on the order of the day. The USA finds itself sucked into one foreign adventure after another. This supposes a never-ending and ultimately unsustainable drain on its resources. Whereas Britain succeeded in plundering its colonies and enriching itself with the proceeds, America's war in Iraq is costing it, on a conservative estimate, one billion dollars a week. Even the richest power on earth cannot sustain such a tremendous hemorrhage for long. The US military is also increasingly overextended, with long deployments and "stop loss" orders driving down recruitment and reenlistments. The problem is that to withdraw will be even more costly. But sooner or later, withdraw they must.

The Bush Administration has learned nothing from the experience of Vietnam. It is said that the manifest destiny of the United States is to be involved in Latin America. But the people of the United States can have no interest in plundering the peoples of the rest of the continent for the benefit of the bank balances of wealthy and irresponsible US corporations. The criminal activities of these corporations, and the oligarchies and dictators backed by them, are continually destabilizing the continent. This instability must sooner or later affect the United States.

Everywhere, the people are rising against oppression. The success of the revolution in any important country in Latin America will have the most profound effects in the USA, where the largest and most rapidly growing part of the minority population is of Hispanic origin. Instead of intervening against the revolution in South America, the US imperialists would be fighting revolution at home.

CHAPTER X

THE SOUL OF AMERICA AND THE FUTURE OF HUMANITY

The Dictatorship of Big Business

All governments are more or less combinations against the people ... and as rulers have no more virtue than the ruled ... the power of government can only be kept within its constituted bounds by the display of a power equal to itself, the collected sentiment of the people.—Benjamin Franklin, in a *Philadelphia Aurora* editorial, 1794

Human consciousness always lags behind the march of history. Tradition, habit, and routine weighs heavily on the minds of men and women, and it is always comforting to look back to a supposedly happier past. Mythology is a powerful force and not only in religion. Ideas can persist long after the material causes that gave birth to them have disappeared.

Nowadays, nothing is left of the old democratic and egalitarian America of which de Tocqueville wrote. Yet in the United States today many people still believe that it is possible to get rich by working hard, and that the old "frontier spirit" can still triumph over adversity. This is pure mythology, but it is in the interests of those who rule America to foster the myth. In the United States and on a world scale, we see a huge and growing gap between rich and poor. The class divide, which according to the official theories should have disappeared long ago, or at least been reduced to insignificance, has reached unheard of proportions. It does not diminish, but rather increases in times of economic boom. Today, the richest 20 percent of Americans own half the country's wealth, while the poorest 20 percent own barely 4 percent.

In that epoch-making document *The Communist Manifesto*, Marx and Engels predicted that free competition would inevitably end in monopoly. For a long time the official economists tried to deny that the concentration of capital predicted by Marx had taken place. Particularly in the last two decades they insisted that the tendency would be in the opposite direction, that is, towards small enterprises, in which the small businessman would come into his own. They even coined a phrase: "small is beautiful."

How absurdly inappropriate these words sound now! The process of the concentration of capital has everywhere reached unheard-of levels. The whole of world trade is now dominated by no more than 200 giant companies—most of them based in the USA, where this process has gone furthest of all. Today, the lives and destinies of millions of Americans are in the hands of a tiny handful of corporations, which in turn are in practice run by tiny handfuls of superrich executives. The sole purpose of this new caste of robber barons is to enrich themselves, and to increase the power of their respective companies. The interests of the vast majority of US citizens are of little interest to them, while those of the inhabitants of the rest of the globe are of no interest at all.

In his recent best seller *Stupid White Men*, Michael Moore gives some very telling facts about the world we now live in:

> From 1979 until now, the richest 1 percent in the country have seen their wages increase by 157 percent; those of you in the bottom 20 percent are actually making $100 *less* a year (adjusted for inflation) than you were at the dawn of the Reagan era.
>
> The world's richest two hundred companies have seen their profits grow by 362.4 percent since 1983; their combined sales are now higher than the combined gross domestic product of all but ten nations on earth.
>
> In the most recent year for which there are figures, forty-four of the top eighty-two companies in the United States did not pay the standard rate of 35 percent in taxes that corporations are expected to pay. In fact, 17 percent of them paid NO taxes at all—and seven of those, including General Motors, played the tax code like a harp, juggling business expenses and tax credits until the government actually owed *them* millions of dollars!
>
> Another 1,279 corporations with assets of $250 million or more also paid NO taxes and reported "no income" for 1995 (the most recent year for which statistics were available) (Michael Moore, *Stupid White Men*, 52–53).

These ladies and gentlemen (for there are quite a few females among them now) are the real rulers of America. The famous democracy of which de Tocqueville wrote has become just a cover for the dictatorship of the big corporations. It really matters little who the people of America elect into the White House or Capitol Hill, since all the important decisions are taken behind closed doors by these tiny, unrepresentative cliques that are in practice responsible only to themselves.

The vested interests of this ruling stratum are backed up by the most powerful military machine in history. It claims the right to intervene everywhere, to topple legally elected governments, to launch wars and civil wars, to bomb and destroy supposedly sovereign states, without let or hindrance. Is it any wonder why *this* America has earned the hatred of millions of people throughout the world? This is really not hard to understand. Yet this is not the real America, or the real people of America who fought British imperialism to win their freedom and then fought a Civil War to extend that freedom (at least on paper) to the black slaves.

Illusions die hard. To many Americans, the USA despite everything remains the land of the brave and the home of the free. They cannot understand why it is that the USA is so unloved by the rest of the world. Yet slowly but surely a realization is dawning that all is not well with America. A recent survey by *Business Week* revealed that seventy-four percent of Americans thought that big business had too much power over their lives. The rest of this interesting survey also showed that beneath the surface of calm and contentment, there is a growing feeling of dissatisfaction with the present state of affairs. The massive demonstrations that began five years ago in Seattle served notice on the ruling class of the USA that something is beginning to stir. This is just the beginning.

Growing Discontent

> *The spirit of resistance to government is so valuable on certain occasions,*
> *that I wish it always to be kept alive. It will often be exercised when wrong,*
> *but better so than not to be exercised at all. I like a little rebellion now and*
> *then*—Thomas Jefferson, letter to Abigail Adams, 1787

The long years of economic upswing that followed the Second World War cut across the revolutionary movement that was developing in the 1930s in the United States and to some extent blunted the class consciousness of the proletariat. But now the world crisis of capitalism is affecting the USA in a serious way. Millions are threatened with closures and sackings. This represents a fundamental change. The USA has not experienced sustained unemployment at the 2000 level since the 1960s. The rate of unemployment now stands at around 5.4 percent with no improvement in sight. The economy must create 150,000 new job positions each month just to keep pace with the growing workforce, yet most months it does not achieve even this paltry figure. Moreover, workers who have lost their jobs have had more trouble finding new ones. A recent article in *The New York Times* (November 28, 2002) pointed out that the proportion of those who have been out of work for more than 27 weeks is very high:

> Now, about 800,000 more workers have been out of work for six months or longer, compared with the number in 2000. That is why extending unemployment benefits is so important.
>
> In addition, the number of part-time workers who would like full-time work has risen by one million. And the increase in the labor force has slowed markedly because many more people have stopped looking for jobs. They do not show up in the unemployment data. In the recessions of the early 1980s and 1990s, the labor force grew far more rapidly, pushing up the unemployment rate.

The boom of the 1990s meant a certain amelioration for many workers and "middle class" people and fabulous fortunes for a small minority. Even at this time the rich gained much more than the poor, whose position improved far more slowly. But since the recession that began four years ago, family incomes are once again falling across the board (even during the so-called recovery). And they are falling most rapidly for those in the bottom 20 or 30 percent. Inequality is increasing, and the contrast between the fat cats at the top and the "have-nots" at the bottom is more glaring than ever.

The wealthy find ways of avoiding the payment of taxes, and the burden of taxation falls heavily on the shoulders of the "middle class" and the working poor. A good example of this is the estate tax, which is, overwhelmingly, a tax on the wealthy. In 1999, only the top two percent of estates paid any tax at all. Paul Krugman in an article in *The New York Times* (October 20, 2002) with the significant title "The Class Wars: The End of Middle Class America," writes:

> Income inequality in America has now returned to the levels of the 1920s. Inherited wealth doesn't yet play a big part in our society, but given time— and the repeal of the estate tax—we will grow ourselves a hereditary elite just as set apart from the concerns of ordinary Americans . . . And the new elite, like the old, will have enormous political power.

Even those who still retain their jobs are unhappy. They have little confidence in the future. Nobody feels secure any more. There is a new volatility and a mood of criticism and discontent at all levels. There is a huge and growing alienation between the people of America and those who rule their lives. And a growing number of Americans are becoming aware of this state of affairs and are dissatisfied with it. Maybe they do not know exactly what they want, but they certainly know what they do not want. The sense of alienation is reflected in the large number of people who do not vote in elections.

There is a groundswell of discontent that comes from the very heart of America. Millions of ordinary men and women are unhappy with the kind of lives they are leading: the long hours, the remorseless pressure, the dictatorial attitudes of management, the chronic insecurity. These moods are beginning to affect even the formerly affluent layers of the working "middle class." And even at a higher level, there are those who are beginning to question the values of a society where the laws of the jungle are held up as a model: dog-eat-dog! Each man for himself and let the devil take the hindmost! Is this what life in the 21st century is really all about?

A few years ago, economist J. K. Galbraith wrote a book called *The Policy of Contentment,* in which he issued a warning to America:

> Recession and depression made worse by long-run economic desuetude, the danger implicit in an autonomous military power and growing unrest in the urban slums caused by worsening deprivation and hopelessness have been cited as separate prospects. All could in fact, come together. A deep recession could cause stronger discontent in the areas of urban disaster in the aftermath of some military misadventure in which, in the nature of the modern armed forces, the unfortunate were disproportionately engaged (J. K. Galbraith, *The Policy of Contentment,* 172–73).

So far, America has avoided the kind of deep recession predicted by Galbraith. But postponement does not signify avoidance. The present rally of the US economy, based as it is on consumption and debt rather than productive investment, may not be long-lasting and may well be just the prelude to an even steeper fall. In any case, the future of the capitalist economy, both in the USA and on a world scale has a somber aspect. New shocks are inevitable, with unforeseen consequences.

The point is that nobody can control the forces that have been unleashed on a global scale over the past ten or twenty years. The fundamental contradictions of capitalism have not been abolished, as some American economists have claimed, but only reproduced on a far vaster scale than ever before. There is no law that says that these market forces will achieve some kind of automatic equilibrium. On the contrary, the anarchic, unplanned character of capitalism must manifest itself in the most tremendous convulsions. Globalization will manifest itself as a global crisis of capitalism—in fact, it is already doing so. George Soros, who is certainly no Marxist but is an expert on the workings of world market, has pointed out that the market does not operate like a pendulum but rather like a wrecking ball—demolishing anything that gets in its way. We have already seen the results of this wrecking ball in the economic meltdown of Argentina. It will not be the last case.

The Rotten Heart of Corporate America

The Enron scandal, and the tidal wave of corporate scandals that followed it, completely exposed the lie that the market economy is the most efficient system, the best way to avoid bureaucracy and corruption, and that it is somehow "more democratic" and allows more people a say on how things are run. The fact of the matter is that inside the big corporations in the USA corruption is rife, tyranny reigns, and the jobs, lives, and pensions of millions are in the hands of powerful and despotic minorities of superrich executives.

It is entirely untrue that the present system works well because it rewards efficiency. There is precious little reward for the vast majority of American workers who are obliged to work long hours under remorseless pressure to earn enough for their families' needs. All too often, they have to take two or three jobs to make ends meet—while others languish on the unemployment line or fall off the social radar as they are no longer even counted as "looking for work." In the last twenty years, productivity in the USA has been hugely increased and vast profits have been made out of squeezing the US workforce. The working week has been lengthened inexorably from 40 to over 50 hours on average. People are feeling the strain. It is undermining their physical and mental health and ruining their family life. This is increasingly the case, not only with blue-collar workers but also with professional people and lower management. What keeps them going is not free choice or incentive to "get on," but relentless pressure to get results (i.e., profits for the bosses), and fear of losing their jobs and homes.

On the other hand, it is equally untrue that the top executives of the big corporations are guided by the principle of greater rewards for greater results. On the contrary, over the past decades, the CEOs have consistently rewarded themselves with the most staggering sums of money, bearing no relation to performance or productivity. Vast fortunes have been made, and are still being made, by people who do next to nothing (and sometimes nothing at all). Even in the present recession, when company profits are falling and workers are sacked or told to make sacrifices, the fat cats continue to plunder the wealth of America in the most shameless manner.

Quite apart from their huge salaries—which are quite unrelated to performance—the CEOs receive a wide range of perks, amounting to corruption on a grand scale. The best example is the notorious system of stock options. Thus, although AOL Time Warner executives were "punished" by the nonpayment of bonuses, they nevertheless received stock options valued at around $40 million a head. Many American workers would be very pleased to receive such "punishment" during a recession, or for that matter even during a boom.

There is also a wide range of perks that do not appear in the normal surveys of bosses' earnings. Coca-Cola demands that both its boss and his wife always travel in the company's jet—a privilege that cost the company $103, 898 last year alone. At AOL Time Warner, Gerald Levin and Richard Parkins, his appointed successor, each got $97,500 in "financial services" (for "tax return preparation and financial planning," the company explained—whatever that might mean). True, some of them have now taken "pay cuts." What do these "cuts" consist of? Stanford Weill, the chief executive of Citigroup, took an 83 percent pay cut recently, which left the poor fellow with a miserable $36.1 million. *The Economist* (6/4/02) commented:

> One worry is that executive pay has risen to such heights that the bad times look rather like the good times used to: the median total compensation in the Mercer survey [a recent survey of 100 big companies by William M. Mercer and the *Wall Street Journal*] was still $2.16 million. Nor has pay fallen by nearly as much as profits have done. The total compensation of chief executives is down by 2.9 percent on a year ago, but after-tax profits fell by nearly 50 percent last year among the companies included in the S&P 500. Some components of bosses' pay such as basic salaries actually rose healthily on the back of this dreadful performance.

The Economist continues:

> Some of the financial services that American companies offer to their top chaps would put regular banks out of business. Compaq, a computer maker, has agreed to forgive a $5 million [!] loan it extended to its boss, Michael Capellas, and is providing him with a new loan to help with the tax bill. Bernie Ebbers, the chief executive of WorldCom, a troubled telecom firm, borrowed a princely $341m from his employer, on which he is paying a little over 2 percent on interest.

When they are employed, these executives, responsible in reality to nobody, enrich themselves shamelessly out of the profits that are the unpaid wages of the working class. It is a condemnation of the system that when layoffs are announced, the value of the stock invariably goes up. When a worker is sacked (which these people rarely are) or retires, they receive a very meager compensation—if they get anything at all. But these ladies and gentlemen continue to act like leeches even when they are formally retired.

> On top of his pension, worth around $9 million a year, Jack Welch, the retired boss of General Electric, is "required" under the terms of his contract to consult with the company for the rest of his life, for which he will charge a daily [yes, that's right, daily] rate of $17,000 (*The Economist*, 6/4/02).

What exactly this "consultation" consists of is not mentioned. But the general picture is pretty clear. What we have here is not the picture of the go-getting, self-made American entrepreneur, so assiduously cultivated by the advocates of capitalism, but the exact opposite. This is a picture of unqualified and unrestrained plunder of the American economy by a tiny, unrepresentative and above all, unproductive group of corporate drones. Comfortably installed in their shiny glass towers, utterly remote from the workforce and the American people, at the head of vast and servile corporate bureaucracies, they quietly determine the fate of millions, both in the USA and on a global scale. This is the real face of corporate America and the reality of the so-called free market economy. Enron was just the tip of a very large, ugly, and dangerous iceberg.

In case anyone thinks that this is just Marxist exaggeration and alarmism, let us leave the last word to that champion of the free market economy, *The Economist*, which we have already quoted. It predicts that on present trends, "by 2021 there will emerge a big American company where the boss is paid more than the firm's entire sales. If that is market forces at work, then market forces had better be ignored."

Socialism and Democracy

The idea that socialism and democracy are somehow incompatible is yet another falsehood. On this question, the defenders of capitalism behave like a squid that defends itself by squirting a large quantity of ink to confuse its enemy. The fact of the matter is this: that the democracy in the USA is a cover for the dictatorship of a handful of powerful corporations run by tiny cliques of unelected and irresponsible people. The latter not only own and control the wealth of America, they also control its press, television and all other means of molding and conditioning public opinion. While in theory there are two parties, everyone knows that the difference between the Democrans and Republicrats is minimal.

Stalinist Russia was a one-party dictatorship (something that neither Marx nor Lenin ever advocated). America boasts a pluralistic democracy. In this democracy everyone can say what they want (well, almost), as long as the banks and big corporations decide what happen. Elections take place regularly, but in fact the electorate have no real choice. Both Democrats and Republicans stand for the interests of big business. There is no real difference between them; what small differences used to exist in the past have all but disappeared. In order to get elected at all, one either has to be a billionaire, or else have access to vast sums of money. And as the proverb goes: "He who pays the piper calls the tune." The Enron scandal merely confirmed what everyone already knew: that the great majority of senators and congressmen and women are in the pockets of big business. No wonder millions of US citizens feel disenfranchised and do not bother to vote.

Marxists stand for democracy. But we advocate a genuine democracy, not a fraudulent caricature. And the first condition for the introduction of democracy in the USA is the overthrow of the dictatorship of big business. The power of the big banks and corporations must be broken, and the commanding heights of the economy nationalized, under the democratic control and administration of the workers themselves. There would be plenty of scope for personal initiative!

The talents of the engineers, managers, scientists, and technicians would play a crucial role in a socialist planned economy. Once private profit was no longer the overriding principle, the way would be open for an unprecedented boom in inventions, innovations of all kinds. Above all, the men and women on the shop floor would be encouraged to participate in discussions and debates on how to improve working practices and conditions. In this way, everyone would have a stake in the running of society. Decision-making would no longer be the privilege of a few wealthy executives, but the common property of all Americans.

In what way does this idea contradict the traditional and dearly held American ideals of democracy and individual rights? It does not contradict them at all, but reaffirms them and takes them to a qualitatively higher level. In fact, at the moment there is really very little scope for the free development of the individual in the USA of the giant corporations. None of the important decisions affecting the lives of the people are taken by the people. They are not even being taken on Capitol Hill, but by unseen individuals behind locked doors on Wall Street, in the Pentagon, the State Department, and above all in the boardrooms of the giant corporations that really rule the USA

The Future of Democracy

This country, with its institutions, belongs to the people who inhabit it. Whenever they shall grow weary of the existing government, they can exercise their constitutional right of amending it, or their revolutionary right to dismember or overthrow it—Abraham Lincoln, April 4, 1861

The celebrated American sociologist C. Wright Mills coined the phrase "the military industrial complex" to describe the union between big business, government, and the military that runs the USA today. The modern American state is a vast bureaucratic monster that exists not to serve the people but to lord it over them in the interests of the big companies that really rule America.

When Thomas Jefferson was made the first Secretary of State, he had just five employees to man his office. Now the state bureaucracy numbers a huge army of hundreds of thousands of bureaucrats. Though they talk incessantly about "cutting government down to size," all administrations have added to this monster, increasing its size and power constantly, at tremendous cost to the economy. "Cheap government" has become a hollow phrase from the distant past. In present-day America, the bureaucratic monster of big business is indissolubly linked to the bureaucratic monster of the state. That is what the military-industrial complex means.

Most people in the USA nowadays take democracy for granted. But this is a dangerous misconception. The history of the United States shows that the common people have always had to struggle to win even the most elementary rights, and that democracy is a very fragile plant. Whenever the ruling oligarchy feels itself challenged it immediately takes steps to limit or even cancel those hard-won democratic rights enshrined in the Constitution and the Bill of Rights. It should be added that the Constitution itself has a number of defects from a strictly democratic standpoint. The powers given to the president are truly immense. Section One of Article Two says simply: "The executive power shall be vested in a President of the United States of America." The president is commander in chief of the armed forces. He has powers to make treaties with the concurrence of the Senate and to make appointments of public officials and employees.

Theoretically, the powers of the executive are limited by a complicated system of checks and balances. But the fact is that the powers of the president have never been used to their full extent. They are important reserve powers that, under certain conditions (e.g., the possibility of a socialist majority in Congress that wanted to nationalize the big corporations) could be used to carry through a legal coup and institute a presidential dictatorship. This possibility is never considered, because it has never been seen, but it is a real danger.

In any situation deemed by the ruling elite to constitute a national emergency it would be possible for the president, with the connivance of a majority of Congress, to virtually set aside the Constitution, vote unlimited authority to the president, and adjourn *sine die*. This may seem unlikely, but if we look at the recent trends we can see an increasing tendency to encroach upon the democratic rights of American citizens and grant ever greater power to the state and its organs of repression. Some even say that the Constitution itself has already been turned into a dead letter.

Real power lies in the hands of a tiny number of boards of directors of the big corporations and banks. These faceless men and women are, in practice, elected by nobody and responsible to nobody. Yet they wield more real power than millions of ordinary Americans. With billions of dollars to play with, they can, and do, buy congressmen and women, judges, lawyers, newspaper editors, parties, and presidents. They decide what you can read, hear on the radio, or see on television. Their psychology is that of Commodore Vanderbilt: *"Law? What law? Hain't I got the Power?"*

What is the attitude of Marxists to democracy? In the first place, we stand for the defense of all the democratic conquests that were won through the struggle of the working class in the past. The working class needs freedom to develop its organizations: the unions, shop stewards committees, and all the other things that represent the embryo of a new society within the womb of the old. We need the maximum freedom of speech, of assembly, and of the press; freedom to strike, demonstrate, and agitate in favor of socialism. We must therefore fight any attempt by the dictatorship of big business to cancel or restrict any of these rights. We will make use of every democratic channel that is open to us to put our case before the people.

We will fight for the creation of a mass party of labor that will fight for the interests of the working class and all oppressed people, and will stand for the nationalization of the big corporations under workers' control and management. Once we have broken the stranglehold of the Democrats over the unions, it will be possible to fight and win elections in a cause that will inspire millions of people with hope. The working class, together with the small farmers, the unemployed, and other nonexploitative sections of society, constitute the decisive majority of the population, will respond enthusiastically, once they see they have a real alternative. It is entirely possible that a labor party could win a majority. But in that case, we have to ask ourselves how the big banks and corporations that really run America would react.

All history shows that no ruling class has ever given up its power, wealth and privileges without a fight, and that has normally meant a fight with no holds barred. We must be prepared to deal with a slaveholders' rebellion in the same way that Abraham Lincoln did. Therefore, while accepting the need to fight to win the majority through elections, we understand that in the last analysis the decisive conflict will be fought outside Congress: in the streets and factories, in the farms, schools, and universities.

The power of the American working class is colossal. Not a light bulb shines, not a telephone rings, not a wheel turns without the kind permission of the workers. This is potentially such a tremendous power that no force can resist it, as long as the working class is organized, mobilized, and united in the struggle to change society. The resistance of the present day slaveholders can be swiftly overcome and reduced to nothing, on one condition: that the workers are determined to fight to the end.

Is Bureaucracy Inevitable?

It is frequently asserted that private ownership is superior to nationalized enterprises because it permits private initiative. But in practice, the big corporations that dominate the US economy are extremely bureaucratic, inefficient, and corrupt. They do not allow much room for initiative—at least as far as the big majority of the workforce is concerned. They are fundamentally undemocratic, being run by a handful of superrich executives whose main aim in life is to make themselves even more wealthy.

The general public good is of no concern to such individuals, except inasmuch as bad publicity may harm sales, and therefore profits. The solution to this problem, however, is not to act in the public interest, but to pay for the services of a slick public relations department which is used to present the company's image in the most favorable light—that is to say, to mislead and deceive the public. The case of Enron is an excellent example of the reality of US corporate practice. It should be noted that this company was so closely connected with the US government at the highest levels that it proved almost impossible to investigate its activities, and even now the whole truth has not come out. And there are many more Enrons which have not yet been exposed.

No less an authority than the classical bourgeois economist Adam Smith already warned of the dangers of monopoly, when he wrote:

> The directors of such [joint-stock] companies[,] being the managers rather of other people's money than of their own, it cannot be well expected that they should watch over it with the same anxious vigilance with which the partners in a private company frequently watch over their own [.] *Negligence and profusion, therefore, must always prevail, more or less, in the management of the affairs of such a company"* (Adam Smith, *Wealth of Nations*, part 3, 112).

The solution to this problem cannot be a return to the era of small businesses, as some people advocate. That period has been relegated to history and will not return. The modern capitalist economy is entirely dominated by big monopolies, and nothing can reverse that tendency. Anyone who doubts this has only to examine the history of anti-trust legislation in the USA. There have been laws against monopolies for a very long time, yet their practical effect has been negligible. Witness the recent tussle between Bill Gates and the Federal authorities. No one doubts that Mr. Gates has created the world's biggest monopoly, and that this is harming the progress of technology in a most vital area. Yet in practice, it is proving impossible to reverse the position.

Since it is not possible to halt the inevitable tendency towards monopolization, there remains only one alternative: to bring these giant corporations—which are at present responsible to nobody but themselves—under democratic control. But here we come up against an insurmountable difficulty. It is not possible to control what you do not own. The answer is very clear: in order to control the monopolies, it is necessary to take them out of private hands altogether—that is, to nationalize them. Only then would it be possible to ensure that the key points of the economy are the servants of society, not its master.

But would this not create the danger of a bureaucracy, as existed in Stalinist Russia? This seems to be a very serious objection, but actually it is not. The bureaucratic degeneration of the Russian Revolution was not the result of nationalization, but of the isolation of the revolution under conditions of frightful backwardness. It should not be forgotten that in 1917 Russia was an extremely backward semifeudal country. Out of a total population of 150 million, there were only four million industrial workers. In a remarkably short space of time, the nationalized planned economy transformed Russia from a backward country like Pakistan is today into the second most powerful nation on earth. For several decades the USSR achieved economic results that have never been equalled by any other country. Nor should we forget the fact that its economy suffered the most terrible devastation in the Second World War when 27 million Soviet citizens perished.

It is not possible to understand what happened in the Soviet Union without considering these facts. Nor is it reasonable to draw an analogy between the fate of the nationalized planned economy in backward Russia and the prospects for a socialist planned economy in the United States. *Bureaucracy is a product of economic and cultural backwardness.* It is not difficult to prove this. If one considers the state of affairs in those countries which are sometimes referred to as the "Third World"—the states of Africa, Asia, and Latin America—then it immediately becomes obvious that bureaucracy is a feature common to every single one of them—whether the means of production are nationalized or not (and even in the advanced capitalist countries it is to be seen).

It is possible to draw a graph showing that the degree of bureaucratization of a given society is in inverse proportion to the level of its economic and cultural development. The same is true of phenomena like corruption, inefficiency, and red tape that are usually connected with bureaucracy. Society tends to free itself of these things to the degree that it lifts itself out of a low level of economic and technological development, and raises the cultural level of the population.

Of course, where a bureaucracy becomes an entrenched ruling caste, as happened in Russia after the death of Lenin, it can hang onto its power and privileges even when the level of economic and cultural development renders it entirely superfluous. But in that case, the bureaucracy will suffocate and destroy the nationalized planned economy—which is precisely what occurred in the Soviet Union. But that is exactly the point. The existence of the bureaucracy in Russia was not only not the product of the nationalized planned economy, but was in complete antagonism to it. Trotsky explained that a nationalized planned economy requires democracy as the human body requires oxygen.

Without democracy and the control and administration of society by the working class, the planned economy eventually seized up, clogged and obstructed by the suffocating control of the bureaucracy.

What About Russia?

Ah, but the Soviet Union collapsed. Doesn't that prove that socialism has failed? Yes, the Soviet Union collapsed after decades of bureaucratic and totalitarian rule, which completely negated the regime of workers' democracy established in 1917. As early as 1936, Leon Trotsky predicted that the Stalinist bureaucracy that usurped power after Lenin's death would not be satisfied with its legal and illegal privileges, but would inevitably strive to replace the nationalized planned economy by privately owned monopolies. The capitalist counterrevolution in Russia, however, offers no way forward to the peoples of the former USSR. It has been accompanied by a horrific collapse of the Russian economy, living standards, and culture, as Trotsky predicted. If there is a country in the world where capitalism stands condemned, that country is Russia.

The prolongation of senile capitalism threatens the future of human culture, civilization, democracy, perhaps even the survival of humanity itself. The world is crying out for a fundamental social and economic transformation. The only hope for humanity consists in the radical abolition of capitalism and the establishment of a harmonious system of production and distribution based on the common ownership of the means of production under democratic workers' control and administration.

The enormous potential of a nationalized planned economy was demonstrated by the Soviet Union, before, during, and in the first 25 years after the Second World War. Despite all the efforts of the bourgeoisie and its hired prostitutes to deny it, the fact is that the USSR (and later China) showed that it is possible to run an economy without private capitalists, bankers, speculators, and landlords, and that such an economy can obtain spectacular results.

The future socialist planned economy of the USA will not be based on backwardness, as was the regime established by the Bolshevik Party of Lenin and Trotsky in November 1917. It will be as different from Russia as computer science is from the wooden plow. American socialism from the very beginning will draw on the colossal advances of industry, science, and technology, which will become the servants of human needs, not the slaves of the profit motive. Once the vast productive capacity of the USA is organized on the basis of a rational plan, the sky will be the limit.

This is not just a theoretical assertion. It has already been proved in practice, and not only in Russia. As we have seen, during the Second World War, when elements of a planned economy and state control were introduced in the USA, the economy grew rapidly and unemployment all but disappeared. That gives us just a glimpse of the tremendous potential that a socialist planned economy in America would unleash. Of course, this was not socialism. The basic levers of the economy remained in the hands of private capitalists. Real planning is not possible under capitalism. And the nationalized industries were run by bureaucrats. But despite these limitations, even these elements of a planned economy gave serious results for a time.

The elements of planning, even on a capitalist basis, gave better results than the free-for-all of the market economy. Just imagine the results that would be possible in a real socialist planned economy in which the benefits of a central plan would be combined with the democratic control and administration by the working people themselves. On the basis of a modern, technologically advanced economy, rational planning will spur production to an unprecedented level.

The Soul of America

In the first part of *Reason in Revolt*, a reference is made to the contradiction between the marvellous advances of science and the extraordinary lag in human consciousness. This contradiction is particularly striking in the United States. In the country that has done more than any other to advance the cause of science in the past period, the overwhelming majority of people in the USA believe in god, or are religious in some way. Thirty-six percent of Americans think the Bible is the literal world of god, and half believe that America enjoys divine protection. After 9/11, 78 percent thought that the influence of religion on public life was growing. Books on the apocalypse became best sellers. This situation is quite different to that of most European countries, where organized religion is dying on its feet (although there is still plenty of superstition and mysticism around).

Strangely enough, the Founding Fathers were not at all religious. These true sons of the 18th century Enlightenment expressed themselves in the most scathing terms about religion in general and Christianity in particular. Founding Fathers George Washington and John Adams, in a diplomatic message to Malta, wrote: "The United States is in no way founded upon the Christian religion." John Adams, in a letter to Thomas Jefferson, went even further when he wrote: "This would be the best of all possible worlds, if there were no religion in it."

Thomas Jefferson, in 1814, commented: "In every country and in every age, the priest has been hostile to liberty. He is always in alliance with the despot, abetting his abuses in return for protection to his own." And the same Thomas Jefferson wrote in 1823:

> The day will come when the mystical generation of Jesus by the Supreme Being as his father, in the womb of a virgin, will be classed with the fable of the generation of Minerva in the brain of Jupiter.

He added: "I do not find in orthodox Christianity one redeeming feature."

Things were no better with Abraham Lincoln, who was also openly irreligious: "The Bible is not my book, and Christianity is not my religion," he said. "I could never give assent to the long, complicated statements of Christian dogma." These views were the natural outcome of the rationalist philosophy that represented the most advanced philosophical ideas of the 18th century Enlightenment. The rejection of religion was always the first step towards a rational view of nature and society. It was the beginning of all modern progress, the basis of both the American and the French revolutions. And it was equally the starting point for the development of modern science and technology, the true foundation for America's greatness. Nowadays the degree of scientific and technological advance in the USA is unequalled by any other country. Here we have a tantalizing glimpse of the future—the staggering potential of human development. But we also see a contradiction. Side by side with the most advanced ideas we see the persistence of ideas that have been handed down, unchanged, from a remote and barbarous past.

The reason for the persistence of religious belief is that men and women feel that their lives are under the control of strange unseen forces. They do not feel in control of their own destinies, as really free human beings should. And in fact, our lives really are determined by forces not under our control. The wild swings of "market forces" on a world scale determine whether millions of people will have a job or not. The equally wild gyrations of the stock markets can ruin millions of families in a matter of days or even hours. There is a general instability and volatility throughout the world that expresses itself in unending wars, terrorist outrages, and other barbarities. This creates a general climate of fear and uncertainty. It is what is called *the new world order*.

In its period of ascent, capitalism based itself on rationalism. That is just what is expressed in the ideas of the Founding Fathers reproduced above. In general, when a particular socio-economic system is in a state of collapse, its decline is expressed in a general crisis of morality, the family, beliefs, and so on. The ideology of the ruling elite becomes increasingly decrepit, its values rotten. People no longer believe in the old ways, and the old "ideals" are met with skepticism and irony. Eventually a new set of ideals emerge and a new ideology that reflects the standpoint of the rising revolutionary class. In the 18th century that was the bourgeoisie, which generally adopted a rationalist standpoint. In the 21st century, it is the working class, which must stand on the basis of scientific socialism—Marxism.

In general, when society enters—as capitalism has undoubtedly entered—into a phase of terminal decline, one can react in one of two ways. One response is to turn inwards, try to escape from a horrific reality by closing all the doors and windows and shutting one's eyes to what is happening in the world outside. The problem with this is that the world outside has an uncomfortable way of intruding into the life of even the most private persons. Sooner or later it will come knocking at your door, and usually at a most uncivilized hour. There is really no escape.

The second way is to look reality squarely in the face, to try to understand it and thus prepare to change it. Hegel said long ago that true freedom is the recognition of necessity, that is to say, if we want to change the circumstances in which we live, we must first understand them. Marxism provides us with a wonderful tool to help us to grasp the nature of the world we live in and to make us understand where we have come from and where we are going to. Unlike religion, which offers the consolation of a vision of future happiness and fulfillment beyond the grave, Marxism directs our eyes, not to heaven, but to the present life, and helps us to understand the apparently mysterious forces that determine our fate.

Since *Reason in Revolt* first appeared, there have been a number of other spectacular advances in science—notably the mapping of the human genome. These results have completely demolished the positions of genetic determinism that we criticized in *Reason in Revolt*. It has also cut the ground from under the feet of the racist "theories" put forward by certain writers in the USA who attempted to enlist the service of genetics to peddle their reactionary pseudo-scientific "theories," that black people are genetically predisposed to ignorance and poverty. They have also dealt a mortal blow to the nonsense of the creationists who want to reject Darwinism in favor of the first chapters of Genesis, and impose this on American schools.

For many Americans, Marxism is a closed book because it is seen as antireligious. After all, did Marx not describe religion as the "opium of the people"? As a matter of fact, just before these famous words, Marx wrote: "*Religious* distress is at the same time the *expression* of real distress and the *protest* against real distress." In essence, religion is an expression of a desire for a better world and a belief that there must be something more to life than the vale of tears through which we pass in the all-too-brief interval from cradle to grave.

Many people are discontented with their lives. It is not just a question of material poverty—although that exists in the USA as in all other countries. It is also a question of spiritual poverty: the emptiness of people's lives, the mind-deadening routine of work that is just so many hours out of one's life; the alienation that divides men and women from each other; the absence of human relations and solidarity that is deliberately fostered in a society that proudly proclaims the law of the jungle and the so-called survival of the fittest (read: wealthiest); the mind-numbing banality of a commercialized "culture." In this kind of world the question we should be asking ourselves is not "is there a life after death?" but rather, "is there a life *before* death?"

The capitalist system is a monstrously oppressive and inhuman system, which means untold misery, disease, oppression, and death for millions of people in the world. It is surely the duty of any humane person to support the fight against such a system. However, in order to fight effectively, it is necessary to work out a serious program, policy, and perspective that can guarantee success. We believe that only Marxism (scientific socialism) provides such a perspective.

The problem a Marxist has with religion is basically this: We believe that men and women should fight to transform their lives and to create a genuinely human society which would permit the human race to lift itself up to its true stature. We believe that human beings have only one life, and should dedicate themselves to making this life beautiful and self-fulfilling. If you like, *we are fighting for a paradise on this earth, because we do not think there is any other.*

Although from a philosophical point of view, Marxism is incompatible with religion, it goes without saying that we are opposed to any idea of prohibiting or repressing religion. We stand for the complete freedom of the individual to hold any religious belief, or none at all. What we do say is that there should be a strict separation between church and state. The churches must not be supported directly or indirectly by taxes or exemption therefrom, nor should religion be taught in state schools. If people want religion, they should maintain their churches exclusively through the contributions of the congregation and preach their doctrines in their own time.

To the degree that men and women are able to take control of their lives and develop themselves as free human beings, I believe that interest in religion—that is, the search for consolation in an afterlife—will decline naturally of itself. Of course, you may disagree with this prediction. Time will tell which of us is right. In the meantime, disagreements on such matters should not prevent all honest Christians from joining hands with the Marxists in the struggle for a new and better world.

Religion and Revolution

Christianity itself began as a revolutionary movement about 2000 years ago when the early Christians organized a mass movement of the poorest and most downtrodden sections of society. It is not an accident that the Romans accused the Christians of being a movement of slaves and women. The early Christians were also communists, as you will know from the Acts of the Apostles. Christ himself worked among the poor and dispossessed and frequently attacked the rich. He said that it is easier for a camel to pass through the eye of a needle than a rich man to enter the Kingdom of God. There are many such expressions in the Bible.

The communism of the early Christians is also shown by the fact that in their communities all wealth was held in common. Anyone who wished to join had first to give up all his or her worldly goods. Of course, this communism had a somewhat naive and primitive character. This is no reflection on the men and women of that time, who were very courageous people who were not afraid to sacrifice their lives in the struggle against the monstrous Roman slave state. But the real achievement of communism (that is, a classless society) was impossible at that time because the material conditions for it were absent.

Marx and Engels for the first time gave communism a scientific character. They explained that the real emancipation of the masses depends on the level of development of the productive forces (industry, agriculture, science, and technology) which will create the necessary conditions for a general reduction of the working day and access to culture for all, as the only way of transforming the way people think and behave towards each other.

The material conditions at the time of early Christianity were not sufficiently advanced to permit such a development, and therefore the communism of the early Christians remained on a primitive level—the level of consumption (the sharing out of food, clothes, etc.)—and not real communism, which is based on the collective ownership of the means of production.

However, the revolutionary traditions of early Christianity bear absolutely no relation to the present situation. Ever since the 4th century CE, when the Christian movement was hijacked by the state and turned into an instrument of the oppressors, the Christian Church has been on the side of the rich and powerful against the poor and oppressed. Today the main churches are extremely wealthy institutions, closely linked to big business. The Vatican owns a big bank and possesses enormous wealth and power, the Church of England is the biggest landowner in Britain, and so on.

Politically, the churches have systematically backed reaction. Catholic priests blessed the armies of Franco in their campaign to crush the Spanish workers and peasants. The Pope in effect backed Hitler and Mussolini. Finally, in the USA today, the religious right, backed by millions of dollars, is conducting a campaign in favor of all manner of reactionary causes. It has at its disposal television and radio stations, where religious charlatans make a fortune by playing on people's fear and superstition.

The Kingdom of God may be reserved for the poor, but these ladies and gentlemen have ensured for themselves a very comfortable life on this earth. Jesus' first act on entering Jerusalem was to drive the moneychangers out of the Temple. But those who presume to speak in his name almost always take the side of the rich and powerful against the poor and oppressed of this earth. They are often the most fervent advocates of welfare cuts and other policies directed against the most defenseless sections of society, such as single parents. Christ defended the woman taken in adultery, but the latter-day Pharisees line up to stone the poor and defenseless.

For such "religious" people, we have nothing but contempt. But for those honest Christians who wish to join us in the fight to change society, we extend a warm and fraternal welcome. We may disagree about philosophy, but we can agree that the present society is unworthy of humanity and ought to be changed. And we know that many devoted and self-sacrificing class fighters in the USA are practicing Christians. This has always been the case, as we see from the following extract from *The Jungle*, that great socialist novel by Upton Sinclair:

> "I am not defending the Vatican," exclaimed Lucas vehemently. "I am defending the word of God—which is one long cry of the human spirit for deliverance from the sway of oppression. Take the twenty-fourth chapter of the Book of Job, which I am accustomed to quote in my addresses as 'the Bible upon the Beef trust'; or take the words of Isaiah—or of the Master Himself. Not the elegant prince of our debauched and vicious art, not the jewelled idol of our society churches—but the Jesus of the awful reality, the man of sorrow and pain, the outcast, despised of the world, who had nowhere to lay His head—"
>
> "I will grant you Jesus," interrupted the other.
>
> "Well then," cried Lucas, "and why should Jesus have nothing to do with His Church—why should His words His life be of no authority among those who profess to adore Him? Here is a man who was the world's first revolutionist, the true founder of the socialist movement; a man whose whole being was one flame of hatred for wealth, and all that wealth stands for—for the pride of and the luxury of wealth, and the tyranny of wealth; who was Himself a beggar and a tramp, a man of the people, an associate of saloon-keepers and women of the town; who again and again, in the most explicit language, denounced wealth and the holding of wealth: 'Lay not up for yourselves treasures on earth!' 'Sell that ye have and give alms!'—'Blessed are ye poor, for yours is the kingdom of heaven!'—'Woe unto you that are rich, for ye have received your consolation!'—'Verily, I say unto you, that a rich man shall hardly enter into the kingdom of heaven!' Who denounced in unmeasured terms the exploiters of His own time: 'Woe unto you, scribes and Pharisees, hypocrites!'—'Woe unto you also, you lawyers!'—'Ye serpents, ye generation of vipers, how can ye escape the damnation of hell?" Who drove out the businessmen and brokers from the temple with a whip! Who was crucified—think of it—for an incendiary and a disturber of the social order! And this man they have made into the high priest of property and smug respectability, a divine sanction of all the horrors and abominations of modern commercial civilization! Jewelled images are made of Him, sensual priests burn incense to Him, and modern pirates of industry bring their dollars, wrung from the toil of helpless women and children, and build temples to Him, and sit in cushioned seats and listen to His teachings expounded by doctors of dusty divinity."

The voice of revolt of the oppressed against injustice and oppression has spoken in this kind of language for at least 2,000 years. What is important is not the language but the meaning. What is important is not the form but the content. The original message of the Christian movement 2,000 years ago was both revolutionary and communist. As has been explained, nobody could be a Christian unless they first gave up all their worldly wealth, renounced private property, and embraced the doctrine of the universal brotherhood (and sisterhood) and equality of all. That revolutionary message was restated by the left wing of the Puritans in the 16th and 17th centuries. It has resurfaced many times since, as an expression of the instinctive revolutionism of the masses. Marxism takes as its starting point this instinctive revolutionism but gives it a scientific and rounded-out expression.

Our first task is to unite to put an end to the dictatorship of capital that keeps the human race in a state of slavery. Socialism will permit the free development of human beings, without the constraint of material needs. As far as the future of religion is concerned, one can say the following: socialism, being based upon full human freedom, will never try to prohibit people from thinking and believing in any way they choose. People should be allowed to hold any religious beliefs they wish—or none at all.

As we have already pointed out above, religion must, of course, be completely separated from the state. Those who wish to practice religion must pay for it out of their own pockets. And there is no place at all for religion in the schools. Once we have established a genuinely free society in which men and women take control of their own lives and destinies, in which they are able to develop to the full all their physical and mental abilities and relate to each other in a really human manner, we believe there will be no room left for the superstitions of the past, and these will gradually disappear.

You do not agree? Well, that is your right. But first of all, let us agree to combine all our forces in a mighty movement dedicated to driving the moneychangers out of the temple, or rather, out of our homes, streets, and workplaces. Let us cleanse this society of all oppression, exploitation, and injustice. Then we can let the future take care of itself.

The Philosophy of the Future

Marxism is a philosophy, but it is quite unlike other philosophies. Dialectical materialism is both a powerful methodological tool to understand the workings of nature, thought, and human society, and a guide to action. As the young Marx put it: "philosophers have only interpreted the world in various ways—the point is, however, to change it."

Now, it may be that you are quite happy with the world in which we live, and do not wish to change it. In that case, you may find this essay educational, or at least entertaining. But you will not have understood it, basically because we will be talking mutually unintelligible languages. However, if ever there was a time when Americans should be seriously reexamining their view of the world and their place in it, that time is now. And in order to obtain a rational insight into this world an understanding of Marxist philosophy is of great importance.

The most essential feature of dialectical materialism is its dynamic character. It sees the world as an ever-changing process, driven by internal contradictions, in which sooner or later things change into their opposite. Moreover, the line of development is not a smooth, linear process, but a line that is periodically interrupted by sudden leaps, explosions that transform quantity into quality. This is an accurate picture of both processes we see in nature and in the process of social development we call history.

Most people imagine that the kind of world into which they are born is something fixed and immutable. They rarely question its values, its morality, its religion, its political and state institutions. This mental inertia, reinforced by the dead weight of tradition, customs, habit, and routine, is a powerful cement that permits a given socio-economic order to continue to exist long after it has lost its rational basis. In the USA, perhaps more than any other country in the world, this inertia exercises a major role and prevents people from realizing what is happening to them.

In actual fact, societies are not immutable. The whole of history teaches us that. Socio-economic systems, like individual men and women, are born, mature, reach a high point in their development, and then at a certain point enter into a phase of decline and decay. When a form of society ceases to play a progressive role (which, in the last analysis, is that point where it is unable to develop the productive forces as it did in the past), people can feel it. It manifests itself in all manner of ways—not only in the economic field. The old morality begins to break down. There is a crisis of the family and personal relations, a growing lack of solidarity and social cohesion, a rise of crime and violence. People no longer believe in the old religions and turn in the direction of mysticism, superstition, and exotic sects. We have seen these things many times in history, and we are seeing the same things now—even in the USA

We are living at a time when many people have begun to ask questions about the world in which they live, and to ask questions is never a bad thing. The terrible events of 9/11 have caused many Americans to think seriously about matters in which they previously showed little interest. They have suddenly realized that all is not well with the world, and that America is deeply involved in a worldwide crisis from which no one can escape, and in which no one is safe. The destruction of the twin towers cast a dark shadow over America. For a time, Bush and the most reactionary wing of the ruling class have had things all their own way. But this situation will not last forever. Sooner or later the thick fog of propaganda and lies will dissipate and people will become aware of the real state of affairs both in the USA and on a world scale.

Although many people feel in their innermost being that something is going badly wrong, they find no logical explanation for it. That is not surprising. The entire way in which they have been taught to think from their earliest years conditions them to reject any suggestion that there is something fundamentally wrong with the society in which they live. They will close their eyes and try to avoid drawing uncomfortable conclusions for as long as they can.

This is quite natural. It is very hard for people to question the beliefs they have been brought up with. But sooner or later, events catch up with them—cataclysmic events that compel them to rethink many things that they previously took for granted. And when such a moment arrives, the same people who stubbornly refused to consider new ideas, will eagerly examine what only yesterday they regarded as heresies, and find in them the explanations and alternatives for which they were searching.

Today, Marxism is seen as such a heresy. Every hand is raised against it. It is said to have no basis, to have failed, to be out of date. But if this is really the case, then why do the apologists of capitalism still persist in attacking it? Surely, if it is so dead and irrelevant, they should just ignore it. The power of Marxist ideas is precisely that they—and they alone—can provide a coherent, rigorous, and, yes, scientific explanation of the most important phenomena of the world in which we live.

It is a matter of great regret that so many people, especially in the USA, have the same attitude towards Marxism as the representatives of the Roman Catholic Church had towards Galileo's telescope. When Galileo begged them to look with their own eyes and examine the evidence, they stubbornly refused to do so. They just "knew" that Galileo was wrong, and that was that. In the same way, many people "just know" that Marxism is wrong, and do not see any reason to investigate the matter any further. But if Marxism is wrong, by studying it, you will be more firmly convinced of its erroneousness. You have nothing to lose, and will have added to your store of knowledge. But the author of these lines is firmly convinced that if more people only took the trouble to read the original works of Marx, Engels, Lenin, and Trotsky, they would soon convince themselves that Marxism really does have a lot of important things to say—and that these things are of great relevance to the modern world.

No More War!

After 1945 the United Nations was set up, supposedly to guarantee world peace. But today, six decades after D-Day, the world is anything but a peaceful place. One war succeeds another in one country after another, on one continent after another. In the modern epoch wars are the expression of the unbearable contradictions that flow from the capitalist system itself. The entire world is dominated by a handful of superrich nations, which in turn are dominated by a handful of superrich and powerful corporations and banks. The actions of these are determined—as they were always determined—by the greed for rent, interest, and profit; for markets, raw materials, and spheres of influence. In the Second World War, fifty-five million men, women and children perished. Millions more will perish in the coming years and decades, not just in wars and other military conflicts, but from starvation and epidemics like malaria, AIDS, and simple diseases caused by the lack of clean drinking water.

The worst thing about all this is that it is objectively unnecessary. In the first decade of the 21st century, when science and technology have performed unheard-of miracles, the majority of the human race faces a grinding struggle to survive. The gap between rich and poor has widened into an abyss, and at the same time the gap between the so-called rich and poor nations has never been greater.

These facts lie behind the tensions and antagonisms that create wars, ethnic strife, terrorism, and all the other horrors that afflict our tortured and turbulent planet. As long as these central contradictions are not resolved, wars and other violent conflicts will continue to sow death and destruction. It is useless to bemoan the results of war, as moralists and pacifists do. It is necessary to diagnose the source of the illness and prescribe a cure.

At bottom, the worldwide turbulence is a reflection of the crisis of a bankrupt socio-economic system that has long ago outlived its usefulness and become a colossal brake on the development of human culture and civilization. A system that subordinates everything to the greed of a handful of superrich barons in control of huge and irresponsible corporations can only signify endless crises, hunger, disease, misery, and wars. In order that humankind might live, this outmoded system must be abolished. There is no other way forward.

In place of the anarchy of capitalist production, what is needed is a planned economy, democratically run by the working class. On that basis, it will be possible in a relatively short time to abolish hunger, homelessness, misery, and illiteracy and all the other elements of barbarism that make life a hell on earth for countless millions of people. In place of the old strife and rivalry between nations it will be possible to unite the productive forces of the whole planet in a socialist commonwealth, where wars will be consigned, along with slavery, feudalism, and cannibalism, to a museum of barbarous relics of the past.

The Sky is the Limit

The development of the productive forces in the USA over the past century has reached vertiginous heights. Industry, agriculture, science, and technique have all been developed to the point where it would easily be possible to make a gigantic leap forward. The productive potential of the USA alone—if it were harnessed in a rational, democratic plan of production—would be sufficient to eradicate poverty, illiteracy, and disease on a world scale.

However, here too we stumble on a dialectical contradiction. In the first decade of the 21st century, millions of people are living on the brink of starvation. A hundred million children each year are born, live, and die on the streets, and they do not know what it is to live in a house. And the worst thing about this is that, for the first time in history, we can say that none of this is necessary. The terrible suffering, the colossal waste of human resources, all these things could be avoided by taking relatively simple steps.

There is no real objective reason why the world in the 21st century is in the state that it is. We are not faced with some vast, incomprehensible catastrophe, the nature and causes of which we are ignorant, and which we are powerless to resolve. All the contradictions we see on a world scale are only a reflection of the impasse of the capitalist system, a system that subordinates the interests of the millions to the rapacious greed of a few.

In its day, capitalism played a revolutionary role. It freed the productive forces from all the petty restrictions imposed by feudalism. It broke down the narrow local barriers, tithes, tolls, and taxes that limited the free flow of goods, and established a national market, the prior condition for the establishment of the national state.

But now the capitalist system has itself become a barrier to the free development of the productive forces. Private ownership of the means of production is now a contradiction in terms, when the means of production have become gigantic corporations that straddle the continents and own greater wealth than many national states. And the national state itself has become as much of a barrier to the free development of the productive forces as were the old local feudal restrictions in the late Middle Ages. In order to break loose from these suffocating bonds, it is necessary to abolish private ownership of the means of production and the nation state. These reactionary barriers must be swept aside if the future of human progress is to be guaranteed.

Freed from the tyranny of the profit motive and a thousand other petty restrictions that cramp the development of the productive forces, science and technology would experience an explosive growth that would transform the lives of millions in a short space of time. The pioneers who opened up the West were inspired by a new and vast horizon of possibilities. But the advent of socialism would open up still vaster horizons for human development on a global scale. What tremendous new vistas would be opened up for humanity!

In recommending the ideas of Marxism to the American public, it is my fervent hope to convince the reader of the correctness and relevance of the ideas of Marx and Engels in the world of the 21st century. If I succeed even partly in convincing you, I will be very pleased. If not, I hope to have dispelled many misconceptions about Marxism and show that it at least has some interesting things to say about the world in which we live. In any event, I hope it will make people think more critically about our society, its present, and its future.

APPENDIX I

IF AMERICA SHOULD GO COMMUNIST

Leon Trotsky

Should America go communist as a result of the difficulties and problems that your capitalist social order is unable to solve, it will discover that communism, far from being an intolerable bureaucratic tyranny and individual regimentation, will be the means of greater individual liberty and shared abundance.

At present most Americans regard communism solely in the light of the experience of the Soviet Union. They fear lest Sovietism in America would produce the same material result as it has brought for the culturally backward peoples of the Soviet Union.

They fear lest communism should try to fit them to a bed of Procrustes, and they point to the bulwark of Anglo-Saxon conservatism as an insuperable obstacle even to possibly desirable reforms. They argue that Great Britain and Japan would undertake military intervention against the American soviets. They shudder lest Americans be regimented in their habits of dress and diet, be compelled to subsist on famine rations, be forced to read stereotyped official propaganda in the newspapers, be coerced to serve as rubber stamps for decisions arrived at without their active participation, or be required to keep their thoughts to themselves and loudly praise their soviet leaders in public, through fear of imprisonment and exile.

They fear monetary inflation, bureaucratic tyranny, and intolerable red tape in obtaining the necessities of life. They fear soulless standardization in the arts and sciences, as well as in the daily necessities of life. They fear that all political spontaneity and the presumed freedom of the press will be destroyed by the dictatorship of a monstrous bureaucracy. And they shudder at the thought of being forced into an uncomprehended glibness in Marxist dialectic and disciplined social philosophies. They fear, in a word, that Soviet America will become the counterpart of what they have been told Soviet Russia looks like.

Actually American soviets will be as different from the Russian soviets as the United States of President Roosevelt differs from the Russian Empire of Tsar Nicholas II. Yet communism can come in America only through revolution, just as independence and democracy came in America. The American temperament is energetic and violent, and it will insist on breaking a good many dishes and upsetting a good many apple carts before communism is firmly established. Americans are enthusiasts and sportsmen before they are specialists and statesmen, and it would be contrary to the American tradition to make a major change without choosing sides and cracking heads.

However, the American communist revolution will be insignificant compared to the Bolshevik Revolution in Russia, in terms of your national wealth and population, no matter how great its comparative cost. That is because civil war of a revolutionary nature isn't fought by the handful of men at the top—the 5 or 10 percent who own nine-tenths of American wealth; this handful could recruit its counterrevolutionary armies only from among the lower middle classes. Even so, the revolution could easily attract them to its banner by showing that support of the soviets alone offers them the prospect of salvation.

Everybody below this group is already economically prepared for communism. The depression has ravaged your working class and has dealt a crushing blow to the farmers, who had already been injured by the long agricultural decline of the postwar decade. There is no reason why these groups should counterpose determined resistance to the revolution; they have nothing to lose, providing, of course, that the revolutionary leaders adopt a farsighted and moderate policy toward them.

Who else will fight against communism? Your corporal's guard of billionaires and multimillionaires? Your Mellons, Morgans, Fords, and Rockefellers? They will cease struggling as soon as they fail to find other people to fight for them.

The American soviet government will take firm possession of the commanding heights of your business system: the banks, the key industries, and the transportation and communication systems. It will then give the farmers, the small tradespeople, and businessmen a good long time to think things over and see how well the nationalized section of industry is working.

Here is where the American soviets can produce real miracles. "Technocracy" can come true only under communism, when the dead hands of private property rights and private profits are lifted from your industrial system. The most daring proposals of the Hoover commission on standardization and rationalization will seem childish compared to the new possibilities let loose by American communism.

National industry will be organized along the line of the conveyor belt in your modern continuous-production automotive factories. Scientific planning can be lifted out of the individual factory and applied to your entire economic system. The results will be stupendous.

Costs of production will be cut to 20 percent, or less, of their present figure. This, in turn, would rapidly increase your farmers' purchasing power.

To be sure, the American soviets would establish their own gigantic farm enterprises, as schools of voluntary collectivization. Your farmers could easily calculate whether it was to their individual advantage to remain as isolated links or to join the public chain.

The same method would be used to draw small businesses and industries into the national organization of industry. By soviet control of raw materials, credits, and quotas of orders, these secondary industries could be kept solvent until they were gradually and without compulsion sucked into the socialized business system.

Without compulsion! The American soviets would not need to resort to the drastic measures that circumstances have often imposed upon the Russians. In the United States, through the science of publicity and advertising, you have means for winning the support of your middle class that were beyond the reach of the soviets of backward Russia with its vast majority of pauperized and illiterate peasants. This, in addition to your technical equipment and your wealth, is the greatest asset of your coming communist revolution. Your revolution will be smoother in character than ours; you will not waste your energies and resources in costly social conflicts after the main issues have been decided; and you will move ahead so much more rapidly in consequence.

Even the intensity and devotion of religious sentiment in America will not prove an obstacle to the revolution. If one assumes the perspective of soviets in America, none of the psychological brakes will prove firm enough to retard the pressure of the social crisis. This has been demonstrated more than once in history. Besides, it should not be forgotten that the Gospels themselves contain some pretty explosive aphorisms.

As to the comparatively few opponents of the soviet revolution, one can trust to American inventive genius. It may well be that you will take your unconvinced millionaires and send them to some picturesque island, rent-free for life, where they can do as they please.

You can do this safely, for you will not need to fear foreign interventions. Japan, Great Britain, and the other capitalistic countries that intervened in Russia couldn't do anything but take American communism lying down. As a matter of fact, the victory of communism in America—the stronghold of capitalism—will cause communism to spread to other countries. Japan will probably have joined the communistic ranks even before the establishment of the American soviets. The same is true of Great Britain.

In any case, it would be a crazy idea to send His Britannic Majesty's fleet against Soviet America, even as a raid against the southern and more conservative half of your continent. It would be hopeless and would never get any farther than a second-rate military escapade.

Within a few weeks or months of the establishment of the American soviets, Pan-Americanism would be a political reality.

The governments of Central and South America would be pulled into your federation like iron filings to a magnet. So would Canada. The popular movements in these countries would be so strong that they would force this great unifying process within a short period and at insignificant costs. I am ready to bet that the first anniversary of the American soviets would find the Western Hemisphere transformed into the Soviet United States of North, Central and South America, with its capital at Panama. Thus for the first time the Monroe Doctrine would have a complete and positive meaning in world affairs, although not the one foreseen by its author.

In spite of the complaints of some of your arch-conservatives, Roosevelt is not preparing for a soviet transformation of the United States.

The NRA aims not to destroy but to strengthen the foundations of American capitalism by overcoming your business difficulties. Not the Blue Eagle but the difficulties that the Blue Eagle is powerless to overcome will bring about communism in America. The "radical" professors of your Brain Trust are not revolutionists: they are only frightened conservatives. Your president abhors "systems" and "generalities." But a soviet government is the greatest of all possible systems, a gigantic generality in action.

The average man doesn't like systems or generalities either. It is the task of your communist statesmen to make the system deliver the concrete goods that the average man desires: his food, cigars, amusements, his freedom to choose his own neckties, his own house and his own automobile. It will be easy to give him these comforts in Soviet America.

Most Americans have been misled by the fact that in the USSR we had to build whole new basic industries from the ground up. Such a thing could not happen in America, where you are already compelled to cut down on your farm area and to reduce your industrial production. As a matter of fact, your tremendous technological equipment has been paralyzed by the crisis and already clamors to be put to use. You will be able to make a rapid step-up of consumption by your people the starting point of your economic revival.

You are prepared to do this as is no other country. Nowhere else has the study of the internal market reached such intensity as in the United States. It has been done by your banks, trusts, individual businessmen, merchants, traveling salesmen, and farmers as part of their stock-in-trade. Your soviet government will simply abolish all trade secrets, will combine all the findings of these researches for individual profit, and will transform them into a scientific system of economic planning. In this your government will be helped by the existence of a large class of cultured and critical consumers. By combining the nationalized key industries, your private businesses, and democratic consumer cooperation, you will quickly develop a highly flexible system for serving the needs of your population.

This system will be made to work not by bureaucracy and not by policemen but by cold, hard cash.

Your almighty dollar will play a principal part in making your new soviet system work. It is a great mistake to try to mix a "planned economy" with a "managed currency." Your money must act as regulator with which to measure the success or failure of your planning.

Your "radical" professors are dead wrong in their devotion to "managed money." It is an academic idea that could easily wreck your entire system of distribution and production. That is the great lesson to be derived from the Soviet Union, where bitter necessity has been converted into official virtue in the monetary realm.

There the lack of a stable gold ruble is one of the main causes of our many economic troubles and catastrophes. It is impossible to regulate wages, prices ,and quality of goods without a firm monetary system. An unstable ruble in a Soviet system is like having variable molds in a conveyor-belt factory. It won't work.

Only when socialism succeeds in substituting administrative control for money will it be possible to abandon a stable gold currency. Then money will become ordinary paper slips, like trolley or theater tickets. As socialism advances, these slips will also disappear, and control over individual consumption—whether by money or administration—will no longer be necessary when there is more than enough of everything for everybody!

Such a time has not yet come, though America will certainly reach it before any other country. Until then, the only way to reach such a state of development is to retain an effective regulator and measure for the working of your system. As a matter of fact, during the first few years a planned economy needs sound money even more than did old-fashioned capitalism. The professor who regulates the monetary unit with the aim of regulating the whole business system is like the man who tried to lift both his feet off the ground at the same time.

Soviet America will possess supplies of gold big enough to stabilize the dollar—a priceless asset. In Russia we have been expanding our industrial plant by 20 and 30 percent a year; but—owing to a weak ruble—we have not been able to distribute this increase effectively. This is partly because we have allowed our bureaucracy to subject our monetary system to administrative one-sidedness. You will be spared this evil. As a result you will greatly surpass us in both increased production and distribution, leading to a rapid advance in the comfort and welfare of your population.

In all this, you will not need to imitate our standardized production for our pitiable mass consumers. We have taken over from tsarist Russia a pauper's heritage, a culturally undeveloped peasantry with a low standard of living. We had to build our factories and dams at the expense of our consumers. We have had continual monetary inflation and a monstrous bureaucracy.

Soviet America will not have to imitate our bureaucratic methods. Among us the lack of the bare necessities has caused an intense scramble for an extra loaf of bread, an extra yard of cloth by everyone. In this struggle our bureaucracy steps forward as a conciliator, as an all-powerful court of arbitration. You, on the other hand, are much wealthier and would have little difficulty in supplying all of your people with all of the necessities of life. Moreover, your needs, tastes, and habits would never permit your bureaucracy to divide the national income. Instead, when you organize your society to produce for human needs rather than private profits, your entire population will group itself around new trends and groups, which will struggle with one another and prevent an overweening bureaucracy from imposing itself upon them.

You can thus avoid growth of bureaucratism by the practice of soviets, that is to say, democracy—the most flexible form of government yet developed. Soviet organization cannot achieve miracles but must simply reflect the will of the people. With us the soviets have been bureaucratized as a result of the political monopoly of a single party, which has itself become a bureaucracy. This situation resulted from the exceptional difficulties of socialist pioneering in a poor and backward country.

The American soviets will be full-blooded and vigorous, without need or opportunity for such measures as circumstances imposed upon Russia. Your unregenerate capitalists will, of course, find no place for themselves in the new setup. It is hard to imagine Henry Ford as the head of the Detroit Soviet.

Yet a wide struggle between interests, groups, and ideas is not only conceivable—it is inevitable. One-year, five-year, ten-year plans of business development; schemes for national education; construction of new basic lines of transportation; the transformation of the farms; the program for improving the technological and cultural equipment of Latin America; a program for stratosphere communication; eugenics—all of these will arouse controversy, vigorous electoral struggle, and passionate debate in the newspapers and at public meetings.

For Soviet America will not imitate the monopoly of the press by the heads of Soviet Russia's bureaucracy. While Soviet America would nationalize all printing plants, paper mills, and means of distribution, this would be a purely negative measure. It would simply mean that private capital will no longer be allowed to decide what publications should be established, whether they should be progressive or reactionary, "wet" or "dry," puritanical or pornographic. Soviet America will have to find a new solution for the question of how the power of the press is to function in a socialist regime. It might be done on the basis of proportional representation for the votes in each soviet election.

Thus the right of each group of citizens to use the power of the press would depend on their numerical strength—the same principle being applied to the use of meeting halls, allotment of time on the air, and so forth.

Thus the management and policy of publications would be decided not by individual checkbooks but by group ideas. This may take little account of numerically small but important groups, but it simply means that each new idea will be compelled, as throughout history, to prove its right to existence.

Rich Soviet America can set aside vast funds for research and invention, discoveries and experiments in every field. You won't neglect your bold architects and sculptors, your unconventional poets and audacious philosophers.

In fact, the Soviet Yankees of the future will give a lead to Europe in those very fields where Europe has hitherto been your master. Europeans have little conception of the power of technology to influence human destiny and have adopted an attitude of sneering superiority toward "Americanism," particularly since the crisis. Yet Americanism marks the true dividing line between the Middle Ages and the modern world.

Hitherto America's conquest of nature has been so violent and passionate that you have had no time to modernize your philosophies or to develop your own artistic forms. Hence you have been hostile to the doctrines of Hegel, Marx, and Darwin. The burning of Darwin's works by the Baptists of Tennessee is only a clumsy reflection of the American dislike for the doctrines of evolution. This attitude is not confined to your pulpits. It is still part of your general mental makeup.

Your atheists as well as your Quakers are determined rationalists. And your rationalism itself is weakened by empiricism and moralism. It has none of the merciless vitality of the great European rationalists. So your philosophic method is even more antiquated than your economic system and your political institutions.

Today, quite unprepared, you are being forced to face those social contradictions that grow up unsuspected in every society. You have conquered nature by means of the tools that your inventive genius has created, only to find that your tools have all but destroyed you. Contrary to all your hopes and desires, your unheard-of wealth has produced unheard-of misfortunes. You have discovered that social development does not follow a simple formula. Hence you have been thrust into the school of the dialectic—to stay.

There is no turning back from it to the mode of thinking and acting prevalent in the seventeenth and eighteenth centuries.

While the romantic numskulls of Nazi Germany are dreaming of restoring the old race of Europe's Dark Forest to its original purity, or rather its original filth, you Americans, after taking a firm grip on your economic machinery and your culture, will apply genuine scientific methods to the problem of eugenics. Within a century, out of your melting pot of races there will come a new breed of men—the first worthy of the name of Man.

One final prophecy: In the third year of soviet rule in America, you will no longer chew gum!

August 17, 1934

APPENDIX II

ADDRESS OF THE INTERNATIONAL WORKING MEN'S ASSOCIATION TO ABRAHAM LINCOLN, PRESIDENT OF THE UNITED STATES OF AMERICA

(Drafted by Karl Marx)

Sir:

We congratulate the American people upon your reelection by a large majority. If resistance to the Slave Power was the reserved watchword of your first election, the triumphant war cry of your reelection is Death to Slavery.

From the commencement of the titanic American strife the workingmen of Europe felt instinctively that the star-spangled banner carried the destiny of their class. The contest for the territories which opened the dire epopee, was it not to decide whether the virgin soil of immense tracts should be wedded to the labor of the emigrant or prostituted by the tramp of the slave driver?

When an oligarchy of 300,000 slaveholders dared to inscribe, for the first time in the annals of the world, "slavery" on the banner of Armed Revolt, when on the very spots where hardly a century ago the idea of one great Democratic Republic had first sprung up, whence the first Declaration of the Rights of Man was issued, and the first impulse given to the European revolution of the eighteenth century; when on those very spots counterrevolution, with systematic thoroughness, gloried in rescinding "the ideas entertained at the time of the formation of the old constitution," and maintained slavery to be "a beneficent institution," indeed, the old solution of the great problem of "the relation of capital to labor," and cynically proclaimed property in man "the cornerstone of the new edifice"—then the working classes of Europe understood at once, even before the fanatic partisanship of the upper classes for the Confederate gentry had given its dismal warning, that the slaveholders' rebellion was to sound the tocsin for a general holy crusade of property against labor, and that for the men of labor, with their hopes for the future, even their past conquests were at stake in that tremendous conflict on the other side of the Atlantic. Everywhere they bore therefore patiently the hardships imposed upon them by the cotton crisis, opposed enthusiastically the proslavery intervention of their betters—and, from most parts of Europe, contributed their quota of blood to the good cause.

While the workingmen, the true political powers of the North, allowed slavery to defile their own republic, while before the Negro, mastered and sold without his concurrence, they boasted it the highest prerogative of the white-skinned laborer to sell himself and choose his own master, they were unable to attain the true freedom of labor, or to support their European brethren in their struggle for emancipation; but this barrier to progress has been swept off by the red sea of civil war.

The workingmen of Europe feel sure that, as the American War of Independence initiated a new era of ascendancy for the middle class, so the American Antislavery War will do for the working classes. They consider it an earnest of the epoch to come that it fell to the lot of Abraham Lincoln, the single-minded son of the working class, to lead his country through the matchless struggle for the rescue of an enchained race and the reconstruction of a social world.

Signed on behalf of the International Workingmen's Association, the Central Council. (Presented to U.S. Ambassador Charles Francis Adams January 28, 1865)

APPENDIX III

THE NEED FOR A LABOR PARTY

Selections from Frederick Engels

To Florence Kelley Wischnewetsky in Zurich[1]

My preface will of course turn entirely on the immense stride made by the American working man in the last ten months, and naturally also touch H.G.[2] and his land scheme. But it cannot pretend to deal exhaustively with it. Nor do I think the time has come for that. It is far more important that the movement should spread, proceed harmoniously, take root and embrace as much as possible the whole American proletariat, than that it should start and proceed from the beginning on theoretically perfectly correct lines. There is no better road to theoretical clearness of comprehension than "*durch Schaden klug werden.*"[3] And for a whole large class, there is no other road, especially for a nation so eminently practical as the Americans. The great thing is to get the working class to move *as a class;* that once obtained, they will soon find the right direction, and all who resist, H.G. or Powderly, will be left out in the cold with small sects of their own. Therefore I think also the K. of L.[4] a most important factor in the movement which

---

1 First published in *Gestamtausgabe.* Written by Frederick Engels, London, December 28, 1886. This text courtesy of the Marxist Internet Archive (marxists. org). Transcribed by Sally Ryan (2000) from *Marx-Engels Selected Correspondence,* International Publishers 1968.

2 Henry George

3 to learn by one's own mistakes

4 *The Noble Order* of *the Knights of Labor: A* working-class organization founded in Philadelphia in 1869. Existing illegally until 1878, it observed a semi-mysterious ritual. That year the organization emerged from the underground, retaining some of its secret features. The Knights of Labor aimed at the liberation

ought not to be pooh-poohed from without but to be revolutionized from within, and I consider that many of the Germans there have made a grievous mistake when they tried, in face of a mighty and glorious movement not of their creation, to make of their imported and not always understood theory a kind of *alleinseligmachendes*[5] dogma and to keep aloof from any movement which did not accept that dogma. Our theory is not a dogma but the exposition of a process of evolution, and that process involves successive phases. To expect that the Americans will start with the full consciousness of the theory worked out in older industrial countries is to expect the impossible. What the Germans ought to do is to act up to their own theory —if they understand it, as we did in 1845 and 1848—to go in for any real general working-class movement, accept its *faktische*[6] starting points as such and work it gradually up to the theoretical level by pointing out how every mistake made, every reverse suffered, was a necessary consequence of mistaken theoretical views in the original program; they ought, in the words of *The Communist Manifesto*, to represent the movement of the future in the movement of the present. But above all give the movement time to consolidate, do not make the inevitable confusion of the first start worse confounded by forcing down people's throats things which at present they cannot properly understand, but which they soon will learn. A million or two of workingmen's votes next November for a *bona fide* workingmen's party is worth infinitely more at present than a hundred thousand votes for a doctrinally perfect platform. The very first attempt—soon to be made if the movement progresses—to consolidate the moving masses on a national basis will bring them all face to face, Georgites, K. of L., trade unionists, and all; and if our German friends by that time have learned enough of the language of the country to go in for a discussion, then will be the time for them to criticize the views of the others and thus, by showing up the inconsistencies of the various standpoints, to bring them gradually to understand their own actual position, the position made for them by the correlation of capital and wage labor. But anything that might

of the workers by means of cooperatives. They took in all skilled and even unskilled trades, without discrimination on account of sex, race, nationality, or religion. The organization reached the highest point of its activity during the eighties, when, under the pressure of the masses, the leaders of the Order were compelled to consent to an extensive strike movement. Its membership at that time was over 700,000, including 60,000 Negroes. However, on account of the opportunist tactics of the leaders, who were opposed to revolutionary class struggle, the Order forfeited its prestige among the masses. Its activity expired the next decade.

5 only true
6 actual

delay or prevent that national consolidation of the workingmen's party—no matter what platform—I should consider a great mistake, and therefore I do not think the time has arrived to speak out fully and exhaustively either with regard to H.G. or the K. of L.

The Labor Movement in America[7]

Ten months have elapsed since, at the translator's wish, I wrote the Appendix to this book; and during these ten months, a revolution has been accomplished in American society such as, in any other country, would have taken at least ten years. In February 1885, American public opinion was almost unanimous on this one point; that there was no working class, in the European sense of the word, in America; that consequently no class struggle between work-men and capitalists, such as tore European society to pieces, was possible in the American Republic; and that, therefore, socialism was a thing of foreign importation which could never take root on American soil. And yet, at that moment, the coming class struggle was casting its gigantic shadow before it in the strikes of the Pennsylvania coal miners, and of many other trades, and especially in the preparations, all over the country, for the great Eight Hours' movement which was to come off, and did come off, in the May following. That I then duly appreciated these symptoms, that I anticipated a working-class movement on a national scale, my "Appendix" shows; but no one could then foresee that in such a short time the movement would burst out with such irresistible force, would spread with the rapidity of a prairie fire, would shake American society to its very foundations.

The fact is there, stubborn and indisputable. To what an extent it had struck with terror the American ruling classes, was revealed to me, in an amusing way, by American journalists who did me the honor of calling on me last summer; the "new departure" had put them into a state of helpless fright and perplexity. But at that time the movement was only just on the start; there was but a series of confused and apparently disconnected upheavals of that class which, by the suppression of negro slavery and the rapid development of manufactures, had become the lowest stratum of American society. Before the year closed, these bewildering social convulsions began to take a defi-nite direction. The spontaneous, instinctive movements of these vast masses of working people, over a vast extent of country, the simultaneous outburst of their common discontent with a miserable social condition, the same

---

7 Preface to the American edition of *The Conditions of the Working-Class in England*, New York, 1887. Written by Frederick Engels, London, January 26, 1887. This text courtesy of the Marxist Internet Archive (marxists.org). Transcribed by Andy Blunden from *Marx-Engels On Britain*, Progress Publishers 1953.

everywhere and due to the same causes, made them conscious of the fact, that they formed a new and distinct class of American society; a class of—practically speaking—more or less hereditary wage workers, proletarians. And with true American instinct this consciousness led them at once to take the next step towards their deliverance: the formation of a political workingmen's party, with a platform of its own, and with the conquest of the Capitol and the White House for its goal. In May the struggle for the Eight Hours' working day, the troubles in Chicago, Milwaukee, etc., the attempts of the ruling class to crush the nascent uprising of labor by brute force and brutal class justice; in November the new Labor Party organized in all great centers, and the New York, Chicago, and Milwaukee elections. May and November have hitherto reminded the American bourgeoisie only of the payment of coupons of US bonds; henceforth May and November will remind them, too, of the dates on which the American working class presented *their* coupons for payment.

In European countries, it took the working class years and years before they fully realized the fact that they formed a distinct and, under the existing social conditions, a permanent class of modern society; and it took years again until this class consciousness led them to form themselves into a distinct political party, independent of, and opposed to, all the old political parties formed by the various sections of the ruling classes. On the more favored soil of America, where no medieval ruins bar the way, where history begins with the elements of modern bourgeois society as evolved in the seventeenth century, the working class passed through these two stages of its development within ten months.,

Still, all this is but a beginning. That the laboring masses should feel their community of grievances and of interests, their solidarity as a class in opposition to all other classes; that in order to give expression and effect to this feeling, they should set in motion the political machinery provided for that purpose in every free country—that is the first step only. The next step is to find the common remedy for these common grievances, and to embody it in the platform of the new Labor Party. And this—the most important and the most difficult step in the movement—has yet to be taken in America.

A new party must have a distinct positive platform; a platform which may vary in details as circumstances vary and as the party itself develops, but still one upon which the party, for the time being, is agreed. So long as such a platform has not been worked out, or exists but in a rudimentary form, so long the new party, too, will have but a rudimentary existence; it may exist locally but not yet nationally, it will be a party potentially but not actually.

That platform, whatever may be its first shape, must develop in a direction which may be determined beforehand. The causes that brought into existence the abyss between the working class and the capitalist class are the same in America as in Europe; the means of filling up that abyss are equally the same everywhere. Consequently, the platform of the American proletariat will in the long run coincide, as to the ultimate end to be attained, with the one which, after sixty years of dissensions and discussions, has become the adopted platform of the great mass of the European militant proletariat. It will proclaim, as the ultimate end, the conquest of political supremacy by the working class, in order to effect the direct appropriation of all means of production—land, railways, mines, machinery, etc.—by society at large, to be worked in common by all for the account and benefit of all.

But if the new American party, like all political parties everywhere, by the very fact of its formation aspires to the conquest of political power, it is as yet far from agreed upon what to do with that power when once attained. In New York and the other great cities of the East, the organization of the working class has proceeded upon the lines of trades' societies, forming in each city a powerful Central Labor Union. In New York the Central Labor Union, last November, chose for its standard bearer Henry George, and consequently its temporary electoral platform has been largely imbued with his principles. In the great cities of the Northwest the electoral battle was fought upon a rather indefinite labor platform, and the influence of Henry George's theories was scarcely, if at all, visible. And while in these great centers of population and of industry the new class movement came to a political head, we find all over the country two widespread labor organizations: the "Knights of Labor" and the "Socialist Labor Party," of which only the latter has a platform in harmony with the modern European standpoint as summarized above.

Of the three more or less definite forms under which the American labor movement thus presents itself, the first, the Henry George movement in New York, is for the moment of a chiefly local significance. No doubt New York is by far the most important city of the States; but New York is not Paris and the United States are not France. And it seems to me that the Henry George platform, in its present shape, is too narrow to form the basis for anything but a local movement, or at best for a short-lived phase of the general movement. To Henry George, the expropriation of the mass of the people from the land is the great and universal cause of the splitting up of the people into rich and poor. Now this is not quite correct historically. In Asiatic and classical antiquity, the predominant form of class oppression was slavery, that is to say, not so much the expropriation of the masses from the land as the appropriation of their persons. When, in the decline of the Roman Republic, the free Italian peasants were expropriated from their farms, they formed a class of "poor whites" similar to that of the Southern slave states before 1861; and between slaves and poor whites, two classes equally unfit for self-emancipation, the old world went to pieces. In the middle ages, it was not the expropriation of the people from, but on the contrary, their appropriation to the land which became the source of feudal oppression. The peasant retained his land, but was attached to it as a serf or villain, and made liable to tribute to the lord in labor and in produce. It was only at the dawn of modern times, towards the end of the fifteenth century, that the expropriation of the peasantry on a large scale laid the foundation for the modern class of wage workers who possess nothing but their labor power and can live only by the selling of that labor power to others. But if the expropriation from the land brought this class into existence, it was the development of capitalist production, of modern industry and agriculture on a large scale which perpetuated it, increased it, and shaped it into a distinct class with distinct interests and a distinct historical mission. All this has been fully expounded by Marx (*Capital*, Part VIII: "The So-Called Primitive Accumulation"). According to Marx, the cause of the present antagonism of the classes and of the social degradation of the working class is their expropriation from all means of production, in which the land is of course included.

If Henry George declares land monopolization to be the sole cause of poverty and misery, he naturally finds the remedy in the resumption of the land by society at large. Now, the socialists of the school of Marx, too, demand the resumption, by society, of the land, and not only of the land but of all other means of production likewise. But even if we leave these out of the question, there is another difference. What is to be done with the land? Modern socialists, as represented by Marx, demand that it should be held and worked in common and for common account, and the same with all other means of social production, mines, railways, factories, etc.; Henry George would confine himself to letting it out to individuals as at present, merely regulating its distribution and applying the rents for public, instead of, as at present, for private purposes. What the socialists demand, implies a total revolution of the whole system of social production; what Henry George demands, leaves the present mode of social production untouched, and has, in fact, been anticipated by the extreme section of Ricardian bourgeois economists who, too, demanded the confiscation of the rent of land by the state.

It would of course be unfair to suppose that Henry George has said his last word once for all. But I am bound to take his theory as I find it.

The second great section of the American movement is formed by the Knights of Labor. And that seems to be the section most typical of the present state of the movement, as it is undoubtedly by far the strongest. An immense association spread over an immense extent of country in innumerable "assemblies," representing all shades of individual and local opinion within the working class; the whole of them sheltered under a platform of corresponding indistinctness and held together much less by their impracticable constitution than by the instinctive feeling that the very fact of their clubbing together for their common aspiration makes them a great power in the country; a truly American paradox clothing the most modern tendencies in the most medieval mummeries, and hiding the most democratic and even rebellious spirit behind an apparent, but really powerless despotism—such is the picture the Knights of Labor offer to a European observer. But if we are not arrested by mere outside whimsicalities, we cannot help seeing in this vast agglomeration an immense amount of potential energy evolving slowly but surely into actual force. The Knights of Labor are the first national organization created by the American working class as a whole; whatever be their origin and history, whatever their shortcomings and little absurdities, whatever their platform and their constitution, here they are, the work of practically the whole class of American wage workers, the only national bond that holds them together, that makes their strength felt to themselves not less than to their enemies, and that fills them with the proud hope of future victories. For it would not be exact to say, that the Knights of Labor are liable to development. They are constantly in full process of development and revolution; a heaving, fermenting mass of plastic material seeking the shape and form appropriate to its inherent nature. That form will be attained as surely as historical evolution has, like natural evolution, its own immanent laws. Whether the Knights of Labor will then retain their present name or not, makes no difference, but to an outsider it appears evident that here is the raw material out of which the future of the American working-class movement, and along with it, the future of American society at large, has to be shaped.

The third section consists of the Socialist Labor Party.[8] This section is a party but in name, for nowhere in America has it, up to now, been able actually to take its stand as a political party. It is, moreover, to a certain extent foreign

---

8   The *Socialist Labor Party* came into existence in 1876 as a result of the union of the American sections of the First International with other working-class socialist organizations in the United States. This party consisted mainly of immigrants, particularly Germans. Its activities were sectarian and its leaders were incapable of heading the mass movement of the American workers, as they refused to work in the trade unions.

to America, having until lately been made up almost exclusively by German immigrants, using their own language and for the most part, conversant with the common language of the country. But if it came from a foreign stock, it came, at the same time, armed with the experience earned during long years of class struggle in Europe, and with an insight into the general conditions of working-class emancipation, far superior to that hitherto gained by American workingmen. This is a fortunate circumstance for the American proletarians who thus are enabled to appropriate, and to take advantage of, the intellectual and moral fruits of the forty years' struggle of their European classmates, and thus to hasten on the time of their own victory. For, as I said before, there cannot be any doubt that the ultimate platform of the American working class must and will be essentially the same as that now adopted by the whole militant working class of Europe, the same as that of the German-American Socialist Labor Party. In so far this party is called upon to play a very important part in the movement. But in order to do so they will have to doff every remnant of their foreign garb. They will have to become out and out American. They cannot expect the Americans to come to them; they, the minority and the immigrants, must go to the Americans, who are the vast majority and the natives. And to do that, they must above all things learn English.

The process of fusing together these various elements of the vast moving mass—elements not really discordant, but indeed mutually isolated by their various starting points—will take some time and will not come off without a deal of friction, such as is visible at different points even now. The Knights of Labor, for instance, are here and there, in the Eastern cities, locally at war with the organized trade unions. But then this same friction exists within the Knights of Labor themselves, where there is anything but peace and harmony. These are not symptoms of decay, for capitalists to crow over. They are merely signs that the innumerable hosts of workers, for the first time set in motion in a common direction, have as yet found out neither the adequate expression for their common interests, nor the form of organization best adapted to the struggle, nor the discipline required to insure victory. They are as yet the first levies *en masse* of the great revolutionary war, raised and equipped locally and independently, all converging to form one common army, but as yet without regular organization and common plan of campaign. The converging columns cross each other here and there: confusion, angry disputes, even threats of conflict arise. But the community of ultimate purpose in the end overcomes all minor troubles; ere long the straggling and squabbling battalions will be formed in a long line of battle array, presenting to the enemy a well-ordered front, ominously silent under their glittering arms, supported by bold skirmishers in front and by unshakeable reserves in the rear.

To bring about this result, the unification of the various independent bodies into one national labor army, with no matter how inadequate a provisional platform, provided it be a truly working-class platform—that is the next great step to be accomplished in America. To effect this, and to make that platform worthy of the cause, the Socialist Labor Party can contribute a great deal, if they will only act in the same way as the European socialists have acted at the time when they were but a small minority of the working class. That line of action was first laid down in *The Communist Manifesto* of 1847 in the following words:

> The communists—that was the name we took at the time and which even now we are far from repudiating—the communists do not form a separate party opposed to other working-class parties.
>
> They have no interests separate and apart from the interests of the whole working class.
>
> They do not set up any sectarian principles of their own, by which to shape and model the proletarian movement.
>
> The communists are distinguished from the other working-class parties by this only: 1. In the national struggles of the proletarians of the different countries they point out, and bring to the front, the common interests of the whole proletariat, interests independent of all nationality; 2. In the various stages of development which the struggle of the working class against the capitalist class has to pass through, they always and everywhere represent the interests of the movement as a whole.
>
> The communists, therefore, are on the one hand, practically the most advanced and resolute section of the working-class parties of all countries, that section which ever pushes forward all others; on the other hand, theoretically, they have, over the great mass of the proletarians, the advantage of clearly understanding the line of march, the conditions, and the ultimate general results of the proletarian movement.
>
> Thus they fight for the attainment of the immediate ends, for the enforcement of the momentary interests of the working class; but in the movement of the present, they represent and take care of the future of the movement.

That is the line of action which the great founder of modern socialism, Karl Marx, and with him, I and the socialists of all nations who worked along with us, have followed for more than forty years, with the result that it has led to victory everywhere, and that at this moment the mass of European socialists, in Germany and in France, in Belgium, Holland, and Switzerland, in Denmark and Sweden as well as in Spain and Portugal, are fighting as one common army under one and the same flag.

APPENDIX IV

SHAYS'S REBELLION AND THE AMERICAN REVOLUTION

John Peterson

The American Revolution shook up the entire world. In the name of "Life, Liberty, and the Pursuit of Happiness," the thirteen British colonies that would become the United States of America fought and won against the most powerful imperial power on the planet. The War for Independence was led by self-styled aristocrats like George Washington, but the actual fighting was done by small farmers, craftsmen and artisans, whites, blacks, and Native Americans, freedmen and slaves alike.

But once the dirty work of the Revolutionary War was finished, what was to replace the rule of King George III? The new oligarchy—including the bankers of the East Coast and the plantation owners of the South—were divided as to how they should rule. Some wanted a republic; others favored a limited monarchy, with George Washington as the prime candidate. Some wanted to ally with the French, others with their old enemy the British. Some wanted tighter centralization, others a looser federation. But on one thing they were all united: all the revolutionary rhetoric about freedom and justice was to apply only to free men who owned significant amounts of property. Slaves, women, poor whites, blacks, and Native Americans need not apply. In order to consolidate their power, a political counterrevolution was necessary. They had to put the "unwashed masses"—who believed they had been fighting for genuine freedom for all—back in their place.

In the years following the American victory over the British, the hopes of the masses were betrayed. As a result, there were many popular movements and uprisings against the squeezing of the poor by the big bankers and corrupt government officials. But none had as big an impact on the psychology of the ruling class and the future structure of the US government as Shays's Rebellion of 1786–87, which some have called "The American Revolution's Final Battle." The Massachusetts uprising of the "Shaysites," as they were called, was a defining moment in US history, an outstanding example of the class contradictions and revolutionary traditions built into the very bedrock of American society. The many similarities and parallels with political struggles and revolutionary movements in our own times are striking.

Every revolution passes through broadly similar stages: from the Great French Revolution, the American Revolution, the Russian Revolution, and the Spanish Revolution, to the ongoing Venezuelan Revolution, whose fate has yet to be determined. A revolution is a dynamic struggle of living forces, with inevitable ups and downs, advances and retreats. During the ascent of the movement, there is a colossal shift to the left, characterized by the active participation of the masses. Here is how Leon Trotsky explained it in the preface to his *History of the Russian Revolution*:

> The most indubitable feature of a revolution is the direct interference of the masses in historical events. In ordinary times the state, be it monarchical or democratic, elevates itself above the nation, and history is made by specialists in that line of business—kings, ministers, bureaucrats, parliamentarians, journalists. But at those crucial moments when the old order becomes no longer endurable to the masses, they break over the barriers excluding them from the political arena, sweep aside their traditional representatives, and create by their own interference the initial groundwork for a new régime. Whether this is good or bad we leave to the judgment of moralists. We ourselves will take the facts as they are given by the objective course of development. The history of a revolution is for us first of all a history of the forcible entrance of the masses into the realm of rulership over their own destiny.

This was clearly the case in the Americans' struggle against the British Empire. The revolutionary-democratic ideas of the Enlightenment and the fiery rhetoric of propagandists like Thomas Paine and Samuel Adams aroused the toiling masses to believe another world was possible and worth fighting for.

However, if the continued ascent of the revolution is blocked, either because the objective conditions simply do not exist for it (as in the case of the French Revolution of the 1790s, a time when the material conditions for socialism were not present), or the role played by the leadership (as in the case of Spain in the 1930s, where the material conditions for the socialist revolution were present, but the leadership was not up to the task, or outright betrayed the masses), a period of tiredness eventually sets in. Those who have risen to the top of society on the crest of the revolutionary wave tire of the storm and stress of the years of revolution, and seek to consolidate the gains they've made for themselves. By degrees, the flooding river of the mass struggle begins to ebb and starts to flow back into the old channels. The newly minted ruling class increasingly puts the brakes on the revolution and, while not reversing the fundamental gains of the struggle (for example, the Americans did not bring back the King of England), they must put the masses "back in their place" before things can return to "normal."

However, when the masses, who have sacrificed life, limb, livelihood, personal comfort, and property, find their aspirations betrayed, they become more than a little dejected. And when they realize that after all their efforts to kick out the old rulers, another exploiting group has encrusted itself atop society, they can embark on more or less desperate attempts to keep the momentum of the revolution going, to try to go beyond the material limitations and/or the leadership.

For example, during the English Revolution of the mid 1600s, there were the "Levelers" and the "Diggers," who envisioned and thought they were fighting for a truly egalitarian society. This, despite the fact that at that time, the only kind of "communism" materially possible was a "communism" of distribution, and not genuine communism of production, distribution, and exchange. In the end, although they had been some of the most fervent anti-monarchists and revolutionary democrats, Cromwell was compelled to crush them, once the economic and political rule of the bourgeoisie over the feudal lords, monarchy, and Catholic Church had been more or less consolidated.

Although we cannot make direct and mechanical historical analogies, the Shaysites in the aftermath of the American Revolution represented a somewhat similar phenomenon. They wanted to go beyond the limits of what was materially possible at that time. They wanted genuine political and economic democracy for all, when the only form of democracy possible at that time was bourgeois democracy, which is limited by its very nature.

Two hundred years ago, capitalism was still in its historically progressive phase. In other words, it was still able to develop the productive forces of humanity, despite being a system based on the exploitation of the many by the few. Increased concentration of wealth, technology, and productive capacity was a necessary phase of human social development, laying the material foundations for socialism, a society in which there must be a high level of technology and productivity to ensure there is more than enough to go around. Therefore, the struggle of the Shaysites, yeoman farmers who represented an earlier, less efficient form of production, was doomed from the start.

After throwing off the British yoke, the embryonic American bourgeoisie set out to consolidate their power and conquer the rest of the continent, starting with the backwoods areas of the original thirteen states themselves. At this stage, the thirteen states were more or less independent of one another, with their own governments and laws. They had banded together in the struggle against the British, loosely bound together by the Articles of Confederation, and overseen by the weak Continental Congress, but there was no consensus as to whether or not and in what form this relationship should continue. Shays's Rebellion would profoundly shape that relationship.

One of the fundamental contradictions in the newly independent United States was the conflict between the East Coast and the Western interior. Even at this early stage of the new republic, clearly conflicting class interests and worldviews were evident in this dichotomy. The commercial interests on the Eastern seaboard, representing nascent capitalism, clashed with the interests of the inland small farmers. As for the question of chattel slavery in the South, that was to be dealt with by Northern capitalism eighty years later, in the Second American Revolution, or what was really the full consolidation of the First: the Civil War. That, however, is the subject of another article.

In the late 1780s, the US was primarily a country of small farmers. An estimated 70 percent of the population were yeomen farmers, free holders cultivating their own land. The rest were mostly craftsmen, artisans, slaves, small shopkeepers, professionals, merchants, bankers, government officials, and the like, not to mention the Native American population. The modern urban working class as we know it today existed only in an extremely embryonic form, working in a relatively small number of rudimentary manufacturing workshops, usually employing only a small number of workers.

Generally speaking, the rural economy was based mostly on barter and exchange of labor, not money. As a result, these small free holders had something of a collective mentality, despite the inherent "rugged individualism" of their lives. While each had their individual properties, they relied on each other to combat the elements, to raise their barns and get in the harvests, and to defend themselves against "hostiles" (Native Americans whose land was being encroached upon). The early democratic traditions of the Puritans, the people's militias, "town hall" and other community meetings still remained in some form or another in many areas, especially in New England. This was quite different from the outlook of the bankers, merchants, government officials, lawyers, clergy, etc. in the coastal cities and inland towns. Their world view was shaped by the individualism of the capitalist market and the need for cold, hard cash.

Between these two increasingly polarized groups were the country retailers, small shopkeepers who would buy goods from the coast and sell at a profit to the interior. The coast was dominated by for-profit production and importation for the market, whereas the small scale subsistence farming and barter of the interior was not. Within the US itself, therefore, we had the phenomenon of "uneven and combined development," of more advanced productive forms (early capitalism) grafted onto and coexisting with earlier, less productive forms (small scale farming). In the final analysis, the more productive and efficient mode of production will predominate, and in time it did; but at that time, the sheer numbers were still in favor of the small producers.

However, momentum and history were on the side of capitalism. The commercial lenders were increasingly penetrating the traditional economy, drawing small producers into market-oriented production by offering manufactured goods in exchange. The interior of the country was in effect a colony of the coast, trading labor-intensive agricultural goods for more expensive manufactured goods, similar to the US relationship with Latin America today. The surplus agricultural produce was then sold on the world market for a profit. A chain of debt was established, whereby the country retailers owed the coastal banks and importers of manufactured goods, and the small farmers owed the local retailer.

When the American colonies were still part of the British Empire, they had enjoyed special trading privileges and access to credit. In addition, there was a bonanza of profiteering and lucrative smuggling during the war. But with the war over, and having to make its own way in the precarious world of the late 18th century, the US economy entered a depression. There was a glut of goods, stockpiled on the basis of high wartime prices and speculation, and prices now collapsed. The banks and merchants put the squeeze on the country retailers who owed them for goods received, and the retailers in turn demanded payment of debts from the small farmers.

Traditionally, the rural population could pay back its debts through barter. For example, for a bag of nails or an axe received from the small retailer in the Spring, the farmer could pay back the debt with a certain number of bushels of wheat delivered in the Fall. But the country retailers now demanded repayment in hard currency, as the banks and merchants on the coast needed the cash to reestablish terms of credit with the British and other trading partners.

The state governments, overwhelmingly representing the interests of the urban elite, were also levying taxes, also to be paid in cash. Hadn't one of the rallying cries of the revolution been "No Taxation Without Representation"? Conflict was inevitable.

As the debts piled up, many farmers had their lands confiscated, and some were even thrown into debtors' prison. Their land was sold to speculators below its value, and thousands of independent farmers feared becoming tenant farmers on their own land. After fighting against the British, they were being subjected to a new kind of tyranny. Even if they were not directly affected, they were angry at the way their family and neighbors were being treated. In fact, a recent survey of documents from the era shows that family connections seem to be one of the most important factors driving participation in the movement.

The class lines were clear: there were no country retailers or rich merchants being jailed, just small farmers, often losing their land, or forced to move even further west. A similar process was repeated in the Dust Bowl in the 1930s, dramatically portrayed in *The Grapes of Wrath*. A similar phenomenon continues across Latin America and elsewhere around the world today.

During the initial stages of every revolution, the masses search for reformist solutions to their problems. In other words, they accept the general framework of society, but think that something must be improved. In the case of what would become the Shaysites, they still trusted the Massachusetts government and hoped to achieve their aims without violence. But in a revolution, events take on a dynamic of their own, often unforeseen by the participants themselves. Henry Knox, Secretary of War under the Articles of Confederation, understood from the beginning how things might unfold: "This business must, and will, progress from one stage to another, until it amounts to a pretty formidable rebellion."

In North and South Carolina, as well as other states, similar "Regulator" movements emerged. Generally speaking, they respected the law, but they wanted to "moderate" or "regulate" the government. They aimed their frustration at the court system, in order to prevent the "too rigorous execution of the law." The Shaysites in Massachusetts started out with similar aims.

But as can be seen in every revolution, even the most minor reforms cannot be tolerated by the ruling class, even if they are in keeping with the existing legislative channels and limits of society. These people are accustomed to ruling in a certain manner, and do not want to change their ways or appear to bow to pressure from below. Like the Russians in 1905, the Shaysites first attempted to petition peacefully for relief. They appealed to the government to lower taxes, to introduce paper money in order to lessen their debt load, and to legalize the use of barter, in order to pay off their debts with agricultural products. They also demanded the closing of the debtors' courts. But the rich creditors rejected all of this; they dominated the government after all, and they blamed the rural population for their "extravagant" spending. The same "blame the victim" policy can be seen time and again in our own times.

In the rural areas they began forming conventions, or committees, very similar to the "Committees of Correspondence" that were formed to organize the rebellion against the British Empire. Ironically, the new rulers of the thirteen colonies now called these committees "seeds of sedition," when they themselves had done the same thing just a few years earlier. The key difference, of course, was that now it was *their* class interests which were being threatened. As someone called "Freeman" wrote ironically in the *Worcester Magazine* in 1786,

> When we had *other* rulers, committees and conventions of the people were lawful, they were then necessary, but since I *myself* became a ruler, they cease to be lawful. The people have no right examine *my* conduct.

Instead of backing off, the government passed even stricter laws and increased the repression and squeezing of the debtors. As so often happens, the "whip of counterrevolution" spurred the movement on further. The rejection of their reasonable petitions for reform further radicalized the movement. There was discontent in urban areas as well, with food riots, as in Paris before the French Revolution of 1789, just a couple of years later.

Many of those being thrown into prison were veterans of the Revolutionary War, and being frontiersmen, had something of a "Wild West" mentality and a tendency to "take things into their own hands." In what could be made into a script for a Hollywood movie, the powers that be "picked on the wrong guy." Daniel Shays was a former captain in the Continental Army and a hero of the Revolution. He was twice brought to court, a humiliation for any hard-working man or woman just looking to get ahead in life, but doubly so for someone who had not long ago received an honorary sword as a gift from the French General Lafayette himself.

The people's committees formed militias and began closing and burning down courthouses. By one estimate, as many as one quarter of the fighting men in New England were involved. But they were careful not to harass the communities that the courts were in; they specifically targeted the courts themselves and the judges. They were organized professionally and were highly disciplined, as "the body of the people assembled in arms."

The class outlook of the Shaysites can be seen in their statements and writings, both before, during, and after the rebellion. One of them said that their aim was:

> [to] put a stop to those iniquitous ways of obtaining wealth, by which a set of plunderers have for years been rioting on the spoils of the industrious.

Another Massachusetts farmer said,

> I am a man that gets his living by hard labor, not by a pension or by monopolizing . . . I believe this country would flourish faster if there were less white shirts and more black frocks. Let us oblige the merchants to shut up their shops and get their living by following the plow.

Like many revolts against early capitalism, most famously the Luddites, the Shaysites' outlook was naïve and utopian. They wanted to go backwards to a precapitalist form of production, to an imaginary society of freedom and plenty for all. Their struggle was therefore doomed from the start; the tide of history was not on their side.

However, this prognosis was unclear to the forces involved in the living struggle. Henry Knox made the following appraisal: "Having proceeded to this length, for which they are now ripe, we shall have a formidable rebellion against reason, the principle of all government, and against the very name of liberty. This dreadful situation, for which our government have made no adequate provision, has alarmed every man of principle and property in New England. They start as from a dream, and ask what can have been the cause of our delusion? What is to give us security against the violence of lawless men? Our government must be braced, changed, or altered to secure our lives and property."

One rich Bostonian had this to say:

> We shall have no security of property. What honest man can live without government—what industrious man can live while his property is at the mercy of knaves and thieves?" Another expressed his horror in these terms: "Property will fall with them, and lie wholly at the mercy of the most idle, vicious, and disorderly set of men in the community.

In a letter to George Washington, Henry Knox summed up what was really at stake:

> Their creed is, "That the property of the United States has been protected from confiscation of Britain by the joint exertions of all, and therefore ought to be the common property of all, and he that attempts opposition to this creed is an enemy to equity and justice, and ought to be swept from off the face of the earth."

The rebellion was still in its reformist phase; it was not yet a full-fledged revolutionary movement aiming to overthrow the status quo. But the reaction of the ruling oligarchy was rabid. They referred to the Shaysites as a party of madmen, and railed about the "fury and madness of the people." They were horrified at the burning down of the courthouses, and launched a sort of "red scare" and panic because the authority of the state was being subverted. They declared that this was anarchy, and they blamed conspiracies by spies or by the British. The Governor of Massachusetts, James Bowdoin, rallied the wealthy to unite against the rebellion in their midst: "Every man ought to show his colors and take his side; no neutral characters should be allowed, nor anyone suffered to vibrate between the two." This too is reminiscent of our recent McCarthyist past.

As so often occurs in history, what was once progressive is transformed into its opposite and becomes reactionary. Whereas at one time they armed themselves against the British, the "Founding Fathers" now armed themselves against the masses and an 18th century version of the Patriot Act was passed.

At this time there was as yet no national army. Each state had to provide and pay for its own security. But in the Massachusetts militia there were mutinies of rank and filers who sympathized with the Shaysites. Some merchants were so terrified by the tide of events that they even considered inviting a foreign monarch or some kind of Napoleonic strongman to come in and restore order and save private property, which is what would eventually happen in France. As one merchant wrote, "Monarchy is better than the tyranny of this mob." Noah Webster of dictionary fame said, "I was once as strong a Republican as any man in America. Now a republic is the last kind of government I should choose. I would infinitely prefer a limited monarchy, for I would sooner be the subject of the caprice of one man, than the ignorance of the multitude." So much for "We, the People"!

No longer perceived as the problem of an individual state, the Continental Congress declared:

> The aid of the federal government is necessary to stop the Progress of the insurgents; that such Aid is earnestly desired by the Governor and Council, tho' particular Circumstances prevent its being applied and in a more formal Manner; and that there is the greatest reason to believe that, unless speedy and effectual measures shall be taken to defeat their designs they will possess themselves of the Arsenal at Springfield, subvert the constitutional government, and not only reduce that Commonwealth [of Massachusetts] to a State of Anarchy and Confusion, but probably involve the United States in the Calamities of a civil war.

They called for 1,340 troops to be raised in order put down the Massachusetts militants. As there was growing sympathy for the rebellion, the government claimed the troops were needed due to "Indian troubles." This was the beginning of the national army in what would become the United States, as opposed to the strictly state-based militias. But since there was no central control over monetary policy, there was no way to compel the states to raise money for the troops. So the Boston merchants took matters into their own hands, paid out of their own pockets for the raising of an army, and sent armed expeditions to punish the Shaysites.

Once again, the whip of counterrevolution drove the Shaysites further. They now adopted an openly revolutionary attitude. They feared the total loss of their freedom and now believed, as one of them later said, "that it was better to die by the bayonet, than by the halter." They kidnapped several country retailers and started forming local committees of the people to run their own government. They adopted guerrilla tactics used in the War of Independence and decided to march on Boston to burn it to the ground. And then, an accident of history took the wind out of the movement. In January of 1787, as they were marching on Springfield, Massachusetts to take over the armory, the Shaysites were caught in a snowstorm and surprised by the troops sent from Boston. A handful of the rebels were killed and wounded by cannon fire, and they dispersed to the north. Over the next few weeks, some 1,000 of the atomized Shaysites were arrested, effectively ending the rebellion.

At his trial, Shays denied being the leader of the movement, not because of cowardice, but because all decisions had been made democratically in popular assemblies. Several rebels were fined and imprisoned, and two of them, John Bly and Charles Rose, were hanged. But such was the sympathy the so-called Shaysites aroused in the population, that by 1788, Shays and most of the rest of his followers had been pardoned and released. Shays eventually moved to the Conesus, New York area where he died in anonymous poverty in 1825. He is buried in the Union cemetery.

But it was more than repression and bad luck that ended the rebellions of the "regulators." Two hundred years ago, there was an important safety valve for the accumulating class contradictions: escape to the West. In the end, many former Shaysites simply left the United States and moved into new territories, out of the reach of the government.

The Shays uprising was just one of many outbursts of the class struggle that helped shape early American history. It had a powerful effect on what was to become the US Constitution. After the events of 1786–87, a majority of the decision makers in the loosely confederated states were won over to the Federalists' arguments in favor of a stronger central government. They had seen in practice the need to pool their resources in order to, among other things, provide for a standing army to put down civil unrest. Their fear of the revolutionary initiative of the masses, and the threat to their property and privilege, trumped all the lofty rhetoric about "liberty and justice for all." In the end, the US Constitution, held up as a model of democracy, order, and stability, was passed by just 1/8th of the population—the "frightened men of property," as author Gore Vidal described them.

It is perhaps fitting to end this brief history of the Shaysites with the following famous words by Thomas Jefferson, written about the Shays uprising while he was serving as ambassador to France: "A little rebellion now and then is a good thing. The tree of liberty must be refreshed from time to time with the blood of patriots and tyrants." Although the right-wing "Tea Party" movement has of late hijacked these lines for themselves, their true meaning is the following: in a genuine democracy, the majority should rule. In modern society, the working class is the overwhelming majority, and should, by rights, be the masters of their own destiny.

February 12, 2010

APPENDIX V

WHEN THE SOCIALIST PARTY WAS A FACTOR IN US POLITICS: LESSONS IN PARTY BUILDING[1]

Tom Trottier

In analyzing the socialist revolution and how it could develop successfully, Lenin put forward the idea that three objective factors and one key subjective factor would need to be present. Lenin explained that the first objective factor was that the ruling class would be split and could no longer rule in their traditional manner. The second factor was the tremendous political vacillations of the middle layers of society, moving to the left, then to the right and back again. The third factor was the willingness of the working class to engage in a struggle to the end in order to change society. These three factors have been present in many countries in the past, and more recently, to one degree or another, in Venezuela and Iran.

However, the final factor which would make a socialist revolution successful was the subjective factor: a Marxist leadership. It was the idea that a disciplined organization of workers and youth with a firm foundation built on Marxist theory could provide the leadership necessary to ensure the working class's efforts led to victory. Leadership is the willingness to make sacrifices and lead by example. It is the willingness to go first, so that others can see the way forward and then join you. Building an effective revolutionary leadership requires the study of Marxist theory and the history of the workers movement

1 This article originally appeared in *Socialist Appeal* #52 (January-February 2010).

internationally so that we can assimilate the lessons. In this manner, the same mistakes do not have to be made again and again. In Russia, this Marxist leadership was provided by the Social Democratic Labor Party (Bolshevik), later renamed the Communist Party. However, in many other countries where this leadership was not built, the fact that the first three objective factors existed, but the fourth did not, meant defeat for the working class.

Therefore, for those interested in building such a leadership in the USA, it would be useful to look at past experiences in the labor and left movements in this country to see the lessons which can be learned so as to avoid making the same mistakes that past socialists have made.

We are grateful to those who have struggled in the past and we believe that they deserve our admiration and respect. Looking at their successes and accurately examining their failures and weak points, in no way disregards their heroic sacrifice. On the contrary, we take them and their lives seriously and therefore we do not forget them, but look to learn from them. Everyone makes mistakes. The only person who does not make mistakes is the person who does nothing. However, from the perspective of those who want to change society, we must be willing to recognize errors and learn from mistakes rather than cover them up and turn men and women from history into gods.

In the 1800s, American capitalism was expanding and the country was developing industry at a rapid pace. It did not develop in a straight line, but dialectically. Vigorous economic booms were followed by serious economic slumps. The growth of industry also meant the growth of the working class.

The working class felt the wrath of capitalism, both during its growth periods and during its depressions. Some workers looked for alternatives to capitalism, leading to the development of the Socialist Party of America.

The Socialist Party of America (SP of A) was set up by socialists dissatisfied with the sectarian politics of the Socialist Labor Party (SLP) of Daniel DeLeon. Although in some ways DeLeon was a great thinker, he tended to view society in a rigid, formalistic way. He tended to have a scholastic way of approaching the working class. Rather than examining objective reality and seeking a way to intervene in it, he led his party to believe that the working class would simply come to the SLP and follow a specific path which he laid out.

The SP of A did not have the rigidity of DeLeon, and as a result, they grew much faster. In 1900, the SP of A had about 4,500 members in more than 200 branches spread over 25 of the 48 states. By 1908, the SP had about 40,000 members. In 1917, the party had grown to more than 80,000 members throughout the country. Socialist newspapers, such as *Appeal to Reason*, ˙ ˙d circulations at times of more than 500,000!

The single most important figure in the SP of A was Eugene Victor Debs. Debs was an example of someone who came to socialism as a result of lessons he learned along the way in fighting to improve life for workers. He started out in the Brotherhood of Locomotive Firemen, a union of those men who would fire the steam engine of a locomotive train. At first, his conception of unions was that of a society, based on one's craft, which would help in mutual support to purchase insurance and other benefits. He did not start out believing in strikes or collective bargaining. In the process, he learned that the capitalists would not treat workers in a humane way and that any gain the workers make comes out of struggle. He also learned the futility of dividing workers into craft unions and tried to build one big union including all railroad workers, called the American Rail Union.

Debs and the SP of A were able to elect a number of state and city officials throughout the US, including a congressman from Milwaukee. In 1912, before women had the right to vote and when most Black men were violently prevented from voting, Debs got 6% of the national vote! As a comparison, in 2000, Ralph Nader got a little more than 2.7% of the national vote. In 1920, Debs got less than 6% of the national vote but almost 1,000,000 votes for President, although he was in jail for opposing US participation in World War I.

The gains of the SP of A showed that even in the USA, the advanced workers would find their way to socialist ideas. However, there were many serious problems with the SP. Above all, the leadership of the SP did not understand the importance of Marxist theory as a guide to action. As a result, a number of political and organizational decisions flowed from this which proved ultimately harmful.

Organization

The SP of A was a broad and loose grouping. It combined Marxists, labor militants, and reformists, including clergy. Debs would tend to run on a program promoting the socialist transformation of the US, while Victor Berger, who was elected to Congress on the Socialist Party ticket from Milwaukee, was a reformist. Berger's narrow outlook was reflected on a number of issues, including the question of race.

Sometimes, the SP appeared as reformers who offered to improve a few small things today. Other times, the party presented itself as wanting to change society with little concern for today's problems. What the party needed was to link the struggles for reforms and improvements in today's working conditions with the struggle to fundamentally change society. This problem was actually a problem throughout the Socialist International at that time. European socialists would fight for a limited "minimum program" of immediate reforms and make speeches about socialism at the May Day parades. Only the Bolsheviks were able to skillfully combine the two objectives.

In addition, the SP was not organized under the principles of democratic centralism. Democratic centralism means that the majority decisions are carried out, but there are many safeguards to allow the minority to be able to express their views throughout the party. Under democratic centralism, the leadership and the party newspapers reflect the democratically decided positions of the organization. However, in the SP, the leadership was usually made up of middle class elements, such as small businesspeople, preachers, and professors, who had the financial ability and spare time to devote to party business. Many workers, lacking money and time, were excluded from leadership bodies. The socialist papers, such as *Appeal to Reason*, were independently owned and reflected the owners' version of socialism, rather than the views of the workers in the party. This tended to produce conflict in the party, and there were times when the SP would lose its working class base because of these internal struggles.

Debs did not play the role in these internal battles that he should have. Unlike Lenin, who would use internal disagreements as a way to politically educate the rank and file of the party, Debs avoided party conflict, giving strength to the reformist right wing of the SP. This resulted in confusion in the ranks rather than political clarity.

Racism

One of the biggest theoretical errors of the SP was on the question of racism. Debs was opposed to racism and racial discrimination but he did not think that racism was a special problem of American capitalism that needed to be addressed. Debs once said that "We [the SP] have nothing special to offer the Negro, and we cannot make separate appeals to all races. The Socialist Party is the party of the whole working class, regardless of color—the whole working class of the whole world" (Ray Ginger, *The Bending Cross*, p. 260). The SP also had elements, such as the above-mentioned Victor Berger, who were out and out racists.

However, if the SP was to become the party of the whole working class, it could only be done on the basis of the reality of American capitalism and all of its horrors. The SP should have recognized the special oppression of black Americans and incorporated the struggle against racism into its program. Certainly, racism can only be eliminated by the establishment of socialism, and this will be brought about only by the united struggle of the working class. However, in order to win over the black workers and youth, the party has to be seen as addressing their problems.

Although many blacks lived in the rural South in the early 1900s, increasing numbers were migrating to Northern cities to work in industry and other occupations. This meant that the SP needed to take a lead in fighting Jim Crow and other forms of segregation, not to mention the battle against lynchings. The capitalists tried to divide the working class by discriminating against black workers, hiring them only as replacement workers during strikes. The SP should have explained that this is why it was vital and in the interest of white workers to fight against the discrimination of the white bosses and for union-controlled hiring halls, which would hire a diverse workforce, as part of their battle for union recognition, higher wages, etc. The position of the SP on racism meant that very little support for the party was gained among black workers, even though they were the most oppressed part of the proletariat.

Industrial Unions

The SP correctly understood the need for American workers to form industrial unions. The American Federation of Labor mostly organized workers by their craft or occupation. In other words, carpenters were in one union, electricians were in another, and so on and so forth. However, the working class can easily be divided in that manner, and the craft unions tended to organize the more skilled workers while leaving the unskilled factory workers, who were becoming a much greater part of the work force, without any union.

However, the SP had different strategies on how to organize the workers into industrial unions. Some SP members believed that it was necessary to work in the AF of L. This would mean raising socialist ideas in the AF of L and raising the idea that the labor federation should organize unskilled workers in industry-wide unions. Early in the 1900s the socialists did have a lot of influence in the AFL. At the 1902 AFL convention, a resolution calling for an end to the wage system by establishing workers' political and economic power got more than a third of the convention's vote! However, a few years later, the left wing of the SP, including Debs, thought that they should work to create new industrial unions, separate from the AFL. He and others then founded the IWW.

Although the IWW should be a subject for a future article, it should be noted that the IWW did not have anywhere near the resources of the AFL and received little help and much hostility from it. Although the right wing of the SP correctly worked in the AFL, it should be noted that much of what they did simply went along with the leadership and did not always present a political alternative to it.

Theory was the key in trade union work as well. It was easy to get demoralized about working in the AFL, having to face a conservative bureaucracy. One of the ways that theory aids militants is that it gives a longer term perspective and orientation when intervening in a particular situation.

In general, when capitalism is in an upswing, the "practical" leaders will be at the apex of their support, as they are able to deliver some crumbs in the form of higher wages and better benefits for the membership. However, when the capitalist system inevitably moves into crisis, these same leaders are no longer as popular as members are laid off and concessions are given to the bosses. Therefore, socialists must have a long-term view and patiently explain the situation to the workers, building points of support. As the times become more desperate, workers looking for answers expand the possible base for socialism. Unfortunately, the left wing of the SP did not use Marxist theory and reacted to events in a "pragmatic" way. The IWW was not able to build industrial unions and ultimately, these industries were organized by the CIO, unions that split from the AFL, in the 1930s.

The Russian Revolution

In late 1917, the socialist revolution triumphed in Russia. This was a beacon to workers and socialists all over the world. Here in the USA, the revolution split the SP. The right wing became opponents of the revolution. Most of the left wing formed the Communist Party. Debs, although a strong supporter of the Bolshevik Revolution, never left the SP. He died in 1926.

The theoretical mistakes in the SP of A led to its demise in the 1920s. Although it grew a little in the 1930s it was never again going to play the role it had played. The largest force on the American left was then the Communist Party USA.

APPENDIX VI

THE 75TH ANNIVERSARY OF THE 1934 MINNEAPOLIS TEAMSTERS STRIKE

David May

The 1934 Teamsters strike in Minneapolis, led by the Trotskyists of the Communist League of America (the forerunner of the Socialist Workers Party), was a decisive moment in the US labor and socialist movements. During the years preceding the strike, few would have expected the upsurge that took place in 1934. Throughout the 1920s there was not a single recognized union in the basic industries. Workers at companies such as Ford were unorganized, similar to workers in other areas of mass production who were without workplace rights of any kind, atomized and seemingly powerless against the bosses. Despite the heroic past struggles of US workers—from the Knights of Labor, the strikes of 1877, and the Molly Maguires to the Industrial Workers of the World (IWW) and the struggle for the eight hour day—the few unions that did exist at the time were small, weak, and limited almost exclusively to skilled workers. Workers were organized along purely craft lines and the unions were dominated by a conservative brand of "business unionism."

During the 1920s the unions belonging to the American Federation of Labor experienced steady growth. But then, like now, this was cut across by the economic crisis. By 1929, the year of the "Great Crash" on Wall Street, the membership of the AFL had been reduced to three million members. The average working day had increased to between 10 and 12 hours and workers were subjected to ruthless increases in the rate and intensity of work. Workers were hired and fired at the employer's will and overtime pay was nonexistent.

Between 1929 and 1933 there was a 48.7% decline in overall production, resulting in more than 17 million workers, nearly a quarter of the working population, being thrown into unemployment. Wage cuts also followed, with average wages falling to just half of 1925 levels. By 1933 the membership of unions had fallen even further—to just two million members—reducing the AFL to less than 50% of the size it had been in 1920.

Minneapolis in 1934 was a largely nonunionized city under the control of the Citizens Alliance, a viciously anti-union employers' organization which was pledged to keeping the city an "open shop." Minneapolis's economy was based on its being a regional agricultural and transportation hub, with a large number of transportation and warehouse workers. The city's truck drivers and warehouse workers were almost completely unorganized, poorly paid, and severely overworked. Against this backdrop, the Minneapolis branch of the Communist League of America decided in the winter of 1933 to launch a union organizing drive among workers at the city's coal yards. The CLA's organizing campaign was led by five workers who, by the time the struggle was over, were to become household names to Minneapolis working people: Vince, Grant, and Miles Dunne, Carl Skoglund, and Farrell Dobbs.

The Teamsters union, then as today, was the traditional union representing commercial transport workers, and this union was chosen for the organizing drive. General Drivers Local 574 was one of the few locals not set up along strictly controlled craft lines, and represented a small number of coal yard workers, cab drivers, and others. The target set for the campaign was to organize every coal yard worker into local 574. The initial organizing campaign had to struggle past every kind of bureaucratic hurdle set up by the Teamsters leadership, from official strike authorizations including mandatory "cooling off" periods, binding and forced arbitrations as required in the union's bylaws, and a monopoly of power held in the hands of the bureaucratic officialdom. Despite this, the organizing campaign moved forward, and more and more coal workers signed up to join local 574. But the coal yard bosses, backed up by the Citizen's Alliance, refused to recognize the union.

This led to the first strike, which began on February 7, 1934, and closed 65 coal yards. Even before the strike began, to get around the conservative local Teamsters officials, the workers set up an elected strike committee, which also selected picket captains responsible to the elected committee alone (and not to the official leadership). The need to set up an elected and rank-and-file–based committee was vindicated when the union's national leadership refused to provide strike pay to the workers, since the strike had been launched without the approval of the union's president.

The strikers recognized from the beginning the need to prevent scab trucks moving coal out of the yards, and developed the tactic of "cruising pickets." These were mobile pickets, where in addition to targeted picketing of the entrances of key yards by workers on foot, other groups of workers would mount cars and trucks which would follow scab trucks out of the yards (and out of sight of the police) and then force them to dump their cargoes. The cruising pickets would stop the scab trucks and first explain to the scab drivers the reasons for the strike, that it was for higher wages, workplace rights and dignity, and relate how the strike was a fight for all unorganized drivers. By this method the union was actually able to recruit many former scabs into the union! But if the scabs refused to voluntarily dump the coal, it was dumped for them by the pickets.

By using such methods to wage a solid strike that allowed no movement of goods, the coal bosses soon buckled under the pressure and agreed to recognize local 574 as the representative of all coal yard workers. From this first success, local 574 then began another, more ambitious campaign: to organize all truck drivers and warehouse workers in the city. Based on the name it had made for itself among working people through waging a militant, class-struggle fight against the coal bosses, the union's organizing campaign was able to recruit 3,000 workers in just two months' time. But this was just the beginning of the struggle. Once it seemed that things had gotten back to normal, the bosses refused to recognize the new local, and a second, even more bitter strike became necessary.

In preparation for the second strike, the workers set up a strike headquarters in a large garage, from which cruising pickets were dispatched. Preparing for expected police violence, a hospital was also set up, along with a commissary to serve hot meals to pickets and a repair shop for picket vehicles. During the course of the strike many workers lived out of strike HQ, sleeping on floors or in doorways. The rank-and-file workers took these initiatives to prepare the strike themselves since the union's leadership did everything in its power to limit the scope of the strike, insisting on strictly legal picketing and abiding by the injunctions issued by the bosses' courts. But in the words of Harry DeBoer, a participant of the strike, the Local 574 rank and file "papered the walls with injunctions."

Local 574's rank and file also did everything possible to build support throughout the labor movement. Under the slogan "Every member an organizer," workers attended the meetings of other area unions and called for support for the struggle of 574, which was the struggle of all working people. Through interventions such as these, workers were able to get the officials of other unions to put themselves on record as in support of Local 574. Later, this led to solidarity strikes by many of these unions, including a strike of 35,000 building trades workers during the course of 574's strike in May.

As opposed to the narrow confines of the official leadership's "business unionism," local 574's rank and file worked to draw the entire working class in the area to support the struggle. This was especially true for women and the unemployed. The union worked with the unemployed councils that had sprung up to fight for jobs, insurance, and payments for unemployed workers. The early American Communist Party had played a leading role in organizing these councils across the country. Unemployed workers joined the struggle as volunteer pickets and acted as scouts, spotting the movements of police, the bosses' Citizens Alliance thugs and scab trucks. For its part, 574 raised the issue of the supporting the unemployed in the wider labor movement, and beyond that was able to press other unions to take up the fight for public works projects to employ the unemployed with union wages and rights.

Local 574 also formed a Women's Auxiliary in order to draw workers' families, and working women generally, into the struggle and to keep the strike going. At this, time all truck drivers and warehouse workers were men, and generally women were employed in only a few areas of industry such as textiles (there would be a huge strike of women textile workers in the Southeast US later in 1934). Women played a key role in the Teamsters strike: from working the telephones dispatching cruising pickets, working in the commissary and hospital set up at strike headquarters, to distributing copies of the strike committee newspaper, to participating in the cruising pickets and in the pitched battles with the police and Citizens Alliance thugs. The Auxiliary also played an important role in building support for the union and the strike, highlighted by a march of 700 women to the Mayor's office to demand the withdrawal of deputy police, the "specials."

The key difference in this strike was that democratic structures for waging the struggle were set up from the very beginning. The specially elected strike committee had executive control over how the strike was conducted, augmented by the "committee of 100," which was a broader body composed of picket captains and strike veterans. Whenever possible, all important decisions were submitted to the committee of 100, and from there to the membership as a whole. This kept the leaders of the strike directly accountable to the rank and file, and later, when key leaders of the strike committee were arrested, allowed the strike to continue. Also, 574 had an elected negotiating committee of two, which was only given the authority to meet with the bosses and the state to propose and receive terms, not to negotiate and reach a deal independently of the membership.

By waging a militant strike using class-struggle methods, the union was able to build broad support, and the city's working class was lined up behind the Teamsters. This was despite all of the forces arrayed against the workers by the local capitalists with their press, police, courts, prisons, and its Citizens Alliance, which was busily deputizing hundreds of petty bosses, office workers, and lumpens.

The strike was met with complete hostility by the capitalist press, but the workers found an answer to this as well. For the first time in a US strike, the workers created a daily strike newspaper, *The Organizer*, which explained the union's struggle and demands, gave reports on the strike's progress, and was distributed widely across the city and region. The bosses recognized the worth of the strike paper by targeting its distributors and printers. Through the paper, the strike committee urged workers to place no faith in the government's impartiality nor that of its arbitrators.

The paper was edited by Max Shachtmann and James Cannon, both national leaders of the Communist League of America.

Unable to break the May strike with injunctions, the bosses tried to break it with clubs instead. "Specials" and police converged on the City Market, with its truck docks and warehouses at the center of the strike, and from May 21 to 22, pitched battles between workers and the police took place. The workers captured the market and won what was called "The Battle of Deputies Run." Not a truck moved in, around, or out of the city without the union's permission. The May strike ended on the 25th, with the union winning recognition, wage increases, and also the condition that no participant in the strike would be victimized after returning to work.

However, from the beginning the employers made it clear that they would not honor the contract, and continued to refuse recognition of warehouse workers not directly connected to the trucks. This led to the third and final strike in July. The bosses had been emboldened by the attack of Teamsters President Tobin on local 574's leadership, whipping up a red scare against them, which was seized on in the capitalist press who called on citizens to "Save Minneapolis from Communism." The bosses were now preparing not to only to beat the workers, but to literally shoot them back to work.

As the cruising pickets went into action, the police were preparing a massacre. On Bloody Friday, July 20, police armed with riot guns opened fire on a truck carrying 10 pickets, killing Henry Ness and John Belar and wounding 55 others. Wounded workers streamed into the strike headquarters, where they were treated by volunteer doctors and nurses. 20 minutes after the police massacre, the National Guard was on the streets and martial law had been declared. But the workers refused to be intimidated: the union revoked its travel permits, stopping all trucks. Police stayed clear of the area around the strike headquarters. 40,000 people attended Harry Ness's funeral procession, during which the police were cleared from the streets and workers took over directing traffic.

Soon afterwards, the leadership of the strike committee was arrested by the National Guard. But the strike continued—the arrests were followed by a march of 40,000 more workers demanding the release of the arrested leaders. Finally, on August 22 the bosses gave in to all of the union's main demands.

The Minneapolis Teamsters strike was a model of class-struggle trade unionism. In subsequent strikes, other workers were to use these same methods in the steel, auto, rubber, textile, and other industries, as well as expanding on them with the sit-down strikes in the auto industry, a form of factory occupation. Later, the creation of the Congress of Industrial Organizations (CIO) union federation would organize the key sectors of the world's biggest industrial economy, changing the balance of forces between the working class and the capitalist class in the US, which allowed for higher wages, better benefits, the 40-hour work week, overtime and vacation pay, health and safety inspection of workplaces, and more, all of which pushed up the workers' standard of living. The 1955 merger of the AFL and the CIO would create the largest union federation in any capitalist country.

It is important to note that the 1934 Teamsters strike was led by Trotskyists, with a key role played by Socialist Workers Party (SWP) militants like the Dunne brothers, Carl Skoglund, and Farrell Dobbs. This raised the authority of the SWP hugely in the unions and it presented an important opportunity for Trotskyism to become a much broader tendency in the US working class. Unfortunately, this opportunity was not fully taken advantage of. Despite winning workers, not by the ones and twos, but by the 10s and 20s, the SWP did not carry out really political work in the unions.

For Marxists, it is necessary to orient to the mass organizations of the working class, which include the unions, because this is where the class will first turn when the class struggle begins to push forward. We always fight shoulder to shoulder with our class, fighting for day to day demands and for class-struggle unionism, patiently explaining that the interests of the bosses and the interests of the workers cannot be reconciled, and keeping alive the memory of our traditions of struggle. But at the same time we offer our union brothers and sisters a political explanation of the crisis of capitalism and seek to win workers and the unions to a revolutionary program.

Instead of doing this, the SWP carried out a largely apolitical trade union policy, not going beyond the bounds of class-struggle trade unionism. Important as this work is and was, it is not enough. Workers must have a political expression for their needs and aspirations, and this, in the final analysis, requires the building of a mass, class independent political party based on the unions. A key role of the Marxists in the unions is to patiently explain this to our class. There is a fundamental difference between doing trade union work in the unions, and doing revolutionary political work in the trade unions.

The SWP was criticized at the time by Leon Trotsky, who had serious concerns that in their methods there existed symptoms that could lead to opportunism, of trying to find shortcuts where none existed. As he put it,

> You propose a trade union policy not a Bolshevik policy. Bolshevik policies begin outside the trade unions. The worker is an honest trade unionist but far from Bolshevik politics. The honest militant can develop but it is not identical with being a Bolshevik.

Trotsky's criticisms were later proved correct, as the SWP continued to adapt itself to sections of the union bureaucracy and ended up losing a whole layer of workers won over in the pitched struggles of the 1930s. Unfortunately, after Trotsky's death, the SWP lost its course on this and a whole series of other domestic and international questions.

Today, the unions are on the defensive. Just 12.4 percent of US workers are unionized, companies like GM are laying off tens of thousands of union workers, and the story is the same elsewhere. Similar to the period leading up to the Teamsters strikes, the unions are dominated by a conservative bureaucracy, tied hand and foot to big business, unable to fight for even basic reforms like the EFCA. They've done nothing serious to answer the attacks of the employers and the government for decades. In fact, they play a key role in maintaining class peace by subordinating the workers' interests to the bosses and keeping them tied to the Democratic Party. But, as the experience of the Minneapolis Teamsters strike proved 75 years ago, the unions can be transformed, practically overnight, when the workers begin looking towards the unions for an answer to their problems, and especially if there are dedicated militants in the unions who can win them to class-struggle methods.

While for the time being the working class largely has its head down under the weight of the recession, as many are worried about just having a job and a roof overhead, when the class begins to feel more secure in its position it can and will strike back with a vengeance. This is why a key task of the US working class is the struggle to transform the unions into real organs of class struggle and to break with the political parties of the bosses.

BIBLIOGRAPHY

Bryant, Arthur, *Triumph in the West, 1943–1946.*

Carroll, P.N. and D.W. Noble, *The Free and the Unfree, a New History of the United States.*

Daugherty, Harry M., *The Inside Story of the Harding Tragedy.*

de Tocqueville, Alexis, *Democracy in America.*

dos Passos, John, *1919.*

————, *The 42nd Parallel.*

————, *The Big Money.*

Dougherty, Carroll, *Labor Problems in American Industry.*

Engels, Frederick, *The Conditions of the Working-Class in England.*

————, *The Origins of the Family, Private Property, and the State.*

Fleming, D.F., *The Cold War and its Origins, 1917–1960, Vol. 1.*

Foner, Philip S., *The Great Labor Uprising of 1877.*

Galbraith, J.K., *The Great Crash 1929.*

————, *The Policy of Contentment.*

Ginger, Ray, *The Bending Cross.*

Grant, Ted and Alan Woods, *Reason in Revolt.*

————, *Russia: from Revolution to Counter-Revolution.*

Huberman, Leo, *We the People.*

Isaacs, Jeremy and Taylor Downing, *Cold War.*

Kuczynski, J., *A Short History of Labor Conditions under Industrial Capitalism.*

Lacy, Dan, *The Meaning of the American Revolution*.

Lenin, V.I., *The State and Revolution*.

London, Jack, *The Iron Heel*.

————, *What Life Means to Me*.

MacNeil, Neil, *An American Peace*.

Martin, Frederick Townsend, *The Passing of the Idle Rich*.

Marx, Karl and Frederick Engels, *The Communist Manifesto*.

————, *Marx-Engels Selected Correspondence*.

Miller, Arthur, *The Crucible*.

Moore, Michael, *Stupid White Men*.

Morgan, Lewis Henry, *Ancient Society*.

Paine, Thomas, *The Rights of Man*.

Preis, Art, *Labor's Giant Step*.

Reed, John, *Ten Days that Shook the World*.

Sinclair, Upton, *The Jungle*.

Sipols, V., *The Road to a Great Victory*.

Smith, Adam, *The Wealth of Nations*.

Steinbeck, John, *Cannery Row*.

————, *Of Mice and Men*.

————, *The Grapes of Wrath*.

Stowe, Harriet Beecher, *Uncle Tom's Cabin*.

Trotsky, Leon, *History of the Russian Revolution*.

Truman, Harry S., *Memoirs, Vol. I, Year of Destiny*.

Trumbo, Dalton, *Johnny Got His Gun*.

Vidal, Gore, *1876*.

————, *Burr*.

————, *Lincoln*.

Woodburn, James A., *Life of Thaddeus Stevens*.

Woodward, W.E., *A New American History*.

NAME INDEX

A

Adams, Abigail 157
Adams, Charles Francis 30, 192
Adams, James Truslow 19
Adams, John 22, 31, 32, 33, 39, 170
Adams, Samuel 17, 18, 20, 21, 22, 25, 29, 36, 68, 203
Adler, Victor 84
Alger, Horatio 75
Allende, Salvador 151
Altgeld, John P. 83
Ames, Oake 74
Amherst, Jeffrey 6
Anderson, Robert (Major) 58
Anneke, Friedrich 66
Antoinette, Marie 39, 120
Aptheker, Herbert vii
Arbenz Guzman, Jacobo 148, 149, 150
Armour, Philip Danforth 74

B

Bacon, Francis 19
Bacon, Nathaniel 14
Baker, Ray Stannard 90
Batista y Zaldivar, Fulgencio 149, 150
Beauregard, P. G. T. 58
Belar, John 223
Berger, Victor L. 109, 215, 216
Berkeley, Martin 136
Blair, Tony xv
Bowdoin, James 210
Bradford, William 11
Brando, Marlon 136

Bright, John 66
Brooke, Allen 128
Brooks, Phillip 64
Brown, John ix, 50, 53, 54
Bryant, Arthur 128
Bryant, Louise ix
Bukharin, Nikolai 42
Burns, James F. 128
Burr, Aaron 35, 39
Bush 177
Bush, George W. vii, x, xiii, xiv, xv, 42, 97, 99, 100, 108, 110, 139, 143, 144, 146, 153, 154
Butler, Smedley D. 104

C

Cannon, James 223
Capone, Al 115
Carnegie, Andrew 74
Carroll, P.N. 3, 5, 28, 40, 41, 44, 110
Castillo Armas, Carlos 149
Castro, Fidel 149, 150, 151
Charles II 10
Chavez, Hugo 153
Churchill, Winston 125, 126, 127, 128, 129
Clausewitz, Carl von 98
Clemenceau, Georges 103, 108
Cleveland, Grover 96
Clinton, George 39
Columbus, Christopher 5
Cooke, Jay 74
Coolidge, Calvin 113, 115, 116
Cooper, Gary 137

229

Cope, John E. 81
Cornwallis, Charles 30
Coughlin, Charles 120
Cromwell, Oliver 10, 19, 29, 204
Custer, George Armstrong 8, 9, 97

D

Daley, Richard J. 146
Darwin, Charles 190
Daugherty, Harry M. 114
Dawes, Charles G. 105
Debs, Eugene ix, 86, 87, 109, 215,
    216, 217, 218
DeLeon, Daniel 214
Dewey, George 98
Diem, Ngo Dinh 142
Dobbs, Farrell 121, 220, 224
Dos Passos, John vii, 107, 108, 110,
    111, 113
Dougherty, Caroll 85
Downing, Taylor 134, 143, 148, 150
Drew, Daniel 75
DuBois, W.E.B. x
Dulles, Allen 148, 150
Dulles, John Foster 148
Dunne, Vincent 220, 224
Dylan, Bob 92

E

Edison, Thomas 113
Einstein, Albert 134
Eisenhower, Dwight D. 148, 149, 150
Eisler, Hans 135
Engels, Frederick iii, v, ix, xiv, 4, 82,
    84, 145, 156, 174, 178, 181,
    193, 195, 228
Everest, Wesley 110, 111, 112

F

Fielden, Samuel 83
Fisk, James 74
Fleming, D.F. 128
Flynn, Elizabeth Gurley ix
Foner, Eric vii
Foner, Philip vii, 79, 80, 81, 82

Ford, Henry 113, 189
Ford, John 137
Frank, Jerome 135
Franklin, Benjamin 22, 155

G

Gable, Clark 137
Gadsden, Christopher 36
Gage, Thomas 17, 18
Galbraith, J.K. 114, 117, 159
Galilei, Galileo 178
Gallatin, Albert 73, 74
Galtieri, Leopoldo 152
Gates, Bill 166
George, Henry 193, 195, 197, 198
George III 24, 67, 202
Gladstone, William 14
Gompers, Samuel 84, 85, 86
Gould, Jay 74, 78
Gowen, Franklin 79
Grant, Ted 1
Grant, Ulysses S. 60, 63, 64, 76
Greenglass, David 134
Greenspan, Alan 117
Green, William 121
Grimm, Warren O. 110, 111
Guthrie, Woody 92

H

Hamilton, Alexander 32, 33, 35, 37,
    39
Hammond, James Henry 51
Hancock, John 25
Harding, Warren G. 109, 114
Hayden, Sterling 136
Hayes, Alfred 91
Hayes, Rutherford B. 80
Haywood, William "Big Bill" ix, 87,
    106
Hegel, G.W.F. 16, 72, 117, 171, 190
Henry, Patrick 36
Hill, James J. 74
Hill, Joe ix, 87, 89, 90, 91, 92
Hitler, Adolf 93, 105, 125, 126, 129,
    174

Hobbes, Thomas 19
Holmes, Oliver Wendell, Jr. viii
Hooker, Joseph (Maj. General) 59
Hoover, Herbert 105, 116, 119, 120, 121
Hoover, J. Edgar 110, 134, 135, 136, 137
Hopkins, Harry 127
Huberman, Leo vii, 6, 35
Hull, Cordell 124
Humphrey, Hubert 145, 146
Huntington, Collis Potter 74

I

Isaacs, Jeremy 134, 143, 148, 150

J

Jackson, Andrew 47, 48, 49
Jefferson, Thomas 15, 16, 19, 22, 23, 24, 27, 32, 35, 37, 39, 40, 41, 42, 43, 44, 73, 157, 164, 170, 212
Johnson, Lyndon B. 142, 143, 145
Jones, Mother ix

K

Kazan, Elia 136
Kelley, Florence 193
Kennedy, John F. 142, 150
Kennedy, Robert 146
Kent, James 47
Kerry, John 153
Keynes, John Maynard 119
King, Martin Luther, Jr. 145
Kinoy, Arthur 135
Knox, Henry 207, 209
Krugman, Paul 158
Kuczynski, J. 45

L

Lacy, Dan 43
Lafayette 208
Laurens, Henry 20

Lee, Robert E. 53, 59, 60, 63, 64
Lenin, V.I. ix, xiii, 1, 4, 12, 58, 67, 85, 93, 104, 106, 110, 145, 162, 168, 169, 178, 213, 216
Lewis, John L. 121
Lincoln, Abraham v, ix, 52, 54, 55, 56, 57, 58, 59, 61, 62, 63, 64, 65, 66, 67, 68, 144, 163, 165, 170, 191, 192
Livingston, Robert R. 22
Lloyd George, David 103, 108
Locke, John 19
Lodge, Henry Cabot 95
London, Jack 92, 93
Long, Huey 120
Louis XVI 39, 66
Luxemburg, Rosa 106
Lynch, Charles 28

M

MacArthur, Douglas 121
MacNeil, Neil 131
Madison, James 32, 37, 39, 44
Martin, Frederick Townsend 77
Marx, Karl v, viii, ix, xiv, 1, 4, 7, 12, 15, 24, 66, 78, 82, 84, 115, 116, 117, 123, 135, 137, 156, 162, 172, 174, 176, 178, 181, 190, 191, 193, 195, 198, 201
Mason, John (Captain) 5
McCarthy, Joseph R. 133, 137
McClellan, George B. 59, 64
McKellar, Kenneth 110
McKinley, William 95, 96, 97, 98
Meany, George 85
Mellon, Andrew W. 74
Miller, Arthur 133
Mills, C. Wright 163
Monroe, James 44
Moore, Michael 69, 156
Morgan, J.P. 74
Morgan, Lewis Henry 3, 4
Morris, Gouverneur 20
Morrison, John A. 90

N

Nader, Ralph 215
Ness, Henry 223
Newton, Isaac 19
Nicholas II 105, 184
Nixon, Richard 133, 145, 146
Noble, D.W. 3, 5, 28, 40, 41, 44, 110
North, Frederick, Lord 24

O

Obama, Barack x
Olney, Richard 86

P

Packer, Asa 79
Paine, Thomas 38, 203
Palmer, A. Mitchell 110
Parsons, Albert ix, 82, 83
Parsons, Lucy 82
Paulus, Friedrich 126
Pepperell, William 27
Pinochet, Augusto 151
Pitcairn, John (Major) 25
Pitt, William 38
Pius XII, Pope 134
Powderly, Terence 193
Powell, Colin 69
Preis, Art 121
Prosser, Gabriel 40

R

Ransome, Arthur 42
Reagan, Ronald 135, 139, 152, 156
Reed, John ix, 106, 107
Revere, Paul 21, 25
Rice, Condoleeza 69
Rich, Robert 136
Robbins, Jerome 136
Robeson, Paul 136
Robinson, Earl 91
Rockefeller, John D. 74, 77
Roosevelt 184
Roosevelt, Franklin D. 119, 120, 121,
    123, 124, 126, 127, 128, 151

Roosevelt, Theodore 95, 97, 99, 100,
    101, 119
Rosenberg, Ethel 134, 135
Rosenberg, Julius 134, 135

S

Sacco, Nicola 110
Schachtmann, Max 223
Seeger, Pete 92
Seward, William H. 56
Shays, Daniel v, x, 33, 34, 35, 36, 202,
    203, 205, 208, 211, 212
Sherman 60
Sherman, Roger 22
Sherman, William Tecumseh 59, 64
Sinclair, Upton 93, 94, 175
Sipols, V. 125
Skoglund, Carl 220, 224
Smith, Adam 166
Smith, William S., Col. 16
Somoza, Anastasio 151
Soros, George 159
Spies, August 83
Stalin, Josef 125, 127, 128, 130
Stanford, Leland 74
Steinbeck, John 118
Story, Joseph 47
Strasser, Adolph 84
Sunday, Billy 110
Sylvis, William ix, 78

T

Thatcher, Margaret 152
Thayer, Webster 110
Thieu, Nguyen Van 147
Thurston, John Mellen 98
Tocqueville, Alexis de 11, 12, 73, 77,
    155, 156
Tolstoy, Leo 99, 100
Townsend, Francis 120
Trotsky, Leon iii, v, ix, x, xiii, xv, 4, 17,
    29, 34, 58, 67, 93, 106, 123,
    127, 131, 153, 168, 169, 178,
    183, 203, 225
Truman, Harry 128, 130

Trumbo, Dalton 136
Trump, Donald x
Turner, Nat ix

V

Vanderbilt, Cornelius 75, 165
Vanzetti, Bartolomeo 110
Vidal, Gore vii, xii, 26, 30, 35, 56, 74, 212
Villa, Pancho 103

W

Washington, George 14, 15, 17, 18, 27, 28, 29, 30, 31, 33, 35, 36, 39, 170, 202, 209
Wayne, John 9, 136, 137
Webster, Noah 210
Weydemeyer, Joseph 66
Williams, Ben 89
Wilson, Woodrow 91, 102, 103, 108, 109
Winthrop, John 13
Woodburn, James A. 61
Woods, Tiger xiv
Woodward, W.E. 6, 21, 22, 25, 26, 27, 33, 36, 44, 48, 53, 63, 66, 72, 73, 75, 96, 103
Worcester, Dean C. 102

X

X, Malcolm 70, 147

Y

Young, Owen D. 105

Z

Zinn, Howard vii
Zola, Emile 93